Leisure Studies in a Global Era

AF173090

Series Editors
Karl Spracklen
Leeds Beckett University
Leeds, United Kingdom

Karen Fox
University of Alberta
Edmonton, Alberta, Canada

In this book series, we defend leisure as a meaningful, theoretical, framing concept; and critical studies of leisure as a worthwhile intellectual and pedagogical activity. This is what makes this book series distinctive: we want to enhance the discipline of leisure studies and open it up to a richer range of ideas; and, conversely, we want sociology, cultural geographies and other social sciences and humanities to open up to engaging with critical and rigorous arguments from leisure studies. Getting beyond concerns about the grand project of leisure, we will use the series to demonstrate that leisure theory is central to understanding wider debates about identity, postmodernity and globalisation in contemporary societies across the world. The series combines the search for local, qualitatively rich accounts of everyday leisure with the international reach of debates in politics, leisure and social and cultural theory. In doing this, we will show that critical studies of leisure can and should continue to play a central role in understanding society. The scope will be global, striving to be truly international and truly diverse in the range of authors and topics. Editorial Board: John Connell, Professor of Geography, University of Sydney, USA; Yoshitaka Mori, Associate Professor, Tokyo University of the Arts, Japan; Smitha Radhakrishnan, Assistant Professor, Wellesley College, USA; Diane M. Samdahl, Professor of Recreation and Leisure Studies, University of Georgia, USA; Chiung-Tzu Lucetta Tsai, Associate Professor, National Taipei University, Taiwan; Walter van Beek, Professor of Anthropology and Religion, Tilburg University, The Netherlands; Sharon D. Welch, Professor of Religion and Society, Meadville Theological School, Chicago, USA; Leslie Witz, Professor of History, University of the Western Cape, South Africa.

More information about this series at
http://www.springer.com/series/14823

Vania L. Sandoval

The Meaning of Leisure

Definitions and Practices among
Migrant and Non-migrant Women
in an Urban Space

palgrave
macmillan

Vania L. Sandoval
Mannheim, Baden-Württemberg, Germany

Plus: Dissertation, Heidelberg University, Faculty of Behavioural and Cultural Studies, *Year 2017. This publication was accepted as a dissertation in 2017 with the title "Multiple Lifestyles? Comparing Leisure Conceptions and Organization among Migrant and Non-Migrant Women in Mannheim, Germany" in the subject Anthropology at the Faculty of Behavioural and Cultural Studies* of Heidelberg University.

Leisure Studies in a Global Era
ISBN 978-3-319-86694-9   ISBN 978-3-319-59752-2   (eBook)
DOI 10.1007/978-3-319-59752-2

Printed on acid-free paper

This Palgrave Macmillan imprint is published by Springer Nature
The registered company is Springer International Publishing AG
The registered company address is: Gewerbestrasse 11, 6330 Cham, Switzerland

For Evis, Omaira, and Hermann

PREFACE

This book was originally written as a PhD thesis on the subject of social and cultural anthropology and based on field research conducted in the city of Mannheim between 2014 and 2015. This edited version seeks to highlight the ethnographic data and to position itself as an ethnography of young women in Mannheim, a city with a decades-old multicultural tradition. The book also focuses on leisure, something that is so palpable in this "carnival city" but that seldom raises scholarly attention, as it is mostly overshadowed by investigations into Mannheim's peculiar dialect.

The book is organized in six chapters. Chapter 1, the introduction, presents an overview of the topic, places it in the context of existing research and literature, and explains the methods used and participants chosen. Chapter 2 deals with the local context in which the research took place, also addressing the importance of the city as actor that can enable or hinder certain leisure channels for inhabitants and for these women in particular. Chapter 3 discusses the concept of leisure from the participants' subjective point of view, including aspects such as conceptualization of leisure in practice and an overall ideal of leisure. This chapter also includes an analysis of sport and physical activities as prominent components of subjective leisure. Chapter 4 deals with leisure in practice: how the conceptualization of leisure translates into leisure practice via planning and organization. This interaction between concepts and practices results in a pace of life divided in to cyclical segments (the week, the weekend, the vacation), which are largely determined by institutionalized work time frames: The week is predominantly a segment for individual leisure while the weekend is predominantly social, and the vacation has immense relevance as it is often the period during which the true realization of overall leisure ideals occurs.

Following, and independent of particularities of origin, Chap. 5 represents an attempt to answer this question: In which situations or regarding which aspects does having a migrant background play a role in the leisure of these women? The chapter addresses issues such as differences in "leisure budget" despite fairly similar socioeconomic positions, discrepancies that have a lot to do with family dynamics in the context of migration. It also shows how ethnic differences present a barrier to a few leisure activities that are associated with other ethnicities, even if these "ethnic specific" activities represent an overall exception in their leisure. An additional aspect highlighted and exemplified through the case of comedy series and comedy content is how some leisure activities that might look the same (e.g., statistically), such as the watching of television series, can contain different identifications for individuals.

In Chap. 6, the concluding remarks reflect on the importance of in-depth research of leisure as an essential part of lifestyle that is a result of socioeconomic conditions, social environment, and individual choices. As such, it considers how understanding leisure might involve finding a middle ground between vertical and subject-oriented paradigms, as leisure is a topic that can help one to understand precisely how this middle ground is found in lived reality by individuals themselves. Furthermore, the chapter reflects on the importance that leisure has for identity construction and how many of the most important identities for the individual are drawn subjectively from leisure activities or experiences, with some identities being particular to the individual and others being shared with others collectively. This chapter readdresses the question of whether leisure can help as a perspective with which to avoid overemphasizing other types of "primordial" identities and their roles in everyday life.

Throughout the book, digressions take the reader nearer to Mannheim and the women of this study, digressions that make their lives and lifestyles more palpable through concrete examples. This book would not have been possible without these women and all the people in this wonderful city who received me as one of their own. Various women and men took the time (from their precious leisure time) to talk to me and generously offer insights into their lives and life in the city. I hope I have been able to shed some light on their decision-making processes and represent them in a manner with which they can identify.

The research and book also profited greatly from the support of Dr. Ulrich Oberdiek, who encouraged me to pursue my own ideas and enriched me with his input, and of Professor Dr. Gregor Dobler, who shared with me his thoughts and knowledge on the subject. Mirjam Lücking helped me with her methodological expertise, and Dripta Nag assisted with comments on my writing. Finally, and not least, I wish to thank two women specifically without whom this project would not have been possible: Evis Rosales and Larissa Domkem, who offered me their constant support throughout this endeavor. Thank you.

CONTENTS

LIST OF FIGURES

CHAPTER 1

Introduction

When I started writing this work in September 2015, one only needed to turn on the TV or the radio while the national or international news was on to hear about the European migrant crisis. Europe, and especially Germany, suddenly seemed to be inundated by refugees fleeing from the Middle East and other conflict regions around the world. On one side were the many reports of the thousands of welcoming and helping hands trying to aid the refugees in this difficult time; on the other were the reports of right-wing radicalism and violent attacks on refugee residences and on individuals with migrant backgrounds. This subject occupied the interest of the public, and it was common to hear voices both condemning the violent attacks and expressing concern about whether successful integration of so many "culturally different" people was possible. During the regional parliamentary elections in the spring of 2016, the newly founded, right-wing Alternative for Germany party obtained a high percentage of the vote, showing that the "migrant issue" was present in the political discourse and on people's minds.

Cultural difference and visions of the "other" have been present long before such events, however. For example, some years earlier, when I began my research project and arrived at the field research site, I had conversations with people about the topic of leisure among diverse people, and everyone reacted the same way. They would say things like: "Well, I'm sure there are a lot of differences," or "Oh, I imagine there are huge differences." The notion that the lifestyles and leisure of individuals with

© The Author(s) 2017
V.L. Sandoval, *The Meaning of Leisure*, Leisure Studies
in a Global Era, DOI 10.1007/978-3-319-59752-2_1

different backgrounds vary, even if they live in the same space, seems to be strongly rooted in public opinion. It seems to be an unquestioned part of common knowledge that the leisure of migrants is different from that of the natives. This book closely considers whether that leisure *actually* does differ and, if it does, *how exactly* does it differ, a topic that has been notably absent from lifestyle and leisure studies within the German ethnographic context.

The research, which concerned culturally diverse women in a German city, is framed in a context of discussion about topics such as migration, integration, and cultural difference. But precisely *because* of these situational characteristics, the aim of the work is to shed light on the everyday life and subjective reality of these women who share a common locality. Even if this book does not focus on the people who are typically direct targets of the media and political and social debates already mentioned, its outcomes can contribute to furthering our knowledge of the lifestyle and leisure of different people in practice beyond stereotypical assumptions.

Furthermore, considering lifestyle as an umbrella concept that contains leisure, as I do in this work, is relevant because these are concepts that connect structural and individual processual aspects, and taking them into account contributes to a better analysis of the similarities and differences among population groups. I will make use of a concept of lifestyle and leisure that is focused on the individual and not as a generalization of lifestyles or "leisure styles." Moreover, I understand leisure from the subjective perspective of the group studied and in differentiation from the concept of work but as closely related to "free time" as a rest period connected to paid work and considered "free" because the individual exercises control over time. As such, leisure is contained in free time, even if the boundaries of both are fluid, as will be seen in the empirical findings. Although many studies on lifestyle remain fixated on the structural aspects of lifestyle and leisure and, to a large extent, on socioeconomic factors that determine them, it is still important to examine how individuals constitute their own lives in their day-to-day actions, taking into account aspects as important as the specific local context in which they are involved. Seeing how leisure is understood and executed in practice by a group of diverse people, in this case women in Mannheim, can help to increase knowledge of diverse populations and their ways of living in other cities as well.

Large cities are generally perfect settings for anthropological research because of the heterogeneity of their populations (s. Miller 2010).

So, Mannheim, even though it is not that large in terms of area and population, provides a fertile ground for such research because of the particular characteristics of the city and the historical processes that have contributed to it becoming a multicultural city. Furthermore, considering a number of women who constitute a relatively homogenous group, in terms of their level of education, household and family composition, age, income, and the like, not only makes the field of study manageable but brings to light how individual differences can express themselves in practice. Additionally, the selection of women of different cultural and ethnic backgrounds mirrors the actual lived world of a city in which high percentages of the population are migrants; it also helps to determine whether such a background is relevant to leisure when other structural characteristics are similar. However, beyond those common characteristics, no specific group markers (such as ethnic or national divisions) were chosen in order to avoid overestimating the importance of culture in lifestyle issues, as Dressler et al. (1996, p. 345) and others have stressed. The focus is therefore not explicitly on the expression of the cultural but on the leisure of individuals who share certain characteristics and a common space. The book seeks to find a middle ground between lifestyle and leisure studies that have placed too much importance on socioeconomic markers and the definition of types and those, mostly anthropological, studies that have focused on the lives of particular ethnic, national, or religious groups. One advantage of the ethnographic method is that it enables the examination of the consequences of socioeconomic markers in practice and highlights how individuals handle and negotiate these markers, including the relation of these markers to individuals' belonging and its meaning in different situations.

In this context, it is important to consider and question the classification of people as migrants or natives and the many different ways in which populations can be classified. For example, Keim (1995, p. 156), in an ethnographic study of Mannheim, considered three population groups: the native population, the German immigrant, and the foreigner. For the purposes of this work, the issue of migrant or native is addressed from the subjective point of view of the participants and is contextualized with the different situations in their lives. Thus, certain identities have gained importance situationally.

The research was designed to tackle this question—How do full-time employed women in Mannheim understand leisure as a concept and constitute their leisure in practice?[1]—and these underlying questions: How does their leisure concept relate do their leisure in practice?; Which channels do they choose for leisure purposes?; How are they influenced by their local context in their leisure?; What are the overall similarities and differences among the women?; Does a migrant background contribute to the differences and, if it does, in which specific situations in leisure does a migrant background exercise an influence?; and, finally: Can any conclusions regarding their lifestyles and identity be drawn from taking a look at their leisure?

Before discussing this study in particular, it is important to highlight the existing literature and studies that deal with similar or adjacent topics. Many academic efforts have already addressed issues relevant for this work, such as lifestyles and leisure and their relation to a myriad of aspects such as ethnicity, migration and gender.

1.1   State of the Art

1.1.1   Approaches to Lifestyle

Studies of lifestyle in Germany have been greatly influenced by the market research of the Sinus Institute. The institute divided the population of Germany in different milieus, which remain the same but are adjusted every year to changes in the population (SINUS 2015). Under this model, people are identified by sociodemographic aspects (age, income, education level, etc.) as well as by values regarding work, leisure, consumption, and so on (ibid.). The population segments are divided accordingly into 10 different milieus. In the year 2015, it was said that the largest milieu was the "hedonistic" one (members of the lower middle class living in the now and having fun, with leisure being the most important part of their lives) and the "*bürgerliche Mitte*," the mainstreamers, those who seek job security, adapt to their conditions, and are fearful of losing status (ibid.).

This classification has also been done for the city of Mannheim. Interestingly, the city has a much higher percentage of population belonging to the hedonistic milieu when compared with the national statistics (the percentages of the hedonistic milieu are even higher for the districts with a larger presence of migrant population) (s. Stadt Mannheim 2011, 2014, p. 15). Even if some knowledge can be gained from the SINUS population classification, such as general tendencies along socioeconomic lines, the results are often taken for granted and considered to be true mirrors of the population. Their influence on policy can be seen, for example, in the official website of the city of Mannheim where the SINUS milieus are presented under the category "Facts and Data" concerning the population:

> Data about the structure of milieus in a city is complementary to the sociodemographic characteristics of the city's population. Together they are the basis for the planning of communal action. (Stadt Mannheim 2016)

The concept of milieu has also been used to predict voters' behavior. Mochmann and El-menouar (2005) found an overlap between lifestyles and party preferences; in their case, individuals with "culture oriented lifestyles" were most likely Green Party voters. For them, the milieu was a consequence of people with similar lifestyles organizing and sharing memberships within the same groups.

In a similar study, Hamm (2003) combined qualitative and quantitative methods and different theoretical approaches, including the SINUS milieus, to segment the market of German youths (14- to 28-year-olds) based on their lifestyles. He evaluated aspects such as music taste and brand preferences and proposed a classification of 10 different groups, some of which mirror the SINUS milieus (e.g., hedonist, open-minded, job-oriented). However, Hamm's groups often plainly mirrored mere differences along age or gender lines. For example, the job-oriented group was mostly composed of individuals in their late 20s. The same point applies to the earlier qualitative study of Lüdkte (1989), who interviewed 100 adults in Germany about their lifestyles. He concluded that there were 12 different styles (traditionalistic, innovative, etc.), which also coincided with the structural characteristics of the respondents. Lüdkte argued that household structure, gender, age, and economic capital all influenced lifestyle in the same proportion.

However, taking for granted the existence of SINUS milieus or other strict classifications is problematic, as the primary goal of the studies is to divide the market into segments for marketing and sales strategies (s. SINUS 2015, p. 1). Otte and Rössel (2011, p. 9) complained that since the 1980s, the German research on lifestyle was based mainly on cluster analysis and classification because of the influence of the SINUS research. Even the SINUS Institute has recognized that "sociodemographic twins" can have different lifestyles and values (SINUS 2011). Zifonun (2010, p. 323), who published ethnographic work on a neighborhood in Mannheim, vehemently argued that there is no empirical evidence supporting the existence of the SINUS milieus as presented for Mannheim. The problem with such studies is that they do not drill further into people's motivations and interpretations of the way they live. Additionally, classifications that have included migrant respondents have often failed to compare migrant groups with native groups that are socioeconomically and educationally similar.[2] In this context, Warneken (2015, p. 255) suggested it is necessary, for example, to study the situation of migrants and native groups from low social classes together.

In lifestyle studies, a key aspect addressed has been participation rates. Gerhards (2008) compared statistical data of the 27 European Union countries to determine the intensity of consumption of "high culture" and found that individuals such as managers, professionals, and business owners had the highest "high culture" consumption. He also found that countries where this type of culture is more institutionalized and incorporated (infrastructure), such as Denmark and the Netherlands, presented the highest participation rates overall. However, just as in the studies mentioned earlier, Gerhards (2008) equated "high culture" to quality and considered people who consumed it as having "legitimate taste." Less focused on participation and more so on meaning, Brunso et al. (2004, pp. 195–203) analyzed statistical data from Germany and Spain to determine food-related lifestyles (values and behaviors related to food) and found that each country presented different food-related values. For example, in Spain the dimension of taste was found to be related to tradition, while in Germany it was related to pleasure. Additionally, convenience (saving time) was important in Germany while in Spain the traditional ways of cooking were more important. However, in terms of lifestyle, within each country, these values were expressed in the same way (pp. 201–202).

Other approaches have taken a national view on lifestyle and its components, such as consumption and values. For example, Becher (1990) took a historical view of the development of a characteristic "German" lifestyle, which presents some common factors among all social classes, such as diet, housing, and leisure activities, including do-it-yourself hobbies. For Becher (1990), this "dominant" lifestyle type is the result of historical processes since the eighteenth century. Similarly, Lamont (1992) found in her study of the French and U.S. American upper-middle classes that there were cultural differences that affected values and symbolism and, in turn, affected lifestyles as well. In Lamont's (1992, p. 189) study, although lifestyle for the French was formed primarily keeping status in mind, for the U.S. Americans, lifestyle was based on material possessions. Even though on a second level material possessions could also have had relevance for status in this case, what the study showed was a different approach to lifestyle construction. The issue of French lifestyle in connection with status is nothing new; in his renowned study, Pierre Bourdieu (1984, p. 49) concluded, based on his ethnographic data, that taste (not only in relation to material possessions) is inseparable from status and that choices made based on taste are merely reflections of social status and people's need to distinguish themselves from other classes.

More recent studies of lifestyles have also focused on the performative aspect of lifestyle and taste. Liu (2008) analyzed thousands of MySpace profiles and argued for the existence of virtual taste neighborhoods. Interestingly, though, profiles of friends within common neighborhoods were not as similar as one would expect. Liu (2008, p. 271) argued that there is a need to perform uniqueness and that individuals fashion their cultural interests into taste performances. This implies that individuals have an agency beyond their own sociodemographic characteristics: they can choose to perform certain tastes and have certain lifestyles. This type of social engagement with issues of authenticity and individuality is also seen in the work of authors dealing with the issue of "hipness" and "hipsters," for example. The ethnographic work of Michael (2015) showed that individuals are concerned with individuality and authenticity by not submitting themselves to any set style while at the same time being open and accepting of other people's tastes. Complying with the ideal of individuality was what was considered being "hip" by the collective and consequently those individuals who did comply enjoyed high social prestige. This was contrary to being a "hipster" because, despite their claim of authenticity, "hipsters" were not perceived to be unique (Michael 2015). Maly and Varis (2015) dealt with online data (discourses and markers) and literature on hipsters in an attempt to understand "hipster culture." They showed how authenticity is evaluated not only in terms of fashion and style and how the label "hipster" is contested but by how the identity of "true hipster" is constituted in ideological terms: "true" hipsters must abide by the "be yourself" rule. Additionally, self-identified "true hipsters" need to deal with the market appropriating subcultural styles and massifying them, thus driving individuals and groups to more complex discourses on authenticity and more complex processes of identity discovery. As a consequence, "true hipsters" discursively distance themselves from the mainstream.[3] Hipsters in this case are seen as an example of a translocal micropopulation in times of "superdiversity," which goes beyond "traditional" identities, such as ethnic ones (Maly and Varis 2015, pp. 13–14). Such overriding identities, which are closely intermingled with performance of the self and which constitute individuals finding a balance between individuality and group belonging, have also been shown among break dancers, for example (s. Langnes and Kari 2016). In the case of break dancers, the lifestyle surrounding the activity of "breaking" was also an expression of rebellion against social oppression related to class, gender, or ethnicity.

Cases such as the hipster show that, despite individual efforts to constitute fully individual lifestyles, lifestyles are also influenced by a myriad of factors, some of which generate commonalities and patterns among individuals. For example, Reuter and Berli (2013) have shown how the lifestyles of museum personnel are greatly determined by their jobs. The cycle of exhibitions with varying workloads and free time results in transitional lifestyles among the personnel because they subjectively assign priority to working life. Similarly, Bourgouin (2012) has shown how African financial professionals develop a similar lifestyle due to the nature of their work, which goes beyond differences in nationality or ethnicity. These professionals develop what they consider a "cosmopolitan" lifestyle, which encompasses expensive drinks; Western-style clothes, cars, and homes; and, often, frequent traveling. Bourgouin showed, in this case study, how individuals are subjectively aware of class differences and emphasize their status by behaviorally and materially expressing their belonging. They use their lifestyle to distinguish themselves from others who are poor and/or locally bound. Bourgouin presented a case in which Bourdieu's (1984) argument of distinction has great validity on a global scale.

1.1.2   *Lifestyle and Leisure*

In establishing a direct relation among lifestyles, leisure, and identity, some authors have approached lifestyle from the perspective of a single leisure activity that holds great meaning for the individual and the way he or she forms social relationships, organizes schedules, and perceives the self as being strongly related to this one activity. Almost 50 years ago, in a study of leisure among the heads of households in the city of Annecy, one of the pioneers of the sociology of leisure, Joffre Dumazedier (1967), considered three types of leisure activities: tourist travel, movies and television, and self-improvement. He sought to understand people's motivation and expectations regarding leisure choices and discovered, among others things, the importance individuals placed on leisure activities, such as movie watching and criminal novel reading, as tools to free the mind from annoying or worrisome issues (p. 141). He highlighted differences in taste between the middle and the working class and considered the consumption of "high culture" more valuable (p. 200). Most important, through his work, Dumazedier recognized the importance of the subject of leisure as the result of the interaction between societal influence and individual reactions to it (p. 230). Yet he did not pay particular attention to the issue of identity in relation to those leisure activities.

More recently, Nadel-Klein (2010, p. 120) argued that far-reaching knowledge can be gained from analyzing specific leisure activities that are contextual to lifestyle, such as gardening, because all activities are social practices: they express and reproduce hierarchies and taste; they are not unattached from aspects such as class and race. Just like Reuter and Berli (2013) and Bourgouin (2012), Nadel-Klein argued for the influence of paid jobs on lifestyle, by stating that how much care people invest in gardening will depend on how much available time they have when they are not at work (p. 111). Particularly prominent in this context is research that deals with sports and physical activities, however. Dumont (2011) described mountain climbing as a lifestyle because individuals organize their activities around this aspect, associate certain values to it, and develop an identity as mountain climbers, individually and as part of a group. In a similar way, Alter (2011) analyzed yoga as lifestyle, as it involves daily practice, intellectual engagement, social relations, and criticism of the status quo. DeLuca (2016) argued that swimming and swim club membership is an essential part of the summer lifestyles of upper-middle-class families in the United States. Both Alter and DeLuca highlighted the importance of social class belonging and its expression and reproduction through such activities. The sole focus on one activity can, however, obscure the importance of other activities and experiences, some of which might embody conflicting values or desires of the individual. Highlighting the importance of one activity, even if it holds great subjective meaning, might over-emphasize the consistency of individual lifestyles and individual decision making.

Additionally, Klein (2009) and others have shown in their studies of physical exercise how some additional aspects might influence lifestyle. Klein found, for example, that an age threshold of 60 years plays a role in the type of physical exercise being practiced and that the higher the educational level, the higher the *consistency* of lifestyle patterns related to physical exercise (pp. 19–21). Furthermore, Klein argued that changing and entering into romantic relationships has a distorting effect on lifestyle, which nonetheless returns to previous patterns after a while (p. 22). Cortis et al. (2008, p. 34) also found, in their study of women's participation in

sports and physical recreation activities, that there is continuity in people's life stories: that women generally engaged in sports with which they
were familiar since childhood. However, they also found that continuity
is dependent on access to facilities, such as public transportation (p. 51).

These are some examples in which leisure activities have been extrapo-
lated to understand individual lifestyles, but there are plenty of studies
dealing specifically with the issue of leisure, in both a qualitative and a
quantitative manner. Taking the approach from a national perspective, for
example, Alesina et al. (2005, p. 9) compared data concerning the United
States with data from European countries and argued that people in the
latter countries work less and have more leisure time thanks to the influence of unions and labor force agreements, which increase, for example,
mandatory paid vacation time. Isengard (2005) analyzed statistical data
concerning Germany between the years 1990 and 2003 to understand
the role of social inequalities in leisure behavior. She concluded that, for
engagement with "high culture" and the subjective value of experiences,
income plays a more important role than level of education. In contrast,
income plays no role in social contacts. Additionally, factors such as time
restrictions and having children greatly influence leisure behavior. Types
have also been defined, specifically in the area of leisure. For example,
Harring (2010) divided youth in Germany into five different types, according to characteristic activities and interests. His results showed that factors
such as migrant backgrounds and gender play a role in leisure of youth.
The "peer-oriented all-rounder" group is a group that does not engage in
just a single activity and is mainly focused on sociability; this group is composed of a small percentage of individuals with migrant backgrounds and
a large percentage of females. In contrast, the highest percentage of youth
with migrant backgrounds and the highest percentage of male respondents can be found in the "organized" group, which is involved in clubs,
organizations, exercise studios, and so on (pp. 145–328). All in all, many
quantitative studies like this fall into the ethnocentric trap of hierarchiza-
tion of lifestyles and leisure behaviors measured by what the researcher or
the society consider high culture.

One of the few studies that deal with the *meaning* of leisure is that of
Fastenmeier et al. (2003), who assessed what people subjectively perceive
leisure to be. They questioned 960 households in Germany and found that,
subjectively, freedom of choice is not as important as the "fun factor" and
that leisure was a complicated concept that permitted "contradictions,"
such as being spontaneous or planned, social or individual. Furthermore,

the questionnaire found that leisure is associated to certain material aspects, such as infrastructure (means of transportation). However, the authors did not find any significant differences stemming from sociodemographic factors (p. 21). On the contrary, from the point of view of urban planning, for example, Zängler and Karg (2003) studied hundreds of households to understand leisure mobility: "Where and when do people go and which paths do they take?" They found that leisure mobility is almost always planned and that being spontaneous has consequences for the planning of transportation means and methods (p. 61). Whillans (2014) investigated the leisure of singles and found there to be similar patterns. She found that, during the week, leisure activities were mostly done alone or in small social circles while the weekends were the primary times of socializing (pp. 193–198). In addition to the argument of Zängler and Karg (2003) that leisure mobility is almost always planned, Whillans showed that one reason behind leisure planning is the social value (perception) of being busy and being with company, so planning can be a form of coping with the uncertainty of other people's time availability.

But the most recent research studies on leisure have dealt with the use of media and technology. For example, Gajjala and Tetteh (2014) researched online leisure activities in Kenya and found that leisure can be achieved through and in technology and that participation in social media must not be considered to be "wasting time" but that it can be a form of leisure that is evidence of empowerment and global participation. Online engagement in discourses about current political situations can be both leisure and proof of individuals making their voices heard in the digital world (p. 41). Jenner (2015) also saw empowerment of individuals thanks to the rapid expansion of the video-on-demand industry, which makes self-scheduling and deliberate watching possible. New forms of leisure, such as TV series binge-watching are on the rise (pp. 4–5).

1.1.3   Leisure and Gender

Furthermore, as this research focuses on women, it is important to highlight existing approaches to leisure and gender issues. Huda and Akhtar (2006) studied the leisure behavior of working women in Bangladesh and found there to be a prevalence of gender-biased leisure conceptions. In this study, women were found to be engaged mostly in home leisure activities and seldom participated in recreation outside their home. Furthermore, it highlighted the role of infrastructure and institutionalized leisure because many preferences, such as art exhibitions and theater visits, could not be translated into practice (pp. 15–16). The study also found that women working in the private sector (mostly Western transnationals) presented less "traditional" lifestyles (mixed-gender meetings, traveling, etc.) and leisure activities than those of their public sector counterparts (p. 20), thus showing that leisure behavior is not detached from cultural conceptions and also that individuals can change or choose to change in the face of global influences.

In an interesting study, Katz-Gerro and Meier Jaeger (2015) looked at the leisure behavior of siblings in an attempt to understand whether the differences between men and women were merely differences that occurred from family to family. The study's results showed that women were more likely to participate in cultural activities (and men in sports) and that socioeconomic factors or household structure had little influence on differences between brothers and sisters. As they found no evidence of gender-specific parental socialization, the authors concluded that gender differences in leisure must originate outside the family. Sayer (2015), when looking at data from chore work in the United States, found that gender disparities concerning amounts of household labor were not exclusive to married women or women with children. Single women living alone also presented much higher levels of chore activities than their male counterparts did, which is why Sayer (2015) argued that chore activities (and consequently reduced leisure time) had less to do with directly providing services for a specific person but more with overall gendered views on womanhood. Carmichael et al. (2015) analyzed data on full-time employed women (50 years of age and older) in the United Kingdom and their participation in physical activity. Their results showed that time shortages were the largest constraint to participation. Yet they also argued that participation is influenced by a myriad of psychological, social, historical, environmental, and economic factors—for example, if someone had a bad experience with a sport at school or was embarrassed while practicing it in the past (pp. 55–57).

Kovac and Trussell (2015, p. 206) investigated women's nightclubbing as leisure and showed how one activity can be liberating by allowing individuals to present identities that vary from that of their everyday lives but at the same time perpetuate gender ideals and heteronormativity, as seen in the policing of dress codes and behavior at nightclubs. Their study showed how alcohol is an important facilitator of the leisure experience even when it can become a major risk factor for women if they are not vigilant in defending themselves from possible male harassment and/or violence. The study also showed gender disparities in leisure experiences due to women having to enforce their own protective measures, such as buddy systems and cautionary tales, to avoid danger and violence (p. 205). Also showing gender disparities, Herridge et al. (2003) explored the relationship between heterosexual women's leisure and their romantic relationships. They argued that romantic relationships can facilitate some forms of leisure but can be a constraint on women's "noncouple" leisure because women often tend to accommodate their partners' needs and wishes before their own. Romantic relationships can therefore have a negative effect on friends' and family leisure. Barnett (2005), who studied the leisure of students in the United States, argued that, while for male students leisure activities had to be challenging in order to avoid boredom and distress, activities for females students had to be foreseeable and planned, for the same reasons. So, gender can influence expectations from leisure activities (pp. 147–148). Nonetheless, Qian et al. (2014) argued that, overall, women were more able than men to free themselves from stress during leisure, showing a quicker psychological recovery. They stated that gender affects how stress is managed, while the meaning of gender decreases in low-stress situations.

Other authors have also considered the issue of gender but in the context of how different genders are affected by weather conditions in the context of leisure. Buchowski et al. (2009) studied women from different ethnic backgrounds and found common seasonal differences in the amounts of physical activity women engaged in during the year, with winter in particular reducing the amount of physical activity during the weekends (p. 258). Indeed, beyond gender issues, weather has been an aspect studied in the context of leisure. For example, Spinney and Millward (2011) argued that atmospheric conditions and patterns of leisure activity engagement go hand in hand. They calculated that the odds of participating in outdoor sports increased by 5% with each degree of temperature increase (based on climate in the southeastern United States) while at the same time decreasing for indoor sports (pp. 138–139). Palutikof et al. (2004) tried to grasp how leisure behavior would change with changing climatic conditions by looking at how people behave when exposed to unusually warm weather. They found changing patterns in outdoor behavior, including means of transportation and nutritional habits. Moreover, their results showed that warm weather can contribute to local holiday plans (p. 56). However, they also argued that many lifestyle changes were related to cultural trends fostered by the media and government—for example, eating more fruit and vegetables and riding bicycles (p. 57). Schmiedeberg and Schröder (2014, p. 387) highlighted that weather conditions can have an overall effect on the response behavior of individuals during interviews and consequently can affect the findings of any given investigation, which is an interesting fact to keep in mind when addressing issues of lifestyle and leisure.

Hancock and Hancock (2014), in contrast, not only saw gender differences but also took into account aspects of the body, such as health, heart rate, and body temperature, to understand how time and life spans are perceived. Interestingly, they found that, with increasing age, individuals also perceive a longer life span left and that women independent of their age perceived to have longer life spans than men. Additionally, individuals who perceive their health to be good perceive time differently. This type of analysis is relevant because subjective long-term perception of time and the elements that constitute that perception influence not only the speed/ pace of living and lifestyle but also the plans individuals might make for the future.

1.1.4   Leisure and Ethnicity

Furthermore, some studies, especially in the US-American academic tradition, have investigated the relationships between race and ethnicity and lifestyles or leisure. An important role in these studies is the issue of restrictions and participation rates. Shinew et al. (2004) aimed to determine whether African Americans had a disadvantaged position regarding access and enjoyment of leisure, their question being whether leisure was racially neutral. Interestingly, their observations led them to conclude that African Americans experience fewer constraints, subjectively, because they have different expectations and are more accustomed to negotiating constraints, something that is critical for overall leisure satisfaction. In a similar manner, Barnett (2005) examined the relationship between ethnicity and leisure experiences. Although she pointed out that there are individual differences and other aspects to consider, such as gender, which can influence the experience (p. 151), she also pointed to the ethnic differences in expectations. She claims that European American students are the only ones distressed by unplanned free time, while their Hispanic and Asian and African American counterparts experience no negative emotional response in this context (pp. 148–150). Spiers and Walker (2009) surveyed 500 people in Canada, seeking to compare Chinese Canadians and British Canadians and measure the effects of ethnicity on leisure satisfaction. They found differences with regard to how happiness is perceived. Although for British Canadians, happiness was associated with personal achievement, for Chinese Canadians, it was associated with the success of personal relationships, the latter presenting an overall lower level of leisure satisfaction. So, a conclusion of the Spiers and Walker study was that leisure satisfaction is directly linked to the concept of happiness and how different ethnicities or cultures might define it (pp. 94–97).

The question of lifestyle, leisure, and ethnicity also has been particularly prominent in studies of sports and physical exercise. Saint and Krueger (2011) investigated the variables of education and racial-ethnic differences with regard to participation in exercise. Their results showed that education plays a role in overall participation but that racial-ethnic differences play a role in which exercise the individual is participating. For example, education in the white population is positively associated with fitness and facility-based sports yet negatively associated with team sports. The authors claimed that racial-ethnic differences must not necessarily decrease with increasing education levels (pp. 205–208). Indeed, other authors have found that education level and cultural capital have a greater influence on biographical consistency in the practice of physical activity, because it concerns discipline and perseverance, while age, ethnicity, and other factors are relevant for the specific type of activity (Klein 2009, pp. 19–21). In a similar manner, Lee and Im (2010, p. 815) pointed out that US statistics show less physical activity for women than men overall and that women of ethnic minorities exercise less than white women. In their study of white, Hispanic, African American, and Asian American women and their participation in physical activity, they concluded that socioeconomic and health factors had no relevance in relation to the understanding of female gender roles but that cultural backgrounds did (pp. 818–822). Lee and Im argued, for example, that Hispanic patriarchal norms discourage women from physical activity (p. 815). Additionally, Sikes and Jarvie (2014, p. 509) argued that, in Kenya, women face important negative consequences if they continue to practice running after marriage, which shows the intersection of gender issues and social views on life stages. However, the success (along with the economic gains) of women athletes has contributed to changes in perceptions of female athletes and gender dynamics in general (p. 516).

1.1.5 *Leisure and Migration*

Beyond issues of ethnicity, few studies have dealt with the issue of migrants and their leisure specifically. All in all, the intersection between migration and leisure studies, especially those of adults, has not attracted too much scholarly attention. When they have intersected, it has been exclusively from the functional perspective of leisure as a means for integration and adaptation of migrants (s. Mata-Codesal et al. 2015, p. 1). It has been shown how organized leisure can contribute to processes of integration. Leisure activities, such as sports and physical exercise, have been some of the major examples in the pursuit of integration by migrants. For example, migrant women in Australia interviewed by Cortis et al. (2008, pp. 26–70) learned to incorporate these activities into their lifestyles as part of leisure and also used these types of activities to make friends in a new environment, even though often they have to overcome cultural barriers (from both the receiving society and their own cultural background [gender roles]) or financial barriers. Taylor (2001, pp. 535–536) conducted a qualitative study of culturally diverse women's leisure in Australia and argued that some activities can serve to assimilate migrants into dominant leisure practices while others can help migrants express their other cultural belongings. Taylor found that migrant women placed a lot of value on leisure activities within their small communities but that, in general, a myriad of aspects intersected to shape their leisure opportunities, including social class, age, cultural background, and ethnicity (p. 548). Furthermore, Walseth (2015, p. 19) has shown how Muslim organizations that offer different leisure activities, including sports, to their youth members contributed to create a mixed "Norwegian Muslim" identity and helped prevent marginalization. Kim et al. (2015a) suggested, however, that not all leisure activities are related to integration in the same manner. In their study of Korean migrants in the United States, they found that, although cultural and volunteer activities contribute to integration or even acculturation, physical activity does not because, in this case, physical activity was organized among ethnically homogenous groups as an intragroup activity. Contrarily, in another study on Canadian and US migrants in South Korea, physical leisure activities were found to contribute to the development of social relations across different ethnic groups as well as the adoption of native practices, such as Taekwondo and hot yoga (Kim et al., 2015b). However, participants of this latter study were invariably high-skilled workers with high levels of education, factors that might have contributed to different results.

Regarding the question of lifestyle and leisure of different ethnicities and migrants in German society specifically, there is still a need to assess how strongly their lifestyles really differ from one another's and which mechanisms are responsible for the differences (Jacob and Kalter 2011, p. 224).

Studies such as those summarized here have addressed this issue only tangentially. Migration can be a process that allows the individual to form new lifestyles that were previously not wanted or not possible. However, migrants must cope not only with social pressures from their direct environment but also with social judgement in their countries of origin (s. Tazanu 2012, pp. 107–126). In the case of the few studies concerning Mannheim that exist, for example, Keim (1995) argued the importance of the neighborhood setting for migrants' lifestyles and for differences along population segment lines with the use of spaces. For example, in the area of Filsbach in Mannheim, leisure venues were used by students, by migrants, or by locals (p. 45). However, Keim pointed out that social relations among migrants are not composed only along ethnic or national lines, as other aspects, such as political views, also play a role (p. 148). She argued, however, for a public perception of "noticeable" and "unnoticeable migrants," the latter being integrated into the "German way of life" (p. 46). Zifonun (2010), in the study of another of Mannheim's neighborhoods, Hochstätt, found that lifestyles and perception of the social environment can be very different, depending on the individual and his or her social situation. For example, some individuals choose not to move because they would lose their local status, which, in the "wider world," would be lower (pp. 317–318). All in all, Zifonun argued that many factors affect lifestyle and worldviews, including ethnicity, social position, and length of stay in Germany, giving rise to different interest groups (p. 319). The inequalities between natives and migrants are more complex than this binary classification would suggest. Aspects such as gender, age, and nationality are indeed relevant for the life situation: "[P]rivileges or discriminations through one criteria can be compensated through another" (Noll and Habich 1990, p. 186).

By taking a look at the different approaches, it is possible to recognize certain tendencies. There is the "vertical paradigm," in which different lifestyles depend on the social situation of the individuals, and the "subject-oriented paradigm," in which lifestyles depend on individual choices (Isengard 2005, pp. 255–256). Within the former can be found the "primordialist perspective," which focuses exclusively on ethnicity, national feelings, or religion (Appadurai 1996, p. 144). Leisure in particular has been referred to as the "structure vs. the subjective perspective" on leisure (Newman et al. 2014, pp. 558–560). Similar tendencies can be noticed among leisure studies: there are some studies supporting the "marginality thesis," which proposes that ethnic groups are restricted in their leisure choices, and others supporting the "ethnicity thesis," which proposes that cultural traditions push ethnic groups to participate in certain activities (Taylor 2001, pp. 537–538). Newman et al. (2014), who analyzed hundreds of research articles dealing with leisure and well-being, found five perspectives from which leisure is mainly being analyzed: detachment-recovery (distraction, cognitive recovery); autonomy (freedom of choice); mastery (learning things); meaning (value and purpose); and affiliation (social activities).

However, it is important to go beyond these perspectives to understand inter-group variance (Taylor 2001, pp. 537–538) and to avoid emphasizing one aspect over others because of the researchers' theoretical preferences (Dressler et al. 1996, p. 345). For example, it is important to avoid overemphasizing differences between ethnically diverse people, as Hudson et al. (2013, p. 156) argue, or overestimating the role of culture within lifestyles, as Dressler et al. (1996, p. 345) point out. Yet differences such as ethnic ones are not always relevant. The analysis needs to consider under which conditions differences are relevant and why, because such differences are social constructs being created and reproduced (Müller and Zifonun 2010, p. 14).

Within this framework, this research sought to understand the leisure of individuals whose socioeconomic status and local context are similar but who have different ethnic, cultural, and individual biographical backgrounds. The aim was to allowing for an examination of people's everyday lives beyond the common denominators found in classifications. The empirical data will show what the link between migration background and ethnicity has to do with phenotypical characteristics and their conjunction and subjective association with cultural traits. This is done, on one hand, by recognizing the importance of sociodemographic factors, not only because of their "objective" existence but also because individuals are aware of structural differences and social positions and their respective belongings (s. Lamont and Aksartova 2010, p. 273), and, on the other, by considering both individual agency and the role the context in which individuals live plays in their formation of leisure and, consequently, their lifestyle. This kind of analysis goes beyond polarizing approaches and without engaging in judgments of value of one leisure activity over another, which is a problem often found in leisure studies (s. Mannell 2014, pp. 3–7).

1.2   THE METHODS

The empirical data used in this book stem from ethnographic fieldwork conducted in the city of Mannheim between August 2014 and August 2015. The ethnographic method is important because it can reveal, in the context of leisure and lifestyle, cultural aspects that quantitative data cannot uncover, such as individual decision-making processes and the way in which local conditions influence those processes. It also can place into context narratives *and* observed behavior. Ethnography is more detail and meaning oriented than mere statistical surveys (Nadel-Klein 2010, p. 107), and fieldwork is a flexible and reflective process that entails collecting and analyzing data, going back to the field and reassessing the data, and analyzing it again in light of new experiences, in order to refine the interpretation (Agar 1980, p. 9). Ethnographic fieldwork requires spending time with and having a deep involvement in the everyday life and lived world of the subjects, which is not always logistically and organizationally simple for the researcher (Gagné 2013, p. 252). Despite its "messiness," in terms of flexible structure and unpredictability, fieldwork can situate complicities, complexities, and ambiguities that otherwise could remain hidden (Breglia 2009, p. 140). It can contribute to the construction of social reality and can even improve it by describing in its results social relations from a different perspective, thus creating a new sense of the social environment (Rapport 2010, p. 79).[4] In a wider context, ethnography can make it possible to present different lifestyles to others beyond stereotypical representations (Agar 1980, p. 27).

Mannheim was a good site for the question of leisure of women with diverse backgrounds for different reasons. Hannerz (1980, p. 312) pointed out that one of the methodological problems of a city is its size and dimensions. Mannheim is a middle-range city, which means a city with less than half a million and more than 100.000 inhabitants, thus it offers a relatively controlled site for fieldwork. At the same time, it is a diverse city in terms of the composition of its population, which makes it possible to find enough informants with diverse backgrounds. Additionally, as a researcher, I was familiar with the city, having spent several years there, and I was acquainted with sites and contacts as well as the city's general dynamics. It also can be said that the selection of Mannheim as a research site was a "judgment sampling" (Bernard 2006, p. 190), in terms of researchers using their judgment to select a site that reflects their interests. This way of selecting the field site can be useful because it enables researchers to draw from their own knowledge and self-narratives (Collins and Gallinat 2010, p. 15);

at the same time, however, it is important to reflect on the ethnographers' positions and how these might influence the findings in general.

The informants were found through various channels. One useful way of finding informants and interview partners is chain referral. Chain referral methods are known to be useful when the population is hard to locate (e.g., when people are scattered over a large area or when potential informants are members of an elite group and do not have a personal interest in the research) (Bernard 2006, p. 192). Within this method, different "seeds," or initial persons, were used, including seeds in respondent-driven sampling (RDS), where key informants acted as seeds to find new people to interview (s. pp. 193–194). Using different seeds was essential to avoid being limited to one extended social network and to avoid making the study merely a study on friendship, for example. Some key informants were found through personal social networks that existed prior to the research. However, in general, finding interview partners with a migrant background was not an easy task, because they were less present in the social networks of the seeds.

Additionally, specialized informants—, those who have particular competence in a given topic (p. 196)—were contacted and either interviewed or engaged in informal conversations regarding themes, such as leisure in the city of Mannheim and the dynamics of its population, including women and the population with migrant backgrounds. Such specialized informants were, for example, city officials in the area of leisure, members of the migration council, and actors relevant to the city's nightlife and social media networks. These type of informants and their knowledge proved particularly important for understanding the context in which leisure is planned and executed from different sources, including how women and migrants are taken into consideration in this context. They also helped the researcher to gain knowledge about hot spots and relevant events in the city and surroundings for participant observation.

The fieldwork was composed of a multiplicity of methods, which is important because people's movements in everyday life are complex, and, at times, the researcher might not have access to all of the areas constitutive of their lifestyle experiences (Brosius 2010, p. 36). One method used was the semistructured interview conducted mostly in German with the informants mentioned previously. Apart from three occasions, when, due to participants' time constraints, the interviews were conducted via phone or Skype, all interviews were conducted face to face in locations chosen by the interviewees. Participants chose different coffee shops in the city center and chose to meet during the week after work hours. Allowing them to choose the place themselves was a good way to avoid further hindrances regarding time constraints and long travel routes. It also fostered a positive environment during the interviews because participants felt comfortable in the chosen space. No compensation was offered for their participation in the interviews; however, some interviewees showed an interest in the research findings and were told they would receive a copy of the final work. Three women who met the profile requirements of interest and who were contacted refused to participate on the grounds of time constraints. In general, when people are employed full time in urban settings, their participation in interviews involves sacrificing their already limited leisure time, which is why some individuals may be unwilling to spend any time in the interview (s. Huda and Akhtar 2006, p. 4).

The interviews developed in an open and casual manner. They took around 40 to 60 minutes to complete and were recorded with the prior consent of the participants. The interviews that did not take place in person tended to be shorter. Schulze (2005, p. 90), in his assessment of milieus, developed questions that tried to understand different levels of lifestyle, such as everyday aesthetics (music, books, TV, etc.), social contacts, work, health, and values. Other authors have emphasized the importance of tackling biographical aspects and using biographic forms of description in order to understand present behavior (s. Redfield 1955, pp. 59–60; Klein 2009). The relevance of conscious choices has been addressed in other studies with questions about ideal models and motivation, such as "Why do you go to the movies?" or "What do you expect from a good film?" (Dumazedier 1967, p. 141). Therefore, lifestyle and, within it, leisure is a complex topic that must be analyzed from different angles. Agar (1980, p. 164) argued that any comprehensive study of lifestyle must include questions about biography, daily routines, and self-evaluations regarding ideals and plans. Despite the fact that participants were very open during the interviews, some topics were very difficult to address, in particular income. For this reason, the researcher drew information about income from secondary data on incomes and job descriptions (as seen in the previous section) in relation to factors such as size of the company where informants worked and questions that placed consumption in the context of percentage of income. For example, one question was: "In which leisure activity do you spend the most part of your income?" The researcher generally was able to compile this information through observations. Another topic that was extremely difficult to address directly but was brought to light in the context of participant observation was drug consumption. As such, then, this work deals only with leisure as narrated to *and/or* observed by the ethnographer.

In this context, the interviews were conducted following a flexible line of questions that allowed the informants to introduce their own topics and interests but that also aimed to assess different levels of response, such as organization, meaning, preferences, and biographical background. After the interview, informants were asked to fill in a questionnaire that provided general sociodemographic information. Semistructured interviews are useful for exploring how people understand and narrate their practices and experiences (Whillans 2014, pp. 189–190). The transcribed responses from the interviews were manually coded by assigning keywords and by classifying them thematically. The transcribed interviews were also sent to the interviewees in order to obtain their further comments and opinions a posteriori. The goal was to see whether participants would provide complementary information or would retract information after reflective reading. However, most interviewees accepted the information and made no further comments. A few inquired about the results of the research in general. In those cases, a response was promised after the research and written work had been finalized.

Eight willing interview partners also completed follow-up, structured diaries that focused on specific time intervals (s. Bolger et al. 2003) during their weekends. Participants could show the range of activities they pursued in a weekend by half hour intervals. Many possibilities were open, such as highlighting suggested activities or including new activities or marking activities taking place at the same time (e.g., cleaning and watching TV). The only reason why these diaries were structured was to save the participants' time, since they often claimed to be short on time. This is why they were asked to fill in the diary only once or twice (s. Jacelon and Imperio 2005; Bolger et al. 2003, p. 592). The benefits of using diaries is that individual reports on fixed intervals can contain more current information from participants' memories and that diaries can help examine specific details that might otherwise be omitted or forgotten during interviews or conversations (Bolger et al. 2003, p. 588) (e.g., activities such as watching a TV series on the computer and chatting on WhatsApp may take place simultaneously at a specific time of day). In cases where the information from the diaries was not clear, short follow-up questions were presented to the participants. In this sense, diaries can help researchers see changes in individual practices and investigate their causes (p. 581). For example, diaries with their follow-ups can enable researchers to understand how activities can change during times of the year, changes that people might not mention in an interview. Diaries and interviews are two tools that can positively complement each other (Agar 1980, pp. 105–106). It is important to understand that the diary method is not always suitable. However, in this study, it was possible to use the diary method due to the composition of the informants, their educational levels, and their backgrounds (s. Zimmerman and Wieder 1977, pp. 481–493).

In addition to conducting the interviews, I engaged in participant observation. In the city, a research strategy that includes participant observation is necessary in order to uncover and explain how the individuals living there accommodate and adapt to the multiple microenvironments they encounter (Low 1999). In general, participant observation is a tool that contributes to gaining an insight, from an emic perspective, to how everyday life in experienced. A strategy can help contextualize and interpret knowledge gained from the interviews as well as to gain new knowledge. Participant observation makes it possible to contextualize information beyond the group being studied. For example, it makes it possible to observe groups that are different or opposing: it is possible to learn about something by looking at its opposite (Brosius 2010, p. xiv). My experience of clerical work in an office in the city allowed me to go through commutes and schedules similar to those of my subjects. Also, by engaging in participant observation in locations suggested by the informants and interviewees, such as outdoor spaces, gyms, cafes, and bars, I was able to gain an insight into the atmosphere and dynamics of the city and to how individuals behave during leisure. I also paid special attention to large events taking place in the city, events with high participation rates, such as summer festivals, Christmas and May markets, parades, and others. In general, every aspect of life in the city had the potential of delivering new knowledge about the topic. A topic like leisure, which is intermingled with so many other aspects of life, requires a great deal of observation. The range of observations must adapt to the topic being studied (Zimmerman and Wieder 1977, p. 480).

Despite the fact that contemporary anthropology might not require a specific length of fieldwork (Faubion 2009, p. 163), the length of fieldwork in this case allowed for the acquisition of detailed information about the changes in leisure across the seasons (e.g., in the use of space, the activities pursued, or the dynamics of social relations). Consequently, the length of participant observation was well suited to the research question being addressed. In part, this type of participant observation blurred the line between the leisure of the researcher and the research topic somewhat. However, the experiences of the self as ethnographer can also be a resource that can be drawn on reflectively (Collins and Gallinat 2010). For example, including the senses and embodied knowledge (in this case, e.g., experiences of gendered bodies) in an ethnography and experiencing and describing smells and sounds is a tool by which social life in the field site can be understood (Grønseth 2010, p. 10). Therefore, the participant observation was accompanied by the taking of field notes and also by many informal conversations within and outside the target group. Field notes helped the recording of observations and experiences, while informal conversations provided new inputs on different topics. Informal conversations are also useful for uncovering possible cases where individuals answered interview questions based on social desirability. But the findings gained by these methods must always be accompanied by reflection on the fact that the ethnographer often might not have the exact same experience as the subjects he or she is seeking to understand. In some ways the researcher will always remain "only" a spectator (s. Geertz 1976, p. 224). The ethnologist's reality is not the native's reality: the final representation is only a reading on such reality (Basso and Selby 1976, p. 4). Despite the difficulties in separating personal roles, I kept the distance in part by pointing out to the persons present in which situations I was an ethnologist and in which I was a private person and by reflecting on the nature of the social relations and their connection to me during particular situations. Even then the experiences of leisure and "work" tasks can be fluid, as will be seen in following sections.

Additionally, due to my length of stay in the city of Mannheim before and after the research, it could be said that this was partly a practice of ethnography at home, in the sense that the researcher is already embedded as a "native" subject in the field site (Breglia 2009, p. 134) ("native" being one of many individuals living their everyday lives permanently in the city). Additionally, anthropology at home can be accompanied by positive aspects, such as having greater accessibility and greater control by the informants themselves (s. Collins and Gallinat 2010, p. 9). Ethnography from within can be useful because the "insider" knows the subtleties and details of lifestyles (Agar 1980, p. 22). It is indeed possible to take a look at the own cultural environment; it just depends on the perspective the researcher chooses to part from (s. Miner 1956). However, when researching one's own environment, it is essential to have doubts and to question things that seem self-evident (Kallmeyer 1995, p. 26), and it might be a difficult task to accomplish because of the constant switching of boundaries and changing positions during the day (Agar 1980, pp. 52–53). Nonetheless, it could be argued that it is not always necessary to differentiate between native and foreign anthropologist because of today's many shifting identities (Narayan 1997). In my case, being both a "native" because I was a permanent resident of the city and being a migrant allowed me to identify with *all* of the women due to a shared local space, and it allowed me to better understand the situation of those women who were migrants as well because of the commonalities in our biographical paths. Shared gender identifications, age group, and family composition also made me an "insider" to the studied group as well and facilitated the women's willingness to meet and their openness during conversations. My position as an "insider" to the group and experiences and knowledge previous to the research project also informed the interest in the topic and the research question, as I believe that, too often, lifestyles of migrants are inaccurately represented. Thus, just like any other research project, this one was not independent of personal interests and motivations, which in turn helped shape the perspective taken in the interpretation.

Finally, despite all the ethnographic methods that have been briefly described here and that were all used as tools to collect and analyze information during the fieldwork, it is important to highlight that "what is distinctively anthropological are ways of problematizing inquiry and conceptually defining its objects" (Marcus 2009). Ethnography is not only methodology; it is an attempt to analyze and describe the experiences of individuals and the symbolic resources they, as members of a society, use to interpret them. The advantage of ethnographic methods is that they help to dig into meanings (Basso and Selby 1976, p. 3) and go beyond looking at variables and hypothesis in isolation (Agar 1980, p. 76).

1.2.1   *The Group*

Besides having an understanding of the methods applied in the local context, it is equally important to have insight into the general characteristics of the women on whom this research focused. First, it is necessary to highlight that the group was selected for the purpose of having some degree of homogeneity, in order that their everyday lives and leisure could be comparable. The group was composed of 25 single women, aged between 25 to 39 years old, with no children.[5] All of them were employed full time (38–40 hours per week), holding various office jobs, generally in the service sector. They have a high level of education among them; most have either an apprenticeship degree (*Ausbildung*) or an undergraduate degree. Most of their qualifications are in areas related to clerical work (e.g., internal sales department, customer service department, finance, etc.) The women also come from similar backgrounds, with their parents having comparable levels of education. Commonly, the parents' careers were in sales. The women's jobs are sedentary, and their typical day-to-day work tasks mostly involve sitting at a desk in front of a computer; talking with clients or colleagues, either in person or via phone; evaluating documents; and utilizing different business applications. They do not manage personnel or hold managerial positions. Due to the nature of their work, none of the women is required to do shift work, so they have a relatively constant working schedule, generally between 8 am and 5 or 6 pm. In harmony with German laws concerning paid vacations, they have between 28 and 30 days of paid vacation each year. Vacations can be taken mostly at will, although longer vacations require longer advance planning and coordination with colleagues. Some companies, it was found, impose constraints on their staff that can restrict approval of vacation requests during December and the summer months in favor of employees with children of school age.

Even though there is certainly income variation among the women who were studied (e.g., due to different industry salary rates) and the income of just a few of the women was made known to the researcher, the average monthly income is around €3000 (gross), with all of them qualifying for the first tax classification (meaning deductions of around 40%). This level of income places them below the national average income level for women;[6] however, this statistically calculated average considers only full-time employees and includes top-earning positions. All in all, due to their socioeconomic characteristics, these women could be considered examples of the German middle class (the majority of the population) (s. Burkhardt et al. 2013).

With regard to their housing situation, the relatively small size of the city and its closeness to neighboring cities generally allows for short commutes to work. Typically, the women's workplaces are located anywhere from 6 to 30 kilometers (about 4–18 miles) from their homes. Almost all of the women who owned a car drive to work, while the others take public transportation (tram) and pay monthly for a transportation ticket, which costs around €70. Most women lived alone, while eight of them lived with their partner (unmarried). Three women mentioned having pets (either dogs or cats), and all of the women lived in apartments with one or two bedrooms. In a city like Mannheim, apartment rent can cost about one third of these women's net income, or a bit less if they live in the adjacent suburbs. The majority of the women live in different neighborhoods of Mannheim, while a few live in nearby cities and work and spend significant amounts of their free time in Mannheim. Mannheim plays a big role in their leisure because of their participation in gyms, or sports clubs, and their enjoyment of the city's nightlife. Many of the women are members of fitness studios, which, in Mannheim, can cost from €20 to €70 a month.

With regard to their backgrounds, of the 25 women interviewed, four are not German nationals, and three were nationalized Germans, while the rest were German nationals since birth, even though some of them had (second-generation) migrant backgrounds. Besides the formal issue of nationality, it is important to highlight that the group was composed of women who self-identify as natives of Mannheim, those who identify as inner migrants (i.e., from other regions of Germany), and others who identify as migrants or persons with migrant backgrounds. However, self-identification with Mannheim often coexisted with identification as migrant, as we consider in later chapters along with the issue of the role ethnicity plays in particular migrant backgrounds. It is important to underline, however, that even though I had contact with a myriad of individuals during the fieldwork, the large migrant minorities, such as the Turkish migrants, were not part of the study group, due to accessibility issues. During the fieldwork I had the opportunity to meet with a representative of the migration council who represents the Turkish community and to discuss with her my difficulties finding informants with Turkish migration backgrounds, among other topics. According to her, such difficulties stem from Turkish migrant women in the age group I was studying already having children and being married. However, I did meet and hold informal conversations with women who would meet the criteria but were not available to be interviewed. The content of such conversations has also been considered as part of the data. As is explained in following chapters, the particularities of cultural backgrounds are not the focus of this study, so the absence of this group in the (formal) interview process is irrelevant for the scope of the research question. Nonetheless, future research most definitely could dig deeper into leisure patterns of a much larger sample of individuals.

To sum up, this book focuses on two main aspects of leisure: subjectively, its abstract conceptualization and its execution in practice. Leisure in practice is composed of a myriad of aspects, not all of which can be addressed in research focusing on aspects that have been observed and identified as important by the group of women interviewed. However, aspects of leisure still remain unstudied. Consider the aspect of sexuality, which can be viewed as a leisure activity/experience but presents unique challenges for studying it empirically. Thus, this work aims to present an overview of some of the main channels chosen for leisure, how they are embedded in the local context, and how shared or individual conceptions of leisure play a role not only in the choosing of those channels but in the interpretation of leisure experiences a posteriori.

As such, the work follows a two-step argument for addressing the issue of diverse women and the research questions. First, the leisure of the women is considered as a whole, viewing the women collectively as individuals who share a living space and are influenced by global dynamics, such as the development of particular technologies, and other structural characteristics. Second, this work considers specifically the situations or contexts in which having a migrant background plays a role for them. This line of inquiry allows for a holistic understanding of the leisure of these women as inhabitants of Mannheim and avoids highlighting difference in the lived reality of individuals when there is none, while the second focus makes it possible to grasp under which circumstances an individuals belonging might gain importance over another and how some leisure aspects might differ because of dynamics related to the migration process in general.

Naturally, these women represent just a tiny fraction of the overall population, and I cannot claim that this is a truly representative study. What I can hope is that I have managed to dig into these women's lives in an appropriate and meaningful manner and have captured their thoughts and motives on leisure and described their way of life in such a way that they might see themselves reflected in this analysis. This analysis profits from being independent from the applied purposes that have been so prominent in previous studies. Hopefully, this research will contribute to the expansion of knowledge about other regions in the field of urban anthropology beyond the current focus on Africa and Latin America (s. Hahn 2012, p. 10) and, in particular, to the issue of urban leisure in a time of "super-diversity" (Maly and Varis 2015).

NOTES

1. The importance of full-time employment is dealt with in the empirical Chaps. 3 and 4.
2. Migrants often are presented as being much more attached to religion and traditions than natives. The question that often remains open is which migrants are taking part in the surveys and whether those migrants are comparable to the native participants.
3. The mainstream is considered the majority or the masses. For example, in the SINUS typology this group is represented by the "bürgerliche Mitte", the middle class.
4. For example as attempted in this study by describing everyday leisure patterns of diverse women beyond sole focus on their ethnicity, culture, etc.
5. "Single" is understood here as unmarried women. Some of the women were, however, involved in relationships.
6. Incomes in Germany still present significant gender disparities for the same task and job. See statistics on income disparities. Available at: https://www.destatis.de/DE/ZahlenFakten/GesamtwirtschaftUmwelt/VerdiensteArbeitskosten/VerdiensteVerdienstunterschiede/Tabellen/Bruttomonatsverdienste.html (accessed June 8, 2016).

REFERENCES

Agar, Michael. 1980. *The Professional Stranger: An Informal Introduction to Ethnography*. New York: Academic Press.

Alesina, Alberto, Edward Glaeser, and Bruce Sacerdote. 2005. Work and Leisure in the U.S. and Europe: Why So Different? In *NBER Macroeconomics Annual 2005*. Vol. 20. http://www.nber.org/chapters/c0073. Accessed November 19, 2014.

Alter, Joseph. 2011. Yoga, Modernity, and the Middle Class: Locating the Body in a World of Desire. In *A Companion to the Anthropology of India*, ed. Isabelle Clark-Decès. Hoboken: Blackwell Publishing.

Appadurai, Arjun. 1996. *Modernity at Large: Cultural Dimensions of Globalization* 1. Minneapolis: University of Minnesota Press.

Barnett, Lynn. 2005. Measuring the ABCs of Leisure Experience: Awareness, Boredom, Challenge, Distress. *Leisure Sciences* 27: 131–155.

Basso, Keith H., and Henry A. Selby. 1976. Introduction. In *Meaning in Anthropology*, ed. Keith H. Basso and Henry A. Selby, 1st ed., 1–9. Albuquerque: University of New Mexico Press.

Becher, Ursula. 1990. *Geschichte des modernen Lebensstils: Essen, Wohnen, Freizeit, Reisen*. Munich: C.H. Beck Verlag.

Bernard, Harvey R. 2006. *Research Methods in Anthropology*. 4th ed. Lanham: Altamira Press. http://www.antropocaos.com.ar/Russel-Research-Method-in-Anthropology.pdf. Accessed December 30, 2013.

Bolger, Niall, Angelina Davis, and Eshkol Rafaeli. 2003. Diary Methods: Capturing Life as It Is Lived. *Annual Review of Psychology* 54: 579–616.

Bourdieu, Pierre. 1984. *Distinction: A Social Critique of the Judgement of Taste*. 2010th edition. London; New York: Harvard University Press and Routledge. Translated by Richard Nice, with a new introduction by Tony Bennett.

Bourgouin, France. 2012. On Being Cosmopolitan: Lifestyle and Identity of African Finance Professionals in Johannesburg. *Ethnos* 77 (1): 50–71.

Breglia, Lisa. 2009. The "Work" of Ethnographic Fieldwork. In *Fieldwork Is Not What It Used to Be: Learning Anthropology's Method in a Time of Transition*, ed. James D. Faubion and George E. Marcus, 129–142. Ithaca: Cornell University Press.

Brosius, Christiane. 2010. *India's Middle Class: New Forms of Urban Leisure, Consumption and Prosperity*. London: Routledge.

Brunso, Karen, Joachim Scholderer, and Klaus Grunert. 2004. Testing Relationships Between Values and Food-Related Lifestyle: Results from Two European Countries. *Appetite* 43 (2): 195–205.

Buchowski, Maciej S., Leena C. Choi, Karen M. Majchrzak, Sari Acra, Charles E. Matthews, and Kong Y. Chen. 2009. Seasonal Changes in Amount and Patterns of Physical Activity in Women. *Journal of Physical Activity and Health* 6 (2): 252–261.

Burkhardt, Christoph, Markus Grabka, Olaf Groh-Samberg, Yvonne Lott, and Steffen Mau. 2013. Mittelschicht unter Druck?

Carmichael, Fiona, Joanne Duberley, and Isabelle Szmiging. 2015. Older Women and Their Participation in Exercise and Leisure-Time Physical Activity: The Double Edged Sword of Work. *Sport in Society* 18 (1): 42–60.

Collins, Peter, and Anselma Gallinat. 2010. The Ethnographic Self as Resource: An Introduction. In *The Ethnographic Self as Resource: Writing Memory and Experience Into Ethnography*, ed. Peter Collins and Anselma Gallinat, 1–22. New York: Berghahn Books.

Cortis, Natasha, Pooja Sawrikar, and Kristy Muir. 2008. Final Report: Participation in Sport and Recreation by Culturally and Linguistically Diverse Women.

DeLuca, Jaime R. 2016. Like a "Fish in Water": Swim Club Membership and the Construction of the Upper-Middle Class Family Habitus. *Leisure Studies* 35 (3): 259–277.

Dressler, William, Dos Santos, José Ernesto, and Mauro Campos Balieiro. 1996. Studying Diversity and Sharing in Culture: An Example of Lifestyle in Brazil. *Journal of Anthropological Research* 52 (3): 331–353.

Dumazedier, Joffre. 1967. *Toward a Society of Leisure*. New York: Collier-Macmillan.

Dumont, Guillaume. 2011. Antropologia multisituada y "Lifestyle-sports": por un examen de la escalada a traves de sus espacios. *Periferia*, 14.

Fastenmeier, Wolfgang, Herbert Gstalter, and Ulf Lehnig. 2003. Was empfinden Menschen als Freizeit?—Emotionale Bedeutung und Definition. In *Motive und Handlungsansätze im Freizeitverkehr: Mit 17 Tabellen*, 13–29. Berlin: Springer.

Faubion, James. 2009. The Ethics of Fieldwork as an Ethics of Connectivity, or the Good Anthropologist (Isn't What She Used to Be). In *Fieldwork Is Not What It Used to Be: Learning Anthropology's Method in a Time of Transition*, ed. James D. Faubion and George E. Marcus, 145–164. Ithaca: Cornell University Press.

Gagné, Natacha. 2013. *Being Māori in the City: Indigenous Everyday Life in Auckland* 41. Toronto: University of Toronto Press.

Gajjala, Radhika, and Dinah Tetteh. 2014. Relax, You've Got M-PESA: Leisure as Empowerment. *Information Technologies & International Development* 10 (3): 31–46.

Geertz, Clifford. 1976. "From the Native's Point of View": On the Nature of Anthropological Understanding. In *Meaning in Anthropology*, ed. Keith H. Basso and Henry A. Selby, 1st ed., 221–237. Albuquerque: University of New Mexico Press.

Gerhards, Jürgen. 2008. Die kulturell dominierende Klasse in Europa: Eine vergleichende Analyse der 27 Mitgliedsländer der Europäischen Union im Anschluss an die Theorie von Pierre Bourdieu. *Kölner Zeitschrift für Soziologie und Sozialpsychologie* 4: 723–748.

Grønseth, Anne S. 2010. Introduction: Mutuality and Empathy. Self and Other in the Ethnographic Encounter. In *Mutuality and Empathy: Self and Other in the Ethnographic Encounter*, vol. 5, 7–20. Wantage: S. Kingston Pub.

Hahn, Hans P. 2012. Introduction: Urban Life-Worlds in Motion. In *Urban Life-Worlds in Motion: African Perspectives*, Global Studies, ed. Hans P. Hahn and Kristin Kastner, 9–27. Bielefeld: Transcript.

Hamm, Ingo. 2003. *Eine lebensstilistische Segmentierung des Jugendmarktes: Inauguraldissertation zur Erlangung des akademischen Grades eines Doktors der Wirtschaftswissenschaften*. Heidelberg: Universität Mannheim.

Hancock, P.A., and G.M. Hancock. 2014. The Effects of Age, Sex, Body Temperature, Heart Rate, and Time of Day on the Perception of Time in Life. *Time & Society* 23 (2): 195–211.

Hannerz, Ulf. 1980. *Exploring the City: Inquiries Toward an Urban Anthropology*. New York: Columbia University Press.

Harring, Marius. 2010. *Das Potenzial der Freizeit: Soziales, kulturelles und ökonomisches Kapital im Kontext der Freizeitwelt Jugendlicher*. 1 Aufl. Wiesbaden: VS Verlag für Sozialwissenschaften.

Herridge, Kristi, Susan Shaw, and Roger C. Mannell. 2003. An Exploration of Women's Leisure within Heterosexual Romantic Relationships. *Journal of Leisure Research* 35 (3): 274–291.

Huda, Sadrul, and Afsana Akhtar. 2006. Leisure Behaviour of Working Women of Dhaka Bangladesh. *International Journal of Urban Labour & Leisure* 7 (1): 1–30.

Hudson, Simon, Gordon Walker, Bonnie Simpson, and Tom Hinch. 2013. The Influence of Ethnicity and Self-Construal on Leisure Constraints. *Leisure Sciences* 35: 145–166.

Isengard, Betinna. 2005. Freizeitverhalten als Ausdruck Sozialer Ungleichheiten oder Ergebnis Individualisierter Lebensführung? Zur Bedeutung von Einkommen und Bildung im Zeitverlauf. *Kölner Zeitschrift für Soziologie und Sozialpsychologie* 57 (2): 254–277.

Jacelon, Cynthia, and Kristal Imperio. 2005. Participant Diaries as a Source of Data in Research with Older Adults. *Qualitative Health Research* 15: 991–997.

Jacob, Konstanze, and Frank Kalter. 2011. Die Intergenerationale Transmission von Hochkulturellen Lebensstilen unter Migrationsbedingungen. In *Lebensstilforschung*, ed. Jörg Rössel and Gunnar Otte, vol. 51, 223–246. Wiesbaden: VS Verlag für Sozialwissenschaften.

Jenner, Mareike. 2015. Binge-watching: Video-on-demand, Quality TV and Mainstreaming Fandom. *International Journal of Cultural Studies* 20: 1–17.

Kallmeyer, Werner. 1995. Ethnographie städtischen Lebens. Zur Einführung in die Stadtteilbeschreibungen. In *Kommunikation in der Stadt: Teil 2. Ethnographien von Mannheimer Stadtteilen*, ed. Werner Kallmeyer, 1–41. Berlin: Walter de Gruyter.

Katz-Gerro, Tally, and Mads Meier Jaeger. 2015. Does Women's Preference for Highbrow Leisure Begin in the Family? Comparing Leisure Participation Among Brothers and Sisters. *Leisure Sciences* 37 (5): 415–430.

Keim, Inken. 1995. Die Westliche Unterstadt. In *Kommunikation in der Stadt: Teil 2. Ethnographien von Mannheimer Stadtteilen*, ed. Werner Kallmeyer, 42–188. Berlin: Walter de Gruyter.

Kim, Junhyoung, Jinmoo Heo, and Chungsup Lee. 2015a. Exploring the Relationship Between Types of Leisure Activities and Acculturation Among Korean Immigrants. *Leisure Studies* 35: 113–127. doi:10.1080/02614367.2015.1055295.

Kim, Junhyoung, Se-Hyuk Park, Eileen Malonebeach, and Jinmoo Heo. 2015b. Migrating to the East: A Qualitative Investigation of Acculturation and Leisure Activities. *Leisure Studies* 35: 421–437. doi:10.1080/02614367.2015.1014929.

Klein, Thomas. 2009. Determinanten der Sportaktivität und der Sportart im Lebenslauf. *Kölner Zeitschrift für Soziologie und Sozialpsychologie* 61: 1–32.

Kovac, Laura, and Dawn Trussell. 2015. "Classy and Never Trashy": Young Women's Experiences of Nightclubs and the Construction of Gender and Sexuality. *Leisure Sciences* 37: 195–209.

Lamont, Michèle. 1992. *Money, Morals, and Manners: The Culture of the French and American Upper-Middle Class.* Chicago: University of Chicago Press.

Lamont, Michèle, and Sada Aksartova. 2010. Der alltägliche Kosmopolitismus einfacher Leute. Strategien zur Überwindung von Rassengrenzen zwischen Männern der Arbeiterklasse. In *Ethnowissen*, ed. Marion Müller, 257–285. Wiesbaden: Springer Fachmedien.

Langnes, Tonje, and Fasting Kari. 2016. Identity Constructions Among Breakdancers. *International Review for the Sociology of Sport* 51 (3): 349–364.

Lee, Seung H., and Eun-Ok Im. 2010. Ethnic Differences in Exercise and Leisure Time Physical Activity Among Midlife-Women. *Journal of Advanced Nursing* 66 (4): 814–827.

Liu, Hugo. 2008. Social Network Profiles as Taste Performances. *Journal of Computer Mediated Communication* 13: 252–275.

Low, Setha M. 1999. Introduction. In *Theorizing the City: The New Urban Anthropology Reader*, ed. Setha M. Low, 1–36. New Brunswick: Rutgers University Press.

Lüdtke, Harmut. 1989. *Expressive Ungleichheit: zur Soziologie der Lebensstile.* Wiesbaden: VS Verlag für Sozialwissenschaften.

Maly, Ico, and Piia Varis. 2015. The 21st-century Hipster: On Micro-Populations in Times of Superdiversity. *European Journal of Cultural Studies* 19: 1–17.

Mannell, Roger C. 2014. Leisure in the Laboratory and Other Strange Notions: Psychological Research on the Subjective Nature of Leisure. In *Contemporary Perspectives in Leisure: Meanings, Motives and Lifelong Learning*, ed. Sam Elkington and Sean Gammon, 3–17. Abingdon: Routledge.

Marcus, George. 2009. Introduction: Notes Toward an Ethnographic Memoir of Supervising Graduate Research Through Anthropology's Decades of Transformation. In *Fieldwork Is Not What It Used to Be: Learning Anthropology's Method in a Time of Transition*, ed. James D. Faubion and George E. Marcus, 1–34. Ithaca: Cornell University Press.

Mata-Codesal, Diana, Esther Peperkamp, and Nina-Clara Tiesler. 2015. Editorial: Migration, Migrants and Leisure: Meaningful Leisure? *Leisure Studies* 34: 1–4.

Michael, Janna. 2015. It's Really Not Hip to Be a Hipster: Negotiating Trends and Authenticity in the Cultural Field. *Journal of Consumer Culture* 15 (2): 163–199.

Miller, Daniel. 2010. *Der Trost der Dinge*. With the assistance of Frank Jakubzik, 1, Auflage 2613. Frankfurt am Main: Suhrkamp.

Miner, Horace. 1956. Body Ritual Among the Nacirema. *American Anthropologist* 58 (3): 503–507.

Mochmann, Ingvill, and Yasemin El-menouar. 2005. Lifestyle Groups, Social Milieus and Party Preference in Eastern and Western Germany: Theoretical Considerations and Empirical Results. *German Politics* 14 (4): 417–437.

Müller, Marion, and Darius Zifonun. 2010. Wissenssoziologische Perspektiven auf ethnische Differenzierung und Migration: eine Einführung. In *Ethnowissen*, ed. Marion Müller, 9–33. Wiesbaden: Springer Fachmedien.

Nadel-Klein, Jane. 2010. Cultivating Taste and Class in the Garden. In *Mutuality and Empathy: Self and Other in the Ethnographic Encounter*, vol. 5, 107–121. Wantage: S. Kingston Pub.

Narayan, Kirin. 1997. How Native Is a "Native" Anthropologist? In *Situated Lives: Gender and Culture in Everyday Lives*, 23–39. London: Routledge.

Newman, David, Louis Tay, and Ed Diener. 2014. Leisure and Subjective Well-Being: A Model of Psychological Mechanisms as Mediating Factors. *Journal of Happiness Studies* 15 (3): 555–578.

Noll, Heinz-Herbert, and Roland Habich. 1990. Individuelle Wohlfahrt: vertikale Ungleichheit oder horizontale Disparitäten. In *Lebenslagen, Lebensläufe, Lebensstile*, Soziale Welt Sonderband 7, ed. Peter Berger and Stefan Hradil, 153–188. Göttingen: Schwarz Verlag.

Otte, Gunnar, and Jörg Rössel. 2011. Einführung: Lebensstile in der Soziologie. In *Lebensstilforschung*, ed. Jörg Rössel and Gunnar Otte, 7–34. Wiesbaden: VS Verlag für Sozialwissenschaften.

Palutikof, J.P., M.D. Agnew, and M.R. Hoar. 2004. Public Perceptions of Unusually Warm Weather in the UK: Impacts, Responses and Adaptations. *Climate Research* 26: 43–59.

Qian, Xinyi L., Careen Yarnal, and David Almeida. 2014. Using the Dynamic Model of Affect (DMA) to Examine Leisure Time as a Stress Coping Resource: Taking Into Account Stress Severity and Gender Difference. *Journal of Leisure Research* 46 (4): 483–505.

Rapport, Nigel. 2010. The Ethics of Participant Observation: Personal Reflections on Fieldwork in England. In *The Ethnographic Self as Resource: Writing Memory and Experience Into Ethnography*, ed. Peter Collins and Anselma Gallinat, 78–94. New York: Berghahn Books.

Redfield, Robert. 1955. *The Little Community: Viewpoints for the Study of a Human Whole*. Uppsala, Stockholm: Almqvist & Wikselis Boktryckeri AB; The Gottesman Lectures.

Reuter, Julia, and Oliver Berli. 2013. Die Kunst zu Arbeiten: Eine Berufsfeldstudie zum Museumspersonal. *Sociologia Internationalis* 51 (1): 1–23.

Saint, Onge, and Patrick Krueger. 2011. Education and Racial-Ethnic Differences in Types of Exercise in the United States. *Journal of Health and Social Behaviour* 52: 197–211.

Sayer, Liana. 2015. *The Complexities of Interpreting Changing Household Patterns*. https://contemporaryfamilies.org/complexities-brief-report/. Accessed May 12, 2016.

Schmiedeberg, Claudia, and Jette Schröder. 2014. Does Weather Really Influence the Measurement of Life Satisfaction? *Social Indicators Research* 117: 387–399.

Schulze, Gerhard. 2005[1992]. *Die Erlebnisgesellschaft: Kultursoziologie der Gegenwart*. 2 Aufl. Frankfurt [Main]; New York: Campus.

Shinew, Kimberly, Myron Floyd, and Diana Parry. 2004. Understanding the Relationship Between Race and Leisure Activities and Constraints: Exploring an Alternative Framework. *Leisure Sciences* 26: 181–199.

Sikes, Michelle, and Grant Jarvie. 2014. Women's Running as Freedom: Development and Choice. *Sport in Society: Cultures, Commerce, Media, Politics* 17 (4): 507–522.

SINUS. 2011. Markt- und Sozialforschung GmbH Heidelberg. *Informationen zu den SINUS Milieus 2011: Stand 04/2011.* http://www.sinus-institut.de/uploads/tx_mpdownloadcenter/Informationen_Sinus-Milieus_042011.pdf. Accessed July 17, 2014.

———. 2015. Markt- und Sozialforschung GmbH Heidelberg. *Die Sinus-Milieus.* http://www.sinus-institut.de/veroeffentlichungen/downloads/. Accessed April 21, 2016.

Spiers, Andrew, and Gordon Walker. 2009. The Effects of Ethnicity and Leisure Satisfaction on Happiness, Peacefulness, and Quality of Life. *Leisure Sciences* 31: 84–99.

Spinney, Jamie E., and Hugh Millward. 2011. Weather Impacts on Leisure Activities in Halifax, Nova Scotia. *International Journal of Biometeorology* 55: 133–145.

Stadt Mannheim. 2011. *Sinus-Milieus 2010 in kleinräumiger Gliederung. Statistische Berichte Mannheim 5/2011.* http://www.sinus-institut.de/uploads/tx_mpdownloadcenter/Informationen_Sinus-Milieus_042011.pdf. Accessed July 11, 2014.

———. 2014. *Sinus Milieus 2010–2013 in kleinräumiger Gliederung: Statistischer Bericht Nr 5/2014.* https://www.mannheim.de/sites/default/files/page/14401/b201405_sinus_milieus_0.pdf. Accessed April 21, 2016.

———. 2016. *Sinus-Milieus in Mannheim.* https://www.mannheim.de/stadt-gestalten/sinus-milieus-mannheim. Accessed April 21, 2016.

Taylor, Tracy. 2001. Cultural Diversity and Leisure: Experiences of Women in Australia. *Society and Leisure* 24: 535–555.

Tazanu, Primus. 2012. They Behave as Though They Want to Bring Heaven Down: Some Narratives on the Visibility of Cameroonian Migrants Youths in Cameroon Urban Space. In *Urban Life-Worlds in Motion*, ed. Kastner Hahn, 101–129. Bielefeld: Transcript.

Walseth, Kristin. 2015. Sport Within Muslim Organizations in Norway: Ethnic Segregated Activities as Arena for Integration. *Leisure Studies* 35: 1–20. doi:10.1080/02614367.2015.1055293.

Warneken, Bernd J. 2015. Spektrum Migration. Ein Kommentar zur Tagung. In *Spektrum Migration: Zugänge zur Vielfalt des Alltags : [… Tagung "Spektrum Migration. Perspektiven auf einen alltagskulturellen Forschungsgegenstand" zurück, die im November 2012 an der Universität Tübingen stattfand]*, 253–257. Tübingen: Tübinger Vereinigung für Volkskunde e. V.

Whillans, Jennifer. 2014. The Weekend: The Friend and Foe of Independent Singles. *Leisure Studies* 33 (2): 185–201.

Zängler, Thomas, and Georg Karg. 2003. Motive der alltäglichen Freizeitmobilität. In *Motive und Handlungsansätze im Freizeitverkehr*, ed. ifmo Institut für Mobilitätsforschung. Eine Forschungseinrichtung der BMW Group, 51–66. Berlin: Springer.

Zifonun, Darius. 2010. Ein 'gallisches Dorf'? Integration, Stadtteilbindung und Prestigeordnung in einem 'Armenviertel'. In *Ethnowissen*, ed. Marion Müller, 311–327. Wiesbaden: Springer Fachmedien.

Zimmerman, Don, and Lawrence Wieder. 1977. The Diary: Diary-Interview Method. *Urban Life* 5 (4): 479–498.

CHAPTER 2

The City of Mannheim

Mannheim is a southern German city located at the confluence of the rivers Rhine and Neckar, the adjacent elements of nature that so often represent life in the city, and the palace grounds, the *Wasserturm*, the church of the Jesuits and the *Paradeplatz* are its main architectural icons. Mannheim's colorful city center comprises 144 blocks and, from above, resembles a chessboard, hence the nickname "Grid City." This particular way of civic construction helps people to orient themselves quickly in the city center, the main location for all types of everyday activities, including work, chores, and leisure.[1]

Mannheim has a total of 331,307 registered inhabitants distributed across 14,496 square kilometers and is considered one of Germany's many "Second Cities" in comparison with the big metropolises of Berlin and Munich (Stadt Mannheim 2015a). However, the city has a higher population density (2011 inhabitants/km^2) than cities with similar population. In fact, it resembles more closely cities such as Duisburg and Wuppertal, cities which like Mannheim are also considered industrial (van Deth 2014). Additionally, it is closely interconnected with its neighboring cities, Heidelberg and Ludwigshafen, as well as the towns and villages of the Rhine-Neckar Region. For example, approximately one third of the working population is inbound or outbound commuters (s. Stadt Mannheim 2015a; Statistisches Landesamt Baden-Württemberg 2013). Mannheim is therefore part of a metropolitan region comprising more than 2 million inhabitants (Metropolregion Rhein-Neckar 2015).[2]

Besides its regional interconnectedness, Mannheim is known as a multicultural city, something that provides public prominence and often is

© The Author(s) 2017
V.L. Sandoval, *The Meaning of Leisure*, Leisure Studies in a Global Era, DOI 10.1007/978-3-319-59752-2_2

promoted as part of the city's identity. The arrival of foreign populations to Mannheim dates back to the 1960s, with the reconstruction of Germany after World War II and the recruitment of guest workers from Mediterranean countries like Italy, Spain, and Turkey, which led to a rapid increase in immigration. Additionally, the establishment post-1945 in the outskirts of the city of a U.S. military base and the presence of thousands of U.S. soldiers influenced greatly Mannheim's society and culture (s. van Deth 2014). Moreover, in recent decades, the city has attracted many students from other regions and countries due to its wide variety of higher education institutions. These students often work and reside in Mannheim and the surrounding region upon completion of their degrees. The city's recognition of the importance of institutions of higher education can be seen in the official change of name in 1967 to "University City Mannheim."

Currently, the city has a total of 130,908 migrants from 170 different countries.[3] The majority of migrants have Turkish (21.4%), Polish (13.7%), or Italian (7.8%) backgrounds and, with regard to gender distribution, about half of all migrants are women. In total, migrants constitute approximately 39% of the population, which is higher than the estimated total of migrants for Germany (approximately 20%) and the Baden-Württemberg province (approximately 26%) to which Mannheim belongs (Stadt Mannheim 2013).

The city's economy is strongly dependent on industry and harbor activities. It receives most of its revenues from the services area, much of which is also connected to industrial production. Statistics show that most people in the city work in the tertiary sector. Furthermore, the city similarly to the countrys rates has an unemployment rate of 5.7%, with 48.7% of the unemployed being women (Bundesagentur für Arbeit Statistik 2015). The unemployment rate among all migrants is higher than among the nonmigrant population (36.2%) (Stadt Mannheim 2015a).

Expanding from the gridlike city center, the city is divided into 17 districts and 24 counties (Kommunale Statistikstelle 2015a).[4] As is the case in other German cities, the migrant population is particularly large in certain districts, such as Neckarstadt-West (66.9%), Innenstadt/Jungbusch (61.3%), Neckarstadt-Ost (49.6%), and Vogelstang (46.6%), even though many of these migrants (43.9%) have German citizenship (Kommunale Statistikstelle 2015b). These districts are also considered "socially noticeable" according to some indicators, such as unemployment and education rates (Stadt Mannheim 2013, p. 40). However, with regard to age groups, the migrant populations of these districts, just as in the overall population, mainly comprise the age groups between 30 and 65 years old. The second largest population group for migrants is that of under 18-year-olds (Kommunale Statistikstelle 2015b).

In terms of everyday life and leisure, the city offers many possibilities. There are 458 sports clubs with a total of 147,618 members, which, makes it the city with the second-highest number of members in the North-Baden Region, behind Karlsruhe. The biggest clubs are DJK Sportverband Mannheim e.V. and TSV Mannheim 1846. People of working age (between 20 and 40 years old) show the lowest rate of participation in sports clubs. In all age groups, women are underrepresented but, when they do participate, they tend to do so within the same categories as men: soccer, handball, track and field, and tennis (Badischer Sportbund 2014). It is important to highlight that, alongside "high culture" policies, such as funding museums, theater and music, sports are the only area of leisure with which the city's administration is actively engaged and developed, even though the entity is called the Department of Sport and Leisure Time (s. Stadt Mannheim 2015b). Additionally, there are a high number of private sports and fitness clubs. In Mannheim alone, search directories show more than 25 fitness centers, each with different themes, customers, and interests. There are, for example, some women-exclusive or health and preventive healthcare gyms.

When considering shopping and consumption, various sources cite Mannheim as one of Germany's best cities in terms of retail businesses and shopping opportunities, because it offers a combination of big retail brands and low-profile businesses, such as for example, bridal shops owned by Turkish migrants (s. Klehr et al. 2007, p. 22; COMFORT 2014; Hartmann 2014a). Cultural variety is also shown in the various ethnic or religious associations that offer leisure activities, such as music and photography (Stadt Mannheim 2015d).

Regarding the environment, as part of the Rhine-Neckar Region, Mannheim has one of the best climatic conditions in Germany, with a yearly average temperature of 13 °C (55 °F), winters that seldom go below −6 °C (21 °F), and summers in which temperatures can reach up to 36 °C (97 °F). In the year 2014, for example, there were 164 rainy days, mostly concentrated in the months of April, July, August, and September, and an average 65% humidity across the year (Rhein-Neckar.de 2015). Therefore, weather conditions play a role in the use of green spaces and pursuit of outdoor activities. The city's natural environment is also central to everyday life, with forests like the Käfertaler Wald, parks like the Luisenpark, and especially the areas close to the rivers, the shores, and boardwalks all used for outdoor social and physical activities. According to the city's official website : "The city on the Rhine plain, between the Palatinate Forest and the Forest of Odes, combines urbanity and leisure opportunities with possibilities of retreat and recuperation" (Stadt Mannheim 2015c).

Nonetheless, despite opportunities for work and leisure, geographical location, favorable climate, and efforts by city officials in cooperation with private partners to impart positive associations with the city, Mannheim tends to have a bad image among those living within and outside the city. It is associated with bad quality of life, pollution, dirt, and social conflict (Zifonun 2010, p. 311). Moreover, in recent times, cases of criminality attracting media coverage seem to have caused additional insecurity and distress in some segments of the population (Ragge 2015). As in most of Germany, despite its long tradition of migration, in Mannheim, the issue of criminality has been discussed in the context of the foreign population, whether it be asylum seekers, refugees, or migrants.[5] All in all, public perception of security or insecurity is an issue that continues to be discussed and that plays a role in everyday life, as we see in the findings sections.

Having a general knowledge of Mannheim as a city is important for understanding the local context in which the lives of the women of this study take place. It must be kept in mind that the city is not an isolated entity but is influenced by regional, national, and global dynamics and that the city is produced and reproduced in everyday life by its population, in both the material and the immaterial space. The city of Mannheim as locality, along with its particular characteristics, has a relevance for the issue of how individual women, both migrant and nonmigrant, perceive, plan, and experience their leisure time. The sociodemographic composition of the city, the infrastructural situation, private and public leisure opportunities, and social conflicts and perception of others all influence the way in which individuals exercise their agency and make use of spaces. Mannheim as locality is forever present in the leisure of these women, not only as context where things take place but also as an agent that molds people's lives.

2.1   Women and Mannheim as Leisure Space

2.1.1   Excursus: Profile Nr. 3

I met M. through one of my seed informants. We met at a bar/cafe that she frequents very often with her friends. The theme or attraction of the venue is its nice selection of "bio craft" beers and wines: a nice place, full of people in their 20s and 30s, many of whom look like hipsters. M.'s looks contrasted with those of most of the other patrons. My first impression of M. was of a very business like and elegant, thin and tall woman; she was not dressed in trendy, laid-back clothes but rather in classic atemporal ones. She could have been a woman from a different decade. She was wearing pearl earrings and a silver necklace, a blazer in a pastel tone, and a flowered scarf. When we started talking, I noticed how she spoke in harmony with her physical appearance, with neither the dialect nor the colloquialisms typical of her generation.

M. is a second-generation migrant with parents from Italy and Holland, but she is also an internal migrant, coming originally from a city around 200 km (124 miles) from Mannheim. Living in a different city is not new to her, though; previously she worked in other cities in Germany and in other European countries as well. However, during our conversation, she constantly stressed how much she liked Mannheim, how she had immediately felt at home in the city, and how she thinks Mannheimers are more talkative and open than people in other German cities. For example, she mentioned how, just one week after starting her new job, a colleague spontaneously asked her to join her in having an ice cream in the city center and that they have been pretty close ever since, going to events and pursuing different activities together. The same happened at her fitness studio, where she met another friend during her workout sessions, a friend who, afterward, introduced her to even more people. All in all, she thinks that Mannheim is easygoing and that its people will start talking to you no matter if you are in a bar, a theater, or at a concert, or if you are alone or in a group. She praises Mannheim's geographical location as being close to the wine region Pfalz as well to big cities, such as Frankfurt and Paris. Yet she also highlighted the fact that she is used to being alone and that she is good at living in this way because her parents were both business owners while she was growing up and, as she had no siblings, she had to make her own leisure activities.

A big part of her leisure consists of going to the gym at least twice a week and also going for outside runs. She likes training in group gym sessions and talking to people but she prefers to be alone when she runs, to so as to concentrate on her own thoughts and not on anyone else. When I met her she was training to participate in a marathon that would take place a couple of months later. Besides physical activity, one of her favorite leisure activities is going to concerts and enjoying live music, mainly by smaller local groups playing rock, indie rock, and pop rock, although occasionally she attends classical music concerts. Sometimes she goes clubbing in Zimmer, but she prefers venues that are not so loud so that you cannot talk to the people you are with or get to know new people.

Yet her life and her leisure have not always been the same. The presence of sports and physical activity in her leisure, for example, dates back two and a half years to the end of a relationship that had driven her to make some changes in her life. She chose to stop smoking and to start doing physical activity, to do less clubbing and pursue more of what she calls "cultural activities," like going to concerts, the theater, and ballet. For her, this has been a positive change that has made her feel more comfortable within herself and with her body. She says that she used to be thin because she wouldn't eat but now she enjoys eating and being strong due to her training.

Her various circles of friends are all-important to her, but they seldom interconnect. Some of these circles comprise colleagues who have developed into friends; others contain friends from sports; while others are made up of friends from childhood. However, most of her friends are migrants, either internal or external, as well. With each circle of friends she pursues different kinds of activities. She visits her childhood friends and family a couple of times a year. When talking about her social life and what she values the most, she stresses how important it is that the people in social relationships take you for who you are and not for what you do. Even though she says that she loves her job, she experiences social discrimination in relation to the perceived status of her job. Indeed, it seems that a big part of the motivation behind her leisure choices is to balance the negative social effects she experiences as a consequence of her job. As someone cultured and physically active, her leisure identity is very important to her. Despite her positive discourse about her working tasks and the challenges they pose, for her, leisure *is* life. It is self-fulfillment. Work, as she says, provides her with the income to be able to live. She says that, in the future, she would like to find a man with whom to build a relationship but that, for now, she is hesitant and concerned about the prospect of losing the freedom in her leisure activities and losing her identity by making such compromises: "What I fear the most in that context is that I meet someone and then forget about myself."

2.1.2 Mannheim: Ugly But Fun?

Mannheim, who likes Mannheim? (Respondent C., December 10, 2014)

One of Mannheim's prominent local bloggers, who also served as one of my expert informants, wrote in an article titled "Is Mannheim Nice?":

Mannheim, a city with really short inner city pathways, a cool grid structure, a lot of affordable housing in the city center and shopping and leisure opportunities, which other midrange German cities don't even get close to having. Culture, nightlife, sport, nature—doesn't matter what you are looking for: you will not be able to tell yourself that you don't have what you need in Mannheim, except for the sea. But even for those sand and beach fetishists there are two rivers and countless lakes close by to get you into a vacation mood practically in your backyard. (Hartmann 2014b)

This blog and the corresponding Facebook page, which are odes to Mannheim and life in the city, have over 26,000 followers, and each article has been shared more than 100 times across different forms of social media.[6] This is but an example of how the image of Mannheim can go beyond negative associations with poverty, pollution, and low quality of life, as described by some (s. Zifonun 2010, p. 311). The reason why Mannheim is the focus of this chapter is that because the local context is hugely importance for leisure, it is necessary to understand how the local context intertwines with the leisure of individuals, specifically to grasp how the locality influences these women's leisure decisions and execution, which in turn can help in the analysis of feelings of belonging and individual identity.

However, the relationship between these women and Mannheim as a space in which they can develop their everyday lives is, like public opinions on the city, ambiguous. On one hand, these women share the negative opinions that are common about the city while, on the other, they enjoy the wide range of activities or possibilities of leisure the city has to offer them. All in all, aesthetics style (i.e., infrastructure), social conflicts, and perceived insecurity weigh in on the negative side while the variety and range of leisure possibilities weigh in on the positive side.

Dealing specifically with the negative associations these women have with Mannheim, there are different aspects to consider. One aspect mentioned was the characteristic of city life as an industrial and polluted city. Furthermore, for some informants, living in Mannheim just presents too many facets of typical city life: they would wish to experience a more rural way of life. For example, in an interview on September 19, 2014, respondent J., a woman from a small village, contemplated her future in this way: "I could never imagine when I get married and have children, to live with them here and that they grow up in Mannheim. That would be a nightmare for me."

However, dreams about a future in small villages often are related to the individual's life history and background: those who wish for a future in a village or small town also have experienced that in the past. For others, particularly women with migrant backgrounds, life in the city, especially a midrange city like Mannheim, was satisfying. They often pointed out that the city was more open to diversity than villages and small towns where people were not used to seeing foreigners. In particular, the issue of race and ethnicity was brought up in comments like this one: "In the village they look at you as if they haven't seen a black person before." Hannerz (1980, p. 113) says that, because in the city the rule is that everyone is a stranger, people tend to be categorized according to external markers, such as ethnicity, class, age, and gender, associations whose meaning can change according to the context. However, this anonymity and categorization does not necessarily cause negative consequences for the individual when the associations are positive or neutral. In this context Latin Americanness evokes positive feelings and is associated with relaxation and vacations. Some categorizations can be less harmful than others.

It could be argued that the nature of all cities, as influenced by the variety of people living in it, is to be particularly open to external influences and to provide space for the fulfillment of new lifestyles and, consequently, worldviews and identities (Hahn 2012, p. 18). The categories according to which strangers are classified could be less based on stereotypes or less related to negative meanings than they would be in rural settings. At least this is how these women perceive it subjectively. Müller and Zifonun (2010) argue that categories help us with orientation, by showing us how to act with strangers: they simplify and structure the world but gain or lose meaning according to the context. This is why it is important to understand how categories are experienced in the lived world (pp. 10–13). In this case, external categorizations of individuals in Mannheim are experienced as less oppressing or less consequential than in rural areas. This is due to the belief in the difference-friendly nature of midrange and large cities in general. This was also the case, for example, for some of the women (migrant and nonmigrant) who expressed their desire to move and live in larger cities, like Berlin or Hamburg, cities that they considered even more open to difference and supportive of a greater variety of worldviews, interests, and channels of leisure.

The internal and external migrant informants mentioned certain aspects explicitly that are seen as positive characteristics of German cities in general, such as fewer gender inequalities and patriarchal norms and freedom with regard to sexual orientation and gender aesthetic ideals. Furthermore, while internal migrants highlighted the issue of social judgment and patriarchal norms in rural areas, external migrants highlighted the protection by law and police and the mentality and tolerance of the population in Germany generally and Mannheim in particular.

Furthermore, Mannheim is not an enclosed entity. The sociopolitical context also plays a role: cities are not isolated from regional and global contexts. As respondent M. said on March 19, 2015: "…yeah, of course it has a charm, it is very central. Pfalz, Odenwald, Heidelberg, Frankfurt, Paris in three hours. It is very quick to get there from Mannheim […] but it is also a feeling, it is a feeling that I cannot explain, I arrived here and felt I had arrived. It just works for me."

Despite the general characteristics that influence the women's relationship with Mannheim in the sense of whether it is more rural or urban, certain aspects are perceived to be particularities of Mannheim and affect how the city is perceived and how leisure is experienced in it. Regarding the issue of openness toward different ethnicities and cultures, for example, and in the context of public discourses on refugees, these women perceived Mannheim to be particularly welcoming. This was presented in a narrative of: "We are all foreigners in this city. No one will notice any more." These kinds of arguments by these women are close to Harman's (1988, p. 6) argument that in the city, the foreigner is the rule, and that the diverse environment is for the inhabitants the normal world, but it is also intertwined with the subjective awareness of the city's particular historical development and composition of the population. All in all, Mannheim is perceived as a space that allows for a variety of "role repertoires" (s. Hannerz 1980, pp. 244–312). It is possible, for example, to be a foreigner *and* a Mannheimer at the same time because of the way the city is imagined as a multicultural city (both by policy makers and by the population). Indeed, most of these women answered the question: "Where do you come from?" with "from Mannheim," even though due to ethnic traits, they might have, in some instances, to answer the following question: "Where do you *originally* come from?" The follow-up question is, however, never constructed in order to invalidate the first answer but is generally a question of curiosity about that person's biography. During my observations, the first answer was quite often accepted as final, especially if another Monnemer posed the question.[7] In this case, Mannheim is experienced and discursively constructed as an enabler of freedom and action because of the lack of social judgment based on external categorizations or cultural belongings. This does not mean that categorizations do not exist, just that they are not always experienced as restrictions. Subjectively speaking, these women's views on Mannheim mirror Velho's (2011, p. 455) stand on the city as producer and enabler of heterogeneity. The women who have come from different regions or countries feel welcome by the social environment. Nonetheless, it is important to emphasize that this welcoming feeling is related to people in the social environment, such as work, leisure, and on the streets (brief encounters); it does not pertain to state institutions, which, on the contrary, are perceived as rather unfriendly and hindering.

Beyond the characteristics that Mannheim might share with other cities regarding openness, Mannheimers are also perceived as having a particular personality that enhances leisure experiences. As respondent M. said on March 19, 2015:

> I feel well here. When you are at a cafe or somewhere someone will start speaking to you, or colleagues, friends, you meet new people and they introduce you to new people, it's a chain. When I feel well I'm relaxed, when you love where you live, because I know I wouldn't feel good in a horrible place, then I wouldn't feel like doing anything. But here it's easy. Mannheimer make it easy, I think. They are easy to engage in conversation with. They'll say something stupid or "hey! Isn't the weather nice?" and smile and start from there. I think it's really easy here.

Despite regional and global connections of all kinds (commuting, migration, technology, etc.), it is important to highlight that, as a city, Mannheim is perceived as a unit. Regarding leisure, even if the Rhine-Neckar Region is very interconnected, and although there many commuters, Mannheim is the main center for leisure, due to the presence, for example, of numerous associations and sports clubs, gyms, swimming pools, movie theaters, bars and nightclubs, and shopping possibilities. As M. stated in the last quote, the women perceive Mannheim to have a higher amount and variety of leisure opportunities than the two neighboring cities of Heidelberg and Ludwigshafen.

Another aspect that is intermingled with perception of the locality and leisure of individuals is awareness. People are aware of leisure opportunities in and surrounding Mannheim. Barnett (2005, pp. 131–132) mentioned the importance of awareness for leisure participation. As such, it is important to recognize the channels that make awareness and through it a wide variety of leisure experiences possible. Awareness does not translate into a leisure experience, but it should present the possibility of choosing something that, generally, is perceived as a better opportunity than being limited by having fewer options. As respondent S. said on May 10, 2015:

> …mmm. I think in general you can do a lot in Mannheim. It has a lot to offer for leisure, it has many museums, it has the SAP Arena where you can go see some handball or ice hockey. There are many sports clubs, you have Jungbusch, which is really cool for going out. I think Mannheim has a lot to offer for leisure. Whether you make use of everything is another question but, if you want something, there is definitely a lot.

Veal (1987, p. 79) argued that, in the context of leisure, there is no evidence that people are happier with a wide range of choices than with fewer choices. However, while the amount of choices might not influence directly the quality of leisure experience after a choice has been made, these women do subjectively relate a wide range of choices to high quality of life and well-being. Awareness of the many leisure possibilities and the knowledge that they could choose a different channel of leisure anytime they would want to is, for them, one of the aspects that cements a positive relationship with the city of Mannheim, even when the women are aware that the city might not offer some leisure opportunities because of characteristics typical of urban areas. As respondent A. said on May 12, 2015:

> Back there I could take the horse when I wanted, ride in the forest. To find something like that again, uncomplicated and cheap, is not possible here in Mannheim, I mean, in cities in general, riding stables are here for tournaments and stuff and that's not my world.

The use of technology for the exchange of information through social media and gathering information through search engines mentioned in Chap. 1 is one of the key aspects that make awareness possible. Information about activities is also exchanged by word of mouth within social circles. However, another key aspect of awareness is the city itself as informative space. Information about leisure opportunities is very present; individuals encounter it constantly in their everyday lives. This is partly due to the fact that the city of Mannheim is full of promotional material concerning leisure opportunities, and public spaces serve as informative and marketing

Fig. 2.1 Advertising column in the city center

spaces. For example, trams have posters with upcoming events of all kinds, from congresses on education opportunities to parties at nightclubs, concerts, theater plays, and city festivals, and promotional posters are also seen around the city, attached to poles or on panels (Fig. 2.1).

So, advertising creates awareness of events and potential leisure experiences. In this context, the city as advertisement site fulfills what Bauman (2013, p. 60) reproached the consumerist society for and what Adorno (1991b, pp. 163–165) reproached the culture industry for: new desires are constantly being created by the market, and individuals are just choosing from the commodities that the culture industry has turned everything into. However, it is important to highlight that the city as an information space also serves for events that are not bound to cost. Leisure experiences that are free also are advertised. For example, it is possible to enjoy the city festival for free. Concerts and performances take place in the street and on stages specially assembled for these events. In this context, consumption might not be exclusively related to financial resources but to consuming experiences similar to that which Schulze (2005) proposed. The value of an event or a leisure opportunity is not related to use or cost but to the potential for leisure experience (p. 59). Moreover, consumption and other meanings can coexist. For example, events organized by city entities and organizations seek to produce and reproduce feelings of belonging among the population as well as to change the city's image. By combining the consumption of alcohol and the leisure experience of a free concert in a Mannheim city festival, for example, it is possible to create feelings of belonging across individuals, regardless of race, social class, and religion, as Lamont and Aksartova (2010, p. 262) and Appadurai (1996, pp. 89–113) point out.

As mentioned, Mannheim is often considered in the context of the two neighboring cities, Ludwigshafen and Heidelberg. Together, the three cities have, subjectively for their inhabitants, an interesting relationship comprising closeness and belonging (Rhine-Neckar Region) and competitiveness. For example, for the women studied, Ludwigshafen, the city closest to Mannheim, on the other side of the Rhine, is viewed as the ugly industrial sister city that one occasionally visits to go shopping at the malls (e.g., on regional holidays when everything is closed in Baden-Württemberg). Heidelberg is often viewed as the idyllic historical student city, which is nice but boring and full of tourists. Generally, when Mannheim is considered in a national or global context, there is a tendency to view the city in a bad light. When considered in the immediate regional context, however, it is seen as the best possible location for leisure. In comparison to Heidelberg, for example, my informants often referred to Mannheim as "real," with "real workers" and "real people," while Heidelberg was "full of students and tourists" and was "artificial." Ludwigshafen was described simply as "ugly" and "industrial," especially now, when the retail and gastronomy in the city center has been practically eradicated by the presence of the shopping mall Rhein-Galerie. Mannheim, on the contrary, is perceived to have more leisure opportunities. As respondent J. explained on May 22, 2015:

> I wanted to live here. I didn't want the life in the village anymore, even though I sometimes notice that I'm really overwhelmed here with all these offers! You can choose between so many things what you could do. Previously in my village there was one party you could go to and either you went or you stayed at home. Here you have so many possibilities. I got used to it and I must say I like Mannheim more than Heidelberg [...] yeah, here there is something for everyone. I like it in Mannheim, even better than in Heidelberg. Heidelberg is not so good for nightlife but in general the region is really good. I'm satisfied.

The presence of leisure opportunities is important because, as Carmichael et al. (2015, p. 53) pointed out, a lack of appropriate facilities is one of the barriers to leisure participation. As access to leisure has consequences for well-being and quality of life, then, having leisure is equated with "really" living. Indeed, the member of the city's leisure and sports committee with whom I talked highlighted the work the committee does in maintaining and developing infrastructure. Each district has a representative on the leisure and sports committee who is in charge of highlighting its needs to the city and gaining the allocation of funds to particular projects. For example, if a soccer field and athletics track need to be renovated, the representative would write a proposal to the city council, whose members then decide on the matter. Additionally, these representatives work closely with associations and clubs, which present their needs or demands to them as well. Wirth (1938, p. 14) pointed out that, in cities, interests were made effective through representation. In the context of leisure and sports development in Mannheim, only the interests of those who are members of associations or clubs are actively represented. Whether sports clubs and other associations represent the wishes of their members is debatable, as many seem more concerned with public image and reputation. For example, many of the women in sports clubs complained that they did not know what the club board was doing or why and suffered under the pressure (from the board) to be a successful team. The boards of clubs ask for example for explanations on teams performance. Because of their focus on their reputation, the clubs work to attract young people to mold into competitive athletes; they do not find adults pursuing sports as a hobby that interesting. In addition, members of the migration advisory board and of the sports and leisure committee pointed out that the city and districts mostly engage in issues of leisure, sports, education, and integration of the youth. Actually, the migration advisory board's main focus is access and changes to formal education to make it friendlier to different cultures, by, for example, providing learning software in different languages at schools. Schools are also the primary target of marketing strategies by the city's cultural associations and sports clubs.

Adult leisure and sport or integration of migrant adults through leisure and sports as pursued, for example, in Australia (s. Cortis et al. 2008) is not a priority, according to these representatives. From their descriptions, it can be concluded that the priority of the city of Mannheim is "preventive leisure services": to make youth socially fit and avoid youth conflicts and criminality, as Veal (1987, p. 166) and Overwien (2004, pp. 56–69) have described. Thus, the city does not focus on the presence of girls or women with different cultural backgrounds, for example with dress codes of sport teams often not allowing heterogeneity. When questioned about what the migrant girls and women in sports clubs told me, the committee member said their participation was low because of "cultural norms" that prevented them from participating; in this way, the committee member's perspective on leisure depends on the culture and/or ethnicity of participants (s. Taylor 2001, pp. 537–538). No active efforts are made to recruit young migrant women into sports clubs as, according to the committee member, it is a "lost cause." Strategies and policies concerning recruitment are important because awareness of the existence of leisure opportunities (Barnett 2005) and feeling welcome (Chavez 2000) are two essential factors of participation. However, in this case, those who do participate do so because of intrinsic motivation and private social networks, not as a response to effective inclusion strategies by the city itself, as these women are not in an age group that is targeted by leisure and sport policies or strategies.

2.1.3 Neckarstadt and Jungbusch: No Risk, No Fun

Except for big events organized by the city and the current infrastructure, adult leisure and sports opportunities are mostly driven by the private sector. These leisure opportunities driven by the private sector are the offers that my informants perceive to be enormous and richer than in the other nearby cities. Nonetheless, there are differences in how neighborhoods are perceived. Some neighborhoods or districts are perceived to be safer and cleaner than others. The majority of informants, for example, perceived the Neckarstadt-West to be chaotic, dirty, and more dangerous than other parts of town, even though a couple of my informants lived there. By way of example, not only my informants but other people often recommended that I avoid walking home alone at night and that I be careful of muggers. An often-told city tale, for example, warns people to avoid the area behind the Penny supermarket at the intersection of the Mittelstrasse and the Humboldtstrasse, an area that constitutes about half of the Neckarstadt-West. This area is considered the "red-light district" of Mannheim. It includes the famous prostitution street, Lupinenstrasse, which is protected by a red gate through which only men can enter, and its red-light windows are recognizable at a distance.

Another neighborhood considered dangerous, even more so than the Neckarstadt, is Jungbusch, the neighborhood immediately to the west of the city grid center. This perception is cemented in public consciousness by media reports on crimes committed there, statistics on crime, and police raids. These types of reports are often directly or indirectly constructed in the context of migration and the high percentage of foreign population in those areas. Orley (2012, p. 37) argued that places retain traces of things that have happened there through the actions of people interacting and encountering them. Events such as the sexual assault and murder of a student in Jungbusch in October 2013 and the murder of a kiosk owner in March 2015 in the Neckarstadt-West received a great deal of media coverage and mention in everyday conversations, which serves to influence and reproduce public perceptions of such spaces. As a researcher and inhabitant of the Neckarstadt-West, in two years I was witness to two large police raids that included helicopters, tracking dogs, and dozens of armored police, and I have received letters in German and in Turkish from the police that appealed for witnesses in attempted murder investigations. Even though those are isolated events and not part of everyday life, they still leave their traces in public consciousness and remain present in collective memory. Furthermore, this perceived danger could affect lifestyle and leisure choices with regard to decisions on the women's own safety and precautions.

Interestingly, though, neighborhoods like Neckarstadt-West and Jungbusch still play a relevant role in the everyday lives and in the leisure experiences of these women. In fact, just like the relationship with Mannheim, the relationship with these neighborhoods is conflicted. There are positives and negative evaluations of them that change depending on situation. This can be contrasted with the neighborhood Schönau, which respondents mentioned only negatively. Just like Ludwigshafen and Heidelberg are used discursively to highlight the positive aspects of Mannheim, Schönau is used to show the Neckarstadt in a better light. An example of this is the often-used (not only by my informants) phrase: "Okay, the Neckarstadt has the foreigners but the Tschänau has the *Asi* [antisocial] Germans."

One reason why Jungbusch and the Neckarstadt are appreciated for leisure is that those areas are important centers for nightlife, such as the Industriestrasse in the northern part of the Neckarstadt-West, where old factory buildings have been reutilized as nightclubs, including Noblesse, 7er Club, and Playa del MA. Jungbusch is known for its many art galleries and exhibition rooms and is associated with alternative lifestyles and pub nightlife. Indeed, Jungbusch is considered to be the city's main area for art and music, hosting many emerging artists in bars, in contrast to the large and renowned concert venues of the city, like Capitol, SAP Arena, and Rosengarten. Jungbusch is open to variety and different worldviews and is perceived to be different. As respondent J. remarked on November 16, 2014:

> I'm often hanging around the bars in Jungbusch. I don't like nightclubs, it's not my thing [...] yeah, I think that the special thing about Mannheim is the multiculturalism, in particular in Jungbusch. I love it, because it shows that multiculti can work, it's open, and no one will look at you in a weird way. Okay, maybe at Kapuzinerplanken. (Kapuzinerplanken is a square in the city)

Jungbusch is often an option for those who find nightlife in Mannheim too "mainstream," as one woman called the type of music and style of clothing of the people there. However, it is also an option for those looking for a more casual and laid-back leisure experience. Respondent A., speaking on May 12, 2015, about nightlife in Jungbusch, compared it to nightlife in the city center, the Kapuzinerplanken: "I think the nightclubs here are too snobbish, people there with a shirt, all pretentious and made up, I don't like that, sometimes it's okay but it's too much."

Despite its association with criminality and its image as a dangerous district, Jungbusch can also be associated with different things, including being an important locale of nighttime leisure. Additionally, respondents compared Jungbusch to other parts of the city, such as Kapuzinerplanken, an area of the city center that the women believe embodies snobbishness and intolerance or even racism. It could be argued that Jungbusch is the hipster center of Mannheim, in the sense that people living and/or spending their leisure time there are defenders of openness, tolerance, and alternative cultural representations (s. Michael 2015). Jungbusch embodies the idea of hipness locally because it is special, with individuals striving for authenticity, creativity, and individuality of leisure experiences.

Important city events, such as the Nachtwandel (a street event that takes place in autumn), occur in Jungbusch. During this event the neighborhood hosts many different activities, such as concerts, exhibitions, and performances. The event is called a "*Wandel*" because the idea is to walk around the streets of Jungbusch and enjoy the different activities taking place. In 2015, organizers reported attendance of more than 25,000 visitors during the two-day festival (Scheuermann 2015). I was advised to go by two of my informants. The event was so crowded it was difficult

Fig. 2.2   Nachtwandel 2015 video exhibition

to move through the streets, and one's senses were almost overwhelmed. One could start by listening to some rockabilly music in a truck parked in one corner while drinking sparkling wine from the neighboring region, Pfalz, then continue to walk and find a photographic exhibition with faces and stories of dozens of Mannheim residents while listening to live traditional Turkish music coming from the building next door before ending up drinking homemade Russian schnapps while watching one of the students of the Popakademie (popular music academy) perform a ballad from the latest charts. Every festival station was as crowded as the streets, and the visitors, in terms of age, language, gender, appearance, etc., were as varied as the festival's program (Fig. 2.2).

Spaces can be experienced and imagined in multiple ways, as explained in regard to Jungbusch. The same applies for the Neckarstadt-West, which has a similar festival called the Lichtmeile (light mile) that takes place in November. During this time, the district is illuminated by different colored lights and hosts concerts, exhibitions, and workshops for children and adults alike.

In fact, the Neckarstadt-West experienced quite a few changes during the time of the fieldwork and the writing of this work. For example, three new art galleries opened, the old bakery was remodeled into a rustic-style cafe, and the closed kiosk at Neumarkt (new market) was reopened by the

Zwischenraum Project, which aims to retake empty city spaces and turn them into spaces of social interaction and art.[8] The center of the neighborhood, which previously was used mostly by older men drinking alcohol and smoking, was overtaken by this entirely new kiosk concept: offering selections of wines, live-music evenings and open-air movie nights. It is possible that these changes are signs of an imminent gentrification of the neighborhood; however, what these descriptions show is that perceived danger and enjoyment can coexist in leisure activities and that individuals and collectives can interact with and within spaces in multiple creative ways. What the publicly available Mannheim statistics concerning percentages of unemployment and migration, especially for particular neighborhoods, fail to show is exactly this multifaceted way in which individuals encounter spaces and each other. They fail to show, for example, that people engage in internal city movements according to the activity they are pursuing and that Neckarstadt and Jungbusch are important centers of leisure for their inhabitants and for inhabitants of other neighborhoods and even cities as well. Some of my respondents lived there; most did not, but they still spent some of their leisure there.

Yet it is also important to remember how the perception of Mannheim and these particular neighborhoods affects leisure because perceived danger affects how spaces are used and how, in practice, leisure is executed. The "buddy system" is one mechanism women used to contrast feelings of insecurity within indoor spaces such as nightclubs. Other countermeasures practiced outdoors by my informants include calling and taking a taxi instead of walking home or walking in groups instead of doing so alone. Calling a taxi can also involve taking one or walking to the house of the person in the group who lives closest and staying the night there. Money for transportation is calculated in the night's budget as part of a risk analysis: it may cost more, but it is safer and more comfortable (second priority). Individuals express agency in that they organize their way around this barrier to leisure. Women often stress the importance of taking a taxi and not walking alone in these neighborhoods and recommend that others to do the same. This is a recommendation also I have often heard men tell women. So, the street, in particular the street at night or dawn, is perceived to be a dangerous space. Although the events of the city or spaces in the city can facilitate leisure, individuals have to surmount what is perceived as the criminality barrier in order to get and come from there. Other spatial barriers to leisure can be, for example, if places are not accessible or not easily accessible using public transportation (Hatzfeld 2001).

This occurs in Mannheim and its surroundings, especially in the case of shopping malls, lakes, wellness spas, and sauna centers, where accessibility is closely linked to car ownership, but not for city events, which mostly take place in central locations. Jungbusch and Neckarstadt are easily accessible by public transportation or even by walking, but they are dangerous at night.

Mannheim, therefore, has many leisure opportunities; some come from the private sector, some from the districts and the city, and some from non-governmental organizations and individuals. Many take place in cooperation with all of these groups. As mentioned earlier, one of the main private activities in which these women participated was the various physical activities offered by gyms and fitness centers. What is important about these larger neighborhood or city wide events is that, through leisure experiences, which include drinking, eating, enjoying music, dancing, and the like, feelings of belonging to the city and the community are being produced and reproduced, which (besides monetary gains) is exactly the organizers' goal. Many such events are planned in the context of community building by the district management centers, or Quartiersmanagement. Indeed, conversations with social workers in charge of such community work cast light on the goal of counteracting the anonymity of the city, of making neighbors known persons instead of strangers. Van Gennep (1977, p. 29) mentioned the importance of such activities for belonging, as part of rites of incorporation. These events show that not only can individually organized leisure in small social circles have different functions and meanings, so can collectively shared leisure experiences, which often are repeated year after year and take form of ritualized practices for attendees.

Despite the fact that evening and nighttime leisure experiences play an important role in the lives of these women, not all leisure takes place after dusk. There are spaces in the city that are particularly important for their daytime leisure and that these women value highly. The rivers Rhine and Neckar, which give the region its name, play an important role in the construction of leisure. They are spaces in which to practice sports, meet socially, read, sunbathe, and participate in events. (There are also activities that take place on ships in the rivers.) These spaces are special because they seem to be used independently of sociodemographic aspects. It is possible, for instance, to observe people of all ages, genders, and cultural backgrounds interacting with and within these spaces, something that is not always the case with other leisure spaces. In contrast, in the other leisure spaces in which these women participate, particular segments of the

Fig. 2.3 Neckar shore in the spring

Fig. 2.4 Rhine shore in the spring (Picture taken Sunday, June 14, 2015, 1757)

population tend to be overrepresented; for example, although the events mentioned are attended by people of all ages and cultural backgrounds, mostly they are people interested in culture and with high education, mainly middle to upper middle class (Figs. 2.3 and 2.4).[9]

The river shores are interesting spaces that are used all year round but by different individuals for different purposes, even though their significance for leisure increases with certain weather conditions and seasons. What I wish to highlight here is that, first, these natural spaces have an immense importance for leisure in the city and, second, different individuals, including the women of this study, make different use of these spaces. For example, although a couple of my informants use the spaces as transitory spaces for running or cycling, others make use of them by having picnics, which might take an entire afternoon. Other favorite interactions for these spaces include dog walking, playing with children, smoking shisha (water pipes), and barbecuing. Additional activities take place, such as buying and selling illicit substances, like marijuana, in particular under the bridges that cross the rivers. Interestingly, these illicit activities do not take place very secretly, as it is quite possible to see customers and dealers completing their transactions in the middle of the day while all the rest of the people continue with their activities. Aitchison (2003, p. 44) highlighted the importance of including illicit activities in leisure analysis. Indeed, a couple of my informants said that smoking weed is similar to alcohol, in terms of it being a part of some leisure experiences: enhancing relaxation and bodily consciousness, but as facilitator and not as a goal itself. However, in conversation, the women indicated that they would not buy from the vendors under the bridge because of trust issues.

The interesting characteristic about the shores, in particular the northern Neckar shore between the Neckarstadt-West and the University Hospital, a distance comprising about four kilometers (2½ miles) of shoreline, is that all these activities and types of individuals coexist (mostly) harmoniously in a relatively small area. Such coexistence of heterogeneous individuals leads to the production and reproduction of local identities through conviviality or, in other words, through cohabitating and interacting in multicultural spaces characteristic of urban areas (Gilroy 2004, p. xi). As the shores are free, in the sense that access to them does not require payment or consumption, and because they are right in the middle of the city, they are very accessible. Spending time and interacting in those spaces is one of the key elements of life in Mannheim and an element that binds all kinds of people together into a common local identity. It could be said that the shores are part of Mannheim's lifestyle, especially spring and summer lifestyles.

Despite the generally smooth coexistence of very diverse people, and the feelings of belonging to the city or its neighborhoods, conflict or problems are not absent from such spaces. When different individuals with different interests meet in the same space, it can potentially give rise to conflict. Differences in power relations play an important role in how leisure dynamics take place (s. Spracklen 2013, p. 175). These spaces, with their cement pathways, their green grass, and sandy areas used as beaches, are special because some social norms might not apply within them, for example, an apparent lack of clothing (women in bikinis, shirtless men, naked children). Thomassen (2012, p. 21) has called beaches and the seaside the "archetypical" liminal landscapes. Liminal spaces can be less controlled by the state institutions, as the open selling of drugs under the Kurpfalzbrücke shows. The absence of control can, in some instances, mean an increased danger. Liminal spaces can be more dangerous than other spaces, which is something that must be addressed in order to better understand them (Andrews and Roberts 2012), but danger must not necessarily be a consequence of liminality; liminality can also imply in this case that there will be an imbalance of power that leads to an unfair resolution of a conflict due to lack of control. As such, one could question whether there is liminality at all.

It has been seen, for example, when discussing physical activities, how in the case of gyms the use of space is gendered. Gender relations also play a role in the context of Mannheim's shores and potential problems. Gender dynamics was one important issue highlighted by my informants when talking about leisure on the shores. It is possible that sexism is less apparent in "nonliminal" environments because it is controlled by norms or even laws preventing it. However, because of the nature of such leisure spaces, sexism can erupt again, and individuals, in this case my informants, must deal with it by themselves. For example, a couple of them complained about sexist comments made by men while they used these spaces for leisure, whether it was running, sunbathing, or reading on the shore. Comments like "Hey there, you look nice. Come have a beer with me" or "Why are you here alone? A woman should not be alone" were perceived as invasions of the private sphere, an interruption of the leisure experience by unwelcomed or even threatening approaches (particularly when involving a group of men). Despite my informants' generally positive discourse about migration topics, gender dynamics in public spaces proved a conflicted issue. These complaints were framed in a discourse on foreign men, migration or refugees, even when the woman making them is herself a migrant. For example, a migrant woman told me in a conversation: "These African guys, they don't let you run in peace. Before [they came] you could do this, but now, they are always bothering you."[10] Another nonmigrant woman said she had stopped making use of these spaces alone and did so only in a group for the same reason. It is important to highlight that these complaints were made long before the events of New Year's Eve 2015, when many women were harassed or assaulted by men in several train stations, and media coverage made an impression on public opinion. However, in the discourse of these women, problems with gender dynamics and use of space on the river shores were directly linked to issues of cultural difference. There is a common perception among these women that sexism is more present in some cultures than in others and that, in the case of leisure on the river shores, they face a type of sexism that is not present in what they associate with "German" culture.

In this case perceptions of "other" men are influenced not only by media discourses but also by their own experiences, including those experiences at the Neckar shore. I cannot dig deeper on the issue of sexism and culture here. However, it is important to understand that sexism in whatever form is an experienced reality during leisure for these women, even if their view on the relationship among sexism, culture, and ethnicity might be a generalization drawn from those singular experiences and preexisting stereotypes about particular cultures or ethnicities. It is possible that those sexist comments and approaches are a particularity of the specific group of men that makes use of the vicinity of the bridge as their leisure space as well. In fact, while running in that same area, I was also the target of sexist comments from what I strongly believe was the same group of men to whom my respondents were referring. All in all, leisure experiences and feelings of safety can be negatively affected by sexist comments and gender dynamics. The same lack of control that permits selling drugs allows harassment of women in public spaces to continue. Conversations also revealed that women consider going to the authorities pointless because "nothing" has happened to them, and the authorities would not react appropriately. One woman went so far as to say that authorities would *never* confront refugees with the consequences of their actions because of the current political climate. Again, as was shown with the streets at night, the shores are public spaces in which women feel solely responsible for their safety, and they take actions to ensure their well-being.

Nonetheless, what must be highlighted is that the interactions within leisure spaces can be conflictive, in the sense that the leisure of one person can be a barrier of the leisure of another, depending on the situation. While some of these women show agency by still being part of these spaces despite the possible issues they might encounter, some others might choose to retreat and find alternative ways to avoid those issues— for example, by choosing to enjoy the Neckar shore with company, by choosing to run another path, by enrolling in "women-only" fitness centers, by attending LGBT-exclusive events, and so on. This is in harmony with Wearing's (1998, p. 141) argument that women-only spaces might enable women to appropriate and take control of spaces outside of the control of men. However, whether these kinds of alternatives perpetuate the status quo instead of changing toward more nondiscriminating or egalitarian environments remains open.

In fact, these women (departing from their narratives and my own experiences of work and leisure in the city) encounter more gender inequality in their leisure than in their work life. Even though most of them deal with gender issues by adapting to them, it is still an issue during leisure. In this sense, social norms and views still apply during leisure and in leisure spaces, which leads me to argue that they are not liminal or in between but, in fact, another area in which heterosexual masculinity has an advantage, as Spracklen (2013, pp. 115–119) argued. Can spaces be liminal to some (who can act outside the rules) while still oppressive for others? Wearing (1998, p. 80) also argued that there is a struggle between men and women over leisure spaces, but this might imply that it is an equal struggle, while, in actuality, it is the women or minorities who must struggle to overcome the barriers put before them. The issue of ethnicity or race can also be a source of inequality and, in the case of leisure, a barrier to overcome. In the particular case of the woman of this study, barriers to leisure were not placed in the context of ethnicity (except for the case of winter sports) while, in the case of public leisure spaces, barriers were explicitly mentioned in the context of gender dynamics. All in all, as Longa and Hylton (2014, p. 388) argued, ethnicity is not a determiner for inclusion in activities and opportunities: it must be considered alongside many other factors, some of which might gain more importance situationally.

What must be emphasized is that there are different kinds of leisure spaces for different purposes in which different individuals interact in the city. These spaces are specific to the locality, such as in neighborhoods like Neckarstadt and Jungbusch and in areas such as the Rhine and Neckar shore. Even though I have emphasized individual leisure at the riverside, these are also important spaces for city events. The natural environment shapes and is shaped by the people living in it (Fig. 2.5).

Fig. 2.5   Neckar shore festival, Lebendiger Neckar (Picture taken June 21, 2015)

All in all, such events, as well as the many leisure opportunities Mannheim offers, contribute to the perceived positive sides of the city. I have highlighted that Mannheim cannot be isolated from the regional context, in which the city is imagined and narrated, and that there are different contexts as well, in which the city's districts or neighborhoods are experienced. Additionally, while there are spaces that can serve multiple functions, there are other spaces, such as the Rhine and Neckar shores, that are predominantly leisure spaces and play an immense role for the leisure of these women (despite problems) and the city's population in general. For those spaces that serve multiple purposes, the city's events transform them during particular periods of time into public leisure spaces. These events not only play a role for these women as individuals but also enfold them in part of a collective that interacts with and within the city. These events, which repeat every year, contribute to the generation of feelings of belonging within the city in general.

To sum up, this section has focused on different aspects of Mannheim as locality, but I have mentioned an additional aspect that plays a role and influences everyday life, including leisure, and that is related to the natural environment: seasons and weather conditions. As I consider next, this aspect not only affects leisure on an individual scale but also influences how leisure, particularly in the form of events, is organized and executed.

2.2   THE ANNUAL CYCLE OF URBAN LEISURE: EVENTS, SEASONAL CHANGES AND WEATHER

Oh my God, in winter? Well, I cook something with my friends at home. I mean, who likes to go out when it's cold outside? So you end up at somebody's place, that's it. (Respondent A., May 12, 2015)

With some exceptions (s. DeLuca 2016), the analysis of lifestyle and leisure incorporates few or no weather conditions and aspects of climate. Even in the case in which DeLuca (2016) mentioned swimming as essential to a certain class and their "summer lifestyles," there is no deeper analysis of how weather and seasons influence the constitution of leisure. In some cases, the absence of environmental conditions in the analysis can be traced back to the exclusive focus on sociodemographic characteristics of the individual (vertical paradigms) (s. Isengard 2005, pp. 255–256); in others, it can be traced back to the absence of external factors influencing individual leisure choices (subject-oriented paradigms). The myriad of aspects that influence the leisure of the individual is considerable, however. The previous section highlighted, for example, that the social context and the locality in which individuals constitute everyday life can be as important as the sociodemographic characteristics of their leisure because the locality is influenced by the multiplicity of individuals living in it and, in turn, exercises an influence on people encountering it and engaging in it as well. It is therefore important to take into account other characteristics of the locality, specifically seasons and weather. Recent ethnographic studies seldom deal with these kinds of aspects together. These factors have come to the foreground mostly in the context of studies on climate change and natural disasters (s. Ulloa 2014, p. 19). Nonetheless, the influence of weather factors has been well researched in the context of their influence on physical activity and health (Spinney and Millward 2011, p. 143).

If we are to dig into the issue of climate and weather, it is important to have some knowledge about the specific environment in which these women experience their everyday life. Search engine results concerning weather in Mannheim often list it as one of the best locations in the country because of the amount of sunlight it receives in comparison with other German cities.[11] However, Mannheim still has four seasons, with a generally snowless and mild winter (average of −1 °C; 30 °F) and an average of 170 days of rain a year (Wetterdienst 2016). General climate data such as this has been used in other contexts, for example, in studies that relate sedentary and low physical activity to lower levels of sunlight and higher levels of rain (Spinney and Millward 2011, p. 134). In this section, I aim to show how climate and weather conditions affect individual leisure patterns by affecting leisure possibilities (including events), perception, and choices.

As considered in previous chapters when dealing with the meaning of leisure, we saw how weather conditions and seasons are interrelated with the perception of leisure in practice and ideal. We saw, for example, how the ideal of leisure is associated with warm weather and sun and that women tended to spontaneously associate leisure in their narratives to activities they pursue outdoor (under certain weather conditions), like barbecuing, walking, sunbathing, and the like. The same occurs when talking about leisure in relation to the locality, in this case, Mannheim. As respondent A. mentioned on May 12, 2015:

> Mannheim, I think, is actually okay at first sight. It's not nice but then it has something. When you have gotten used to it, leisure opportunities are big, especially when the weather is nice. There are the two rivers Rhine and Neckar, you have the Strandbad, you can go there and barbecue. Yeah, I think it's varied here. Or Luisenpark is also there. You can chill or barbecue there, just like that.

As the quote shows us, what is highlighted as positive things are leisure activities in the outdoor spaces of the city. The perception of the city is interrelated with the leisure opportunities perceived for both indoor and outdoor activities. The precise moment of an interview or a conversation can also affect which kinds of activities are mentioned because recent experiences are fresher in the memory.[12] Yet, in general, the women primarily associate leisure with certain weather conditions, sunny but not too hot (over 30 °C; 86 °F) or too cold (below 17 °C; 42 °F). In this context, the discourse on the leisure opportunities of the city are primarily focused on outdoor leisure activities. In practice, the individual interacts with the locality and its weather characteristics, an interaction that tends to form everyday life and leisure patterns. Therefore, the leisure of the individual is not isolated from the environment, both social and physical, yet the amount of influence such conditions can have on lifestyles can be an issue of discussion. Gramsci (1992, pp. 356–357) argued that urban and rural areas are affected differently by the seasons and weather conditions, in part because of the nature of work being done in them. Additionally, others argue that it is the infrastructure of the city that allows its population to be less affected by the seasons and weather conditions, with leisure in the city being less affected by bad weather conditions than leisure in rural areas (Böecker et al. 2013, p. 75).

Earlier I showed how my informants relate to Mannheim as the main space in which they constitute their everyday lives. The locality, with its social and physical components, is influenced by and influences individuals' formation of lifestyle in general and leisure in particular. For example, I highlighted the importance of the riversides for leisure in the city, but these areas (and the people interacting within them) are also affected by weather conditions and seasonal changes. It is not uncommon to see the grass field of the shores disappear in spring and summer days, flooded by rain or melting snow from other regions. As a consequence, flooding of these areas impacts the leisure activities that normally take place in them, meaning that runners, bikers, and dog walkers, for example, have to find alternative leisure spaces. The same happens with strong summer storms, which can end up flooding the popular city beaches, bars, and lounges, all of which disappear under water for a couple of days.

The example of the river shores shows that urban areas and their inhabitants are not exempt from the influence of seasonal changes and weather conditions. However, because of urban infrastructure and leisure opportunities, it is possible that the extent of how much individuals living in urban areas are affected by weather, just depending on the type of activity (outdoor activities are in fact more linked to warmer seasons and weather). What the fieldwork made clear is that seasonal changes and weather conditions play a role in regard to leisure, both on the collective and the individual level. On a collective level, leisure is closely related to local events and the cyclic nature of seasons; on an individual level, it is important to see how the individual adapts to the local conditions in everyday life and forms her own cyclic rhythm of leisure. As Freitas (2015, p. 58) pointed out, individuals are not passive actors in the face of weather, but they can adapt by changing activities, avoiding areas, shortening stays, using umbrellas, and so on.

It is important to highlight that weather conditions (present and future) and seasons are an important part of everyday conversations. The anthropologist Kate Fox (2014, pp. 25–40) half ironically, half seriously addressed the issue of "weather talk" as one of the main features of the English society, this type of talk serving, according to her, to fulfill different social functions, such as breaking the ice with strangers or filling uncomfortable silences. Weather talk is, in this case also, a socially approved tool used to engage in conversation. Indeed, such weather talk was often observed and engaged in during the fieldwork. However, I cannot dig deeper into the dynamics of weather talk and whether or not they are a leisure experience here per se. What is interesting is how weather talk and leisure planning coincide in conversations. It can be witnessed, for example, in phrases, such as: "If the weather is good on Saturday we can do [...]" or "We can do [...] on Sunday; the weather will be good." There is an awareness of present and future weather conditions and a constant exchange of information about them, which is used to plan activities individually or collectively. Once more, technology plays a role in this exchange through weather apps, WhatsApp groups, and the like. Additionally, the local weather conditions are perceived to be generally bad and are often compared discursively to "better," sunnier places in southern Europe or the Caribbean in absense of an analysis of the infrastructural, socioeconomic or political conditions of those places. Good weather is considered to be the exception, and weather predictions are generally received skeptically, because weather is believed to be constantly and unforeseeably changing. Outdoor activities require special, careful consideration, and this is why they are planned using vague time frames to account for weather variations. Often they include alternative indoor backup plans. Yet the presence of "good" weather is not just one of the conditions of ideal leisure; it also makes possible another ideal. It gives rise to *spontaneity* because good weather is often unexpected. For example, friends will call each other to go swimming or to have a drink together on a terrace on a sunny day. As respondent A. said on February 3, 2015:

> Yeah, yeah. You know, in the summer you can just make a plan after work, right? "Let's go have a drink, go to a Biergarten, go to the Neckar shore to sunbathe awhile, let's do a barbecue, cook something in the terrace or garden." You actually *feel* like doing something after work, something that doesn't happen in winter. In winter, everyone wants to get home because it's cold. I mean, okay, you can do stuff inside, like some classes or stuff, but, in the summer, you want to get some fresh air after six months of indoors and jacket.

Beyond weather playing a role in communication and being a topic about which individuals wish to be informed, seasonal changes and their repetition year after year bring a cyclic rhythm to individuals' leisure. Their effect, however, might not be the same for all individuals. Seasons have an effect on nightlife, for example, but the effect might not be the same for everyone. One woman mentioned that she went clubbing more often in colder seasons while in the summer she typically pursued activities outdoors. In contrast, another woman stated that she went partying more often in the summer because she felt more like it than she did in the winter. The use of spaces differs and changes with seasonal changes, and this is true not only in public spaces but for private ones (home leisure) as well. For those women who have balconies or gardens at their homes, their use of their home space and home leisure activities changes as well. More time is invested, for example, in gardening, reading in the sun, and sunbathing instead of watching TV series.

Seasonal changes also affect one of the most important of leisure activities: sports and physical activities. For those informants who practice sports all year around, physical activity, particularly outdoor activities like swimming, running, riding the bike, and beach volleyball, increases in spring and summer. Mostly they are pursued as well as the activities pursued in other seasons. They do not work as substitutes but are complementary. A few women mentioned practicing winter sports, like snowboarding and skiing, but because the nature of those activities requires traveling, they are planned for as part of winter vacations or extended weekend trips. Respondant S. explained on May 10, 2015:

> My vacations? Well, my last vacation was in February or March. We went skiing, I do that every year, snowboarding and, ehm, yeah, I like to do that kind of activity in my vacations, or in the summer. Last year I went surfing in the summer. I also like to do that, so you have the activity, a little sport, but you can also lay cozy at the beach. A mix then.

This shows that external conditions foster variation of activities, in that the individual adapts to them and participates in leisure in that given context. Because seasons are not totally random, certain individual patterns repeat themselves with the passing of time. As the quote shows, it is common for individuals to have vacation patterns that are formed by different aspects such as preferred weather, destination, pricing, and so on. The section on vacations in the chapter on leisure practices will describe how women decide either to spend their vacation time at home or they decide to travel. Seasons and weather conditions are two of the important aspects that influence the how, when, and where of vacations, as respondent J. explained on May 22, 2015:

> So I did that this year too, so it's that I travel in January to gain something back from the winter, and load a little bit of sun: It's a good time to travel, the summer is also nice here so I must not be in Spain or so, I can go when it is gray and rainy here [...] I like to travel but in the case that I can't because I don't have any money then I'll go to the lake or swimming pool, make some day trips with my friends, or go in the city and shop, that's what we do yeah.

The vacation pattern can also often be the result of interplay between seasons and the composition and context of social relations. So, while the woman from the last quote to spend the summer in Mannheim and spend her leisure with friends, another woman, like respondent A. (interviewed February 3, 2015) might enjoy the local summer less because of the social conditions:

> I mean, it depends because many people go on vacation in the summer, so the city is kind of alone. This time I didn't go but all my friends were gone, to Mallorca or, I don't know, some went to Mexico, and I was alone, working. At work there weren't many people either because those who have kids leave in the summer. So, the city is empty, right? So, I did see my friends more often than I do in winter, but only those who were there, people leave in the summer I think, and there are parties but they are not as full because people want to be outside and not inside a club.

Leisure, then, is affected not only by the characteristics of individuals and of their social network and the locality but also by seasonal changes, which are local but also shared on a regional or national level. However, some authors argue that there can be gender differences regarding weather conditions and their effect on outdoor activities, with women being more affected by "bad" weather conditions, such as rain, for example (Böecker et al. 2013, p. 75). Yet, among my informants, perceived bad weather had a relatively low influence on physical activity because most of them either engage in indoor activities in fitness studios and/or are committed to specific training schedules. It is therefore not so much that "bad" weather is a barrier but that good weather fosters even more physical activity for them. This can be seen in the light of some studies that link urban and rural aspects to barriers to physical activities, with urban women perceiving bad weather as less of a barrier than women in rural spaces, partly because of the facilitating infrastructure (s. ibid.). Indeed, the wide availability of indoor leisure activities in Mannheim, along with a good transportation system (or car ownership) and relatively short travel distances, contributes to overcoming barriers posed by bad weather conditions.

Yet beyond individual plans and preferences, the locality itself has a rhythm of life and leisure that interplays with external conditions and, like individual leisure, shows a divide between indoor and outdoor activities. The big events of the city are closely linked to seasonal changes. Some of them stem from centuries-old traditions or historical processes often related to the dynamics of trade and politics, such as the Christmas market in winter, the carnival, the spring and autumn fairs, and the Maimarkt in April/May.

Other, more recent events are also linked or organized around seasonal changes and weather factors, such as the city marathon midspring,[13] the feast of the city at the beginning of summer, and the Christopher Street Parade midsummer. It could be said that the outdoor event period of Mannheim starts with the Maimarkt at the end of April and ends mid-September with the Schlossfest on the grounds of the University of Mannheim, with many large, medium, and small events taking place in between.

However, events like the Christmas market, the carnival, and the already mentioned Nachtwandel and Lichtmeile offer a break from the indoor activities of the colder seasons. All these events are characteristic of life on the local level: they influence life for all residents regardless of attendance because they "occupy" the city. Due to the size of the city, the presence of such events is particularly obvious: tram routes cease temporarily or are rerouted; thousands of participants congregate in small spaces; and music, food, and alcohol is available on the street in trucks or built-in kiosks. For example, conversations often brought to light the fact that, for those who do not like the carnival, the period of its duration is time best spent avoiding the city center or even traveling to regions with no carnival tradition. However, these types of events, which are crowded with thousands of people, are part of the common understanding of life in the city. Choosing to participate in them is not only related to leisure experiences but also forms in a sense of belonging that is produced and reproduced year after year (Figs. 2.6, 2.7, 2.8, and 2.9).

Orley (2012, p. 37) argued that places remember events and that they are interactive, retaining traces of what has happened there; they continue the interaction with people who encounter them and bring those traces to life. As such, beyond everyday life, these events are examples of how individuals interact with and in Mannheim, producing and reproducing the city itself. Orley also said that it is possible to see all places as liminal, as transitory because what they are depends on what is happening at that moment (p. 39). Despite the fact that events and situations can change and that the city can be in constant transition, some transitions repeat in cyclical form. Therefore, in order to understand patterns, it is necessary to look beyond a moment, beyond an event, to grasp how a locality and the individuals therein interact over larger periods of time.

However, it is also important to clarify that not all events are the same. Despite the fact that the events just mentioned are the main events of the city in terms of attendance numbers, promotional efforts, official involvement, and support of the city's institutions, participant observation allows

Fig. 2.6   Christmas market at Wasserturm (Picture taken December 7, 2014)

Fig. 2.7   MonnemAhoi! Carnival celebrations (Picture taken February 15, 2015, Mannheim city center)

Fig. 2.8   Mannheim Marathon (Picture taken May 9, 2015. Estimated number of spectators: 100,000. Estimated number of participants: 12,000 (SRH Dämmer Marathon Presseinformation 2015)

Fig. 2.9   Mannheim city festival (Picture taken May 29, 2015, Mannheim city center)

for an understanding of the differences among them: differences regarding general atmosphere and visitors as well as the kind of leisure experience they provide. These events are visited by a multitude of people of different ages, genders, and ethnicities, but there are some observable tendencies. For example, largely families with children visit the carnival parade to watch the parade and catch the candies and giveaways thrown to the crowd. Adults who attend without children tend to congregate around the (mostly alcoholic) beverage stands and remain there after the parade has finished. Festivals, such as the city festival and the Schlossfest, which are primarily music festivals with a wide range of music styles, attract a youthful majority, students and adults under 40, and a great variety of people speaking different languages and having different physical appearances as well. In contrast, the Maimarkt, the only one of these events that does not take place directly in the city center, attracts a significant part of the senior population. Interestingly, children were seldom found in the crowds of the Christmas market, nor were people of different ethnicities, despite the fact that all of my informants themselves were regular visitors to these markets. More interest-driven events, such as the marathon or the Christopher Street Day (CSD) parade, presented the most varied crowd in terms of age, gender, and ethnicity. In all of these events, except for the marathon, where alcohol consumption is very low among spectators and a few runners after they cross the finish line, alcohol consumption is a constant companion to the experience. There are, of course, individuals who do not consume alcohol at such events due, for example, to their being designated drivers, undergoing medical treatment, their personal taste, or religious grounds, but these people are often exceptions to the rule. Alcoholic beverages, whether beer, cocktails, shots, or wine, are not only a companion to these specific leisure experiences, they are highly symbolic of and associated with the events and the leisure experience itself. In particular, the carnival is associated in public opinion with high alcohol consumption. Indeed, inebriated (sometimes in costumes) people are a common sight in the city during those days.

2.2.1   *It's the Most Wonderful Time of the Year!*

In order to show how these events relate not only to the leisure of the city as a whole but to the women of this study in particular, I will take the case example of the Christmas market, an event that is highly relevant for the outdoor winter leisure of these women. The Christmas market in Mannheim, as in many other German cities, takes place between the end of November and December 23 every year. It is dispersed across different locations in the city center, all of which have different names. The main location, for instance, is Wasserturm, with the market called Weihnachtsmarkt. The market held directly in the city center, Märchenwald, is particularly interesting for families with children during the afternoon and early evening because it is built like an enchanted forest, which presents different fairy tales. Because of its location, it is also well visited during the day by people employed in the vicinity. It is a space in which to take a short break and to eat or drink something. Kapuzinerplanken, an area mentioned previously as a posh area, also has a market. The market at Kapuzinerplanken is different because it focuses on handmade crafts, sold by the creators, and it is where wine makers sell a non-mass-produced product mulled wine called Winzerglühwein, at high prices in harmony with the high-end stores surrounding the Kapuzinerplanken. Notably, here, senior and well-off citizens dominate the demographic in attendance.

In the case of my informants, they all attended the main Christmas market as well as other markets in the region. For all of the interviewees, Christmas markets are a central part of leisure during the weeks in which they take place. The informants visited these markets multiple times, with colleagues, with friends, and/or with family. The experience of the Christmas market is often framed in a discourse of happiness and joyfulness and in the context of a nice atmosphere. Although all informants noted the atmosphere, the aesthetics were specifically highlighted by migrant interviewees as impressive, despite the fact that they have been in Germany for more than three years and so these types of markets are not a novelty for them. As respondent A. said on February 3, 2015:

> It is pretty, the stands, the lights. It is the nice thing about Christmas. After the market the winter is very sad [...] so it's nice to go listen to the music, see the people, drink something, buy something, stay for a while enjoying a different Christmas than what I was used to in Latin America. There, you don't have those stands, the people in jackets, so it's different: it's nice and pretty. Normally, I go here in Mannheim but I've [also] been to the ones in Nürnberg, Lübeck, and Hamburg.

The Christmas market experience is something that is repeated during the weeks in which the market lasts and year after year. Respondent C. explained on December 10, 2014:

> I love the Christmas market. I always go with my best friend. I also go to the one in Heidelberg near the castle, that one is also nice, and I love Glühwein. When it's really cold outside, then the Glühwein is the best. You don't

> notice anything [laughs] and then, mmm, so delicious. It goes cold quickly so I think, okay, let me have another, and then, wow, okay, I can't drive anymore, eh? So, yeah, that's Christmas market, but it depends on who you are with. It has to be with the right people. I mean, I wouldn't go with my grandma to the Christmas market. I could, but no.

As mentioned, Mannheim and its individuals are not isolated entities. The city is intertwined in regional, national, and global contexts. This can also be seen in the case of Christmas markets and the leisure activity of hopping from one to another. Just as respondent A. indicated in the last quote, my informants visited not only the Mannheim Christmas market but many other markets in the region. However, besides changing the location, just as with any other leisure activities, the experience of the Christmas market depends on whom the individual is with and how they perceive or are emotionally attached to those social relations.

Yet Christmas market visits are also a common activity to pursue with colleagues. People often arrange to go have some drinks together at the Christmas market on a day after work, one example of the "nonideal" leisure experience. As has been seen, it does not mean that the women would not have a good time but that there are constraining factors to the leisure experience (e.g., expected behavior). Additionally, sports teams or language classes also organize joint visits to the Christmas markets. In these cases, the individual is part of a variety of groups that can but must not intersect with each other (s. Wirth 1938, p. 16). The interesting fact about events that last many days, such as Christmas markets, is that they are spaces in which the women share exactly the same setting with different groups and have different experiences as a consequence: leisure or leisure-like. This example can be placed in the context of Schulze's (2005, pp. 545–548) conclusion that one can buy the experience offered but that the experience itself is entirely subjective and created by each person him- or herself. One can, for example, choose the person(s) with whom to go to the Christmas market. All of these experiences have importance for the individual, as we will see in the chapter on the meaning of leisure: they can fulfill certain social functions, and they can give the individual the desired variety in leisure. Additionally, Christmas markets and other events offer a high probability for groups to meet tangentially due to the likelihood of bumping into someone familiar in the same space. In those cases, people greet each other briefly but generally remain (separated) with the group they arrived with.

All in all, a ritual characteristic could be recognized in this Christmas market activity: it is repetitive; it marks the beginning of the winter and the Christmas festivities; it involves eating and drinking together; and it generates group cohesion whether it is with friends or colleagues. It also instills wider collective belonging on a citywide, regional, or national scale because it is perceived to be a common national tradition. So, some of these events could be considered seasonal rituals as they are important parts of the life cycle of the inhabitants (s. Turner 1982, p. 110), who allow for a disruption to their routines. For example, Sundays are generally family days or stay-at-home days. However, for the Christmas markets an exception is made. As respondent I. said on December 16, 2014: "At the moment I go very often to the Christmas market because it is there. Otherwise I leave my Sundays free."

Zifonun (2010, p. 320) pointed out that locality plays a key role in how collective identities are perceived and negotiated and that the setting of the locality can determine how collectives—for example, the status of a certain ethnicity—are perceived. The events mentioned here are important elements of Mannheim as locality, and the participation or absence of minorities also has an effect on the perception of such groups. Indeed, the events of the city of Mannheim show a balance of what Taylor (2001, pp. 535–536) called assimilating leisure activities and leisure activities that celebrate cultural differences. While participation by migrants in Christmas markets or carnivals could be a form of assimilation into dominant cultural practices (s. ibid.), events such as the city festival and Nachtwandel focus precisely on the expression and celebration of cultural differences. In contrast, events such as the CSD focus on the expression and celebration of differences regarding gender and sexuality. Such collective events help to go beyond the selective exposure of milieus, as argued by Schulze (s. Schulze 2005, p. 267), by exposing individuals to a higher variety of people and by providing the possibility of communicating with them, thus departing from people's own "reality model."

However, ritual and tradition are not the only motivating factors behind the women's Christmas market attendance. The visit to the Christmas market was also framed in a discourse of alternatives. Colder months are perceived to have fewer leisure opportunities; the Christmas market is a welcomed leisure experience in a leisure drought period because it is an exception to the indoor activities. Additionally, because of the ritual aspect and its importance, uncomfortable cold weather conditions are overcome. As respondent A. explained on February 3, 2015:

I mean, [it] is the only outdoor thing you can do in the winter, [to] go to the Christmas market and have a drink and then go back home under your blanket. So, yeah, you have no option. You cannot travel because you can't spend the day walking around. The landscapes don't look as pretty. For example, I was in Copenhagen one month ago. I had been there a year and a half ago in the summer and it was a beautiful city—I loved it: my favorite European city—and then I went in January and I was, like, no, this can't be. This is such a horrible city in the winter.

Moreover, the cold itself is actually part of the Christmas market experience, with some women complaining about mild winters and the fact that the market just wouldn't be the same if it was not cold enough (minus temperatures). Furthermore, for some women, the experience of the Christmas market is a goal per se, or an isolated leisure experience, while, for others, it is one of a series of events, a sort of "warm-up" activity before going to a bar and/or clubbing. Even though the Christmas market is a collective event, on an individual level, the interaction with space, and therefore with Mannheim as space, is constructed as a flow of events in a single night, as described by Corsin Jimenez (2003, p. 148) in the case of evenings in a Brazilian avenue. A Saturday evening in December for these women can start at the Christmas market with some friends having a Glühwein and a bratwurst, followed by some cocktails at a bar in the city center, then to a nightclub at around midnight, all activities taking place in a two-kilometer (1¼-mile) radius. Even though each stage could be considered separately, such leisure experiences are often remembered and reflected upon a posteriori as *one* great (or not) night in Mannheim. One of the things making them great is often the successful construction of a flow without drastic pace changes or interruptions.

Events like the Christmas market embody what can be called seasonal rituals because they do not involve change in status for the participants, but the participants "have been ritually prepared for a whole series of changes in the nature of the cultural and ecological activities to be undertaken and of the relationships they will then have with others" (Turner 1974, p. 57). The Christmas market marks the beginning of the cold season and helps build up the mood of the Christmas and New Year's celebrations. Events such as this exemplify how individual leisure intersects and overlaps with rituals of the locality as space and as network of (social) networks (s. Hannerz 1980, pp. 244–312).

2.2.2   World's Mega-events on Site

Until now, this chapter has addressed events that are important for the construction of the city as leisure space and that follow seasonal patterns. However, a special event I would like to mention because of the immense influence it had on city dynamics and individual leisure is the soccer World Cup, which took place in the summer of 2014. Even though it took place shortly before the fieldwork officially started, I was already immersed in the field in an exploration phase and was able to observe and participate during these events. In part, this event could also be considered a seasonal event because it repeats every four years and is recognized as an important part of the summer. The special characteristic about this event is that, although it does not formally take place in this specific city, in practice, it does: it is a global event that influences people and localities around the globe, regardless of where it is taking place physically.

In the case of Mannheim, during those weeks the city was filled with different sounds. It was common to hear crowds cheering from inside bars or on terraces, screams coming from balconies or living rooms, and car horns blowing in celebration. During matches, the streets were empty. For Mannheim, this did not mean that people were only watching the German team's matches with special attention. The diversity of people in the city, many of whom come from countries participating in this global event, made for a collective interest in the tournament. Yet overlapping and changing belongings (s. Zifonun 2010, pp. 312–313) were particularly visible during this time as individuals who owned different team's T-shirts would wear them on the appropriate match days and would hang two flags denoting competing teams over their apartment balcony or have the flags painted on their faces. The Neckarstadt-West, for example, where the majority of the population consists of migrants with Italian, Greek, or former Yugoslavian backgrounds (Kommunale Statistikstelle 2015b), was always the location for an event because of the matches played by Italy, Greece, Croatia, and Bosnia-Herzegovina. All of this was accompanied by a fervent support for the German team, especially after the other teams had been eliminated (Fig. 2.10).

During the tournament, the city was in constant tension, experiencing joy, frustration, and sadness, and the smell of sweat and beer seemed to be forever present. Appadurai (1996, p. 2) said that modernity is a "embodied sensation," and this idea could also be applied to the World Cup, as the body interacts with the smells, sounds, sights, and tastes of the city.

Fig. 2.10 Fans during 2014 soccer world championship. End of the match, Germany vs. USA. *Alte Feuerwache event center* (Picture taken Thursday, June 26, 2014, 2016)

The soccer World Cup became the main topic of conversation as, all of a sudden, strangers talked to each other more frequently. This was World Cup talk similar to the weather talk that allows social approaches. My informants, with whom I talked about it months later, often mentioned (without prompting) that this event had been a big part of their summer leisure. For some, soccer plays a big role in their lives, not only because they play it themselves but because of the time they spend watching it on TV or live in a stadium. Yet the World Cup had different proportions. Even though it was not an event that took place in the city, the city was definitely part of the event experience. This citywide experience was magnified during the final phases of the tournament and the success of the German team and reached its peak after the team's victory in the final. People poured out on to the streets, in cars and on foot, to celebrate Germany's triumph. The city's streets were blocked, and horns and fireworks accompanied the celebrations. Strangers high-fived or hugged each other in an emotional state that was truly contagious.

The euphoria of the World Cup could be explained by the evident, insatiable need for sensation to be drawn from mass events (s. Huizinga 1940, p. 331) or the increasing need of outer stimuli to achieve an inner leisure experience (s. Schulze 2005, pp. vii–xx). Appadurai (1996, pp. 89–113) used the example of cricket in India to show how a sport and its events can help fans and players experience a classless and religious-free community, at least in that particular situation. The phenomenon of the World Cup and its resulting mass events has been widely studied. Most attention has been given to the consequences for the countries hosting the tournament, in terms of related socioeconomic factors (s. Schulke 2007) and community-building issues (s. Ndlovu-Gatsheni 2011), but the case of Mannheim shows that spaces and events go beyond territorial boundaries: they are interconnected, and they find expression in the local dimension of nonhost localities as well, bringing to light different belongings and generating mass-shared leisure experiences that stay in the memories of individuals and collective memories.

In the weeks leading up to and surrounding the World Cup, an example of community building was evident when differences that in everyday life have consequences for inequality, such as nationality or ethnicity (s. Bolte 1990, p. 30), became differences with no negative consequences. What arose was a kind of "soccer community." Sabelo Ndlovu-Gatsheni (2011) wondered skeptically about how long the South African national unity on the issue of equality, which was created by the collective support of the national team, would last. Beyond national levels, Kimberly Schimmel (2014) pointed out the importance of understanding how sports events interact with the host city and how events such as the Brazil 2014 World Cup can generate interpersonal attachment or bring to light conflicts and inequalities. Urban spaces are not homogeneous units that benefit as a whole from sporting events. It follows, then, that the state of mind of the population in which those differences are welcomed during such events, and the sense of community or belonging found through an interest in soccer, as in the case of Mannheim, might be ephemeral. In contrast, Strümpell (2008) highlighted that this sense of belonging is not so much ephemeral but that it is theme-centered cohesion: equality achieved by conviviality (sharing a space) and commensality (eating together) is not an all-encompassing equality, it is situational. It is possible to be equals only in respect to one identity, for example, as sports fans during a tournament. These identities can overshadow others temporarily, but they do not replace them (Strümpell 2008, pp. 65–66). These kinds of identities are important though because they offer at least some common ground and some shared experiences for individuals who might otherwise not share anything but the local space.

In this context, it could be argued that the World Cup was for Mannheim, as it probably was for many other places in the world, a liminal state—not necessarily because what comes after is different from that which was before but because of the suspended state of transience were "normality" does not apply (s. Turner 1982, p. 113). Who plays and who is the audience does not matter, as all accept that same system of practices, rules, and parts of the ritual (p. 112). It is a ritual that could be considered outside of the normal structure of life (antistructure), and thus what people were experiencing was a form of *communitas* because it was outside of daily life and it was open to outsiders, allowing a state of equality and togetherness among participants (s. Turner 1989, pp. 96–116).

For example, alcohol (the leisure symbol and companion), which is normally present during the weekends for these women, had a much higher presence during this time because leisure experiences related to the World Cup also took place during the week. The identity as soccer fans and, by the end, German supporters was placed temporarily in the foreground, and nothing else mattered. Similar mass experiences (albeit on a smaller scale) can occur in the context of other kinds of sports (e.g., the main sport associated with Mannheim, ice hockey). As I wrote in a field note on April 23, 2015:

> I was traveling with the tram in the afternoon. It was around 4:30 pm on a Thursday. The city center was blocked and the trams were circulating with delay but, contrary to many delays I have experienced before, where people normally start making annoyed faces and wondering out loud what is wrong, no one said anything. It was pretty clear why the center was closed and what was causing the delay. The display information boards of the transportation company, which normally announce waiting times for each line, read: "Championship Celebration, delay in all lines." The previous day Mannheim's ice hockey team, the Adler, had won the national championship and on this day they were coming back to celebrate with the fans. When I finally managed to get out of the tram at Paradeplatz, I encountered a multitude [of people]. The team and the crew were there with the cup on the top of cars and pickups, some on foot signing autographs. Many in the crowd were wearing the team's uniform; some others seemed to be spontaneous spectators. The majority in the fan uniforms were men but there were also many children and women cheering the team. As I was standing there, I overheard someone ask their companion "what is going on?," seemingly oblivious to the success of one of the most prominent icons of Mannheim's

identity, which is present in billboards all over the city, in spots at the cinema, tickets raffled on the radio, mugs in souvenir shops, not to mention the masses in their large blue hockey T-shirts pouring in public transportation towards the SAP Arena every time there is a home match. The Adler are a symbol of the city, just like soccer teams are for other cities. Even for nonfans it is difficult to experience life in the city without crossing paths with the Adler, especially the year they've won the nationals.

According to different press releases, there were around 1500 fans gathered when the team showed the cup from the balcony at the town hall (s. Sport1 2015).[14] Indeed, the absence of a successful soccer team in higher divisions might contribute to the importance placed on the ice hockey and handball Rhein-Neckar Löwen teams for the city's identity. Yet, in the case of ice hockey, it might also be due to presence of US soldiers and what has been called the influence of "American" culture on Mannheim (s. Führer 2013, pp. 155–158). All in all, events such as the World Cup and ice hockey celebrations have similarities and differences regarding the type of identity they might help to produce and/or reproduce. Ultimately, the collective leisure experience they create locally would repeat itself, for example, with the subsequent European Football Championship in France in 2016.

On a local level, which is to be considered as a whole and not in isolation, these special, one-time global and national events are integral parts of the city, as are the events that repeat themselves more frequently and directly in the city. However, they all have a pivotal role in the construction of locality, the relationship between it and its individuals and how they keep constructing and reproducing it by celebrating together, sharing a space of celebration and leisure, and sharing an experience. The importance of such events, both the ones taking place every year and events such as the World Cup, is that they are sources of harmony. Just as Corsín Jiménez (2003, p. 150) argued that, for families, everyday life in the household can bring up conflicts while special occasions on the public sphere can release tensions, so can these events surmount everyday social conflicts and release tensions. As has been shown in other local contexts (s. Schwab 2015, pp. 174–178), ritualized experiences of the city bring people together and offer a stage in which to perform identity and thus reproduce it.

On an individual level, such events are important elements of leisure as they provide leisure experiences that are often highly emotional and part of the individual's memory and perception of his or her own biography, in which the locality is a feature. Thomassen (2012, p. 31) said that the lines between liminal and ordinary spaces are blurry and that it is necessary to understand how exactly individuals experience liminality and how they act in the face of it instead of focusing too much on the abstract concept itself. These types of city events show that the city can be both liminal and ordinary: it is in constant change, influencing people's lifestyles and leisure and being influenced by the people as well.

2.3   EXCURSUS: SUNDAY RUN ON THE NECKAR SHORE

On Sunday the third of May 2015, I woke up without an alarm and proceeded to put on my running outfit. Like some of my informants and many other inhabitants of the city, I had decided to go for a Sunday run despite the fact that the weather was cloudy and windy, threatening to rain, and the temperature just 14 °C (40 °F). I left the house at 12:30 and, like most runners in Mannheim, headed for the pathways on the riverside. I parted from the Neckarstadt on the northern side of the shore in an eastward direction toward Feudenheim. At this moment I was reminded of something I had read, in which it was written that leisure researchers like to research topics that they themselves find interesting or enjoyable (Spracklen 2013, p. 180), and I felt glad that the women I was researching also like running (even though they were not selected according to this criterion). In fact, it would be difficult to ascertain whether I was having a leisure experience myself or whether I was conducting some participant observation. Perhaps I was doing both, which would mean that I was in *Muße*.

The path took me past the university hospital, a restaurant, a large fitness center, and the athletic club MTG Mannheim. Being a spring day, and because it had rained the night before, I could smell the flowers and wet earth, which give me a nice refreshing feeling. Along the way, I passed a couple of dog walkers, three elderly men taking a walk and having a conversation, and multiple runners. Along the four-kilometer (2½-mile) route eastward, I crossed paths with four female runners and three male runners, all of whom were running alone. Judging by their looks, they were all between the ages of 24 and 50, white, in good shape, and with the latest functional running clothes. When the weather is nicer, you encounter more runners and walkers, people of all ages, genders, ethnicities. Their sporting attire is often less up-to-date and can be varied, which leads me to believe that bad weather filters out the "serious runners" (s. Allen-Collinson 2011, pp. 307–308) from the rest. Half of the people I came across were wearing earplugs, presumably listening to music. None of us said hello to each other while passing. Despite the fact that runners are aware of one another, the unspoken protocol is to look straight ahead, keep running, and not pay attention to the other runners, or other people for that matter. Dog walkers and walkers shift to the side when they see or hear a runner coming. The same applies when a bicycle is approaching. As with the runners, the amount of bike traffic increases with sun and warmth, and most bike riders will be in casual clothes on sunny days, while the more technical biking attire is predominant on bad-weather days.

I reached the bridge over the Neckarkanal and crossed it to turn around and head back. It took me to the southern shore, where I then ran in the opposite direction, westbound. The Hans-Renschke shore is always more crowded than its northern counterpart. Many people were riding their bikes in each direction, or running or walking on the cemented pathway, and the dog walkers were mostly on the grass field just below, closer to the water. This side is also noisier: you cannot hear birds or smell the earth there as you can on the other side. You hear the tram pass by every 10 or 15 minutes, hear cars driving by, hear the voices from the soccer matches taking place at the Carl-Benz-Stadion or the field hockey matches near the Luisenpark. This southern side of the shore requires more effort and is more challenging if you are running eastward because you typically have the wind against you and, if it is sunny, you receive less protection from the trees. In general, many of the runners did a round similar to mine, and we crossed paths on both sides of the shore (Fig. 2.11).

Fig. 2.11   Southern Neckar shore (Picture taken Sunday, April 12, 2015, 1217)

However, while on the other side I saw people running alone, here I passed two female students running and talking about their exams, two men running together, a mixed group of two men and a woman, a couple running with their baby carriage, as well as several single runners. It seemed to me that their ages also ranged from 20 to 50. From my mobile point of observation, I gathered that the fitness and thinness of the person often related to the tightness and functionality of their clothes. Some of the people running alone were wearing earplugs while the ones running in groups were talking.

Besides a few very small children in baby carriages or in child seats on their parents' bikes, I saw no children. On sunny days there are often children riding their bikes or skates, or walking or playing with their families. The time of day also affects the number of people you will encounter. Going out on a Sunday morning before nine, one will come across fewer walkers but more or less the same number of runners. Early on Saturday and Sunday mornings, I have also encountered drunk men on their bicycles, who are more likely to engage with other people by saying something. On a couple of occasions, I have heard them offer encouraging comments to runners, who in turn have ignored them and kept running.

All in all, compared to other Sundays during the year, there were more people running on this day. Perhaps it had something to do with the fact that in the following week, on May 9, the Mannheim marathon and half marathon would take place. As I approached the end of my route, close to the Kurpfalz Bridge, I come across the OEG Lounge and the Neckar Strand, which are popular on sunny days but which, today, due to the weather, were closed. I crossed the bridge and saw a man dressed in running clothes standing on a corner, seemingly waiting for someone. I kept on running toward home and stopped as I completed 10 kilometers (about 6 miles). The feeling after running is one of being tired but at the same time energized and motivated. It goes beyond good bodily feeling. Knowing this, I can understand my interviewees' descriptions of how they feel when they run or exercise. This is something that must be shared by all men and women who decide to engage in these activities—not only the 20 or so individuals with whom I crossed paths in the course of one hour and 10 minutes but also by many more, as the thousands of participants each year in the city's marathon and half marathon prove.

NOTES

1. Google Earth provides a nice overview of Mannheim's gridded city center.
2. For an overview of the Rhine-Neckar Region, access: https://www.m-r-n. com/fileadmin/user_upload/Image/05_Meta/Mediacenter/Karten/ Rhein-Neckar_Bundeslaender.jpg
3. Migrants, or *Einwohner mit Migrationshintergrund*, are considered those who were born in a foreign country, whether they are naturalized German or not, as well as those with at least a migrant parent.
4. For an overview of Mannheim's districts, access: https://www.mannheim. de/sites/default/files/page/2400/17_stadtbezirke_2013.pdf
5. This can be confirmed by searching for online or printed news on Mannheim for the last two years.
6. For more information, visit: http://mannheim.at/ and https://www. facebook.com/mannheimatblog/
7. "Monnemer" is the equivalent of "Mannheimer" in the local dialect. The term often is used purposefully in dialect to express belonging and emotional attachment.
8. For more information, visit: http://www.zwischenraum-ma.de/
9. This assessment is based on observations and participant observation that allowed me to gather knowledge about job descriptions, language use, physical appearances, manners, and the like.
10. Migrant women often reacted more emotionally in these situations, explaining their reaction as a consequence of frustration. They felt they had "escaped" these types of encounters through the migratory process, only to face them again in their current place of residence.
11. For more information, see, for example: Donnerwetter (2016): *Wetter-Ranking der Großstädte*. Available at: http://www.donnerwetter.de/ aktion/wetter-ranking/
12. In this regard, conversations or diary entries that took place days, weeks, or months after the interviews, as well as direct questions about leisure in other seasons, were helpful to understanding how leisure activities might change for the same individual.
13. The marathon likely organized was to have ideal weather conditions for running, with temperatures around 14 °C (57 °F).
14. The number of spectators probably would have been higher if it had not been during early afternoon on a weekday.

REFERENCES

Adorno, Theodor W. 1991. Free Time. In *The Culture Industry: Selected Essays on Mass Culture*, ed. Theodor W. Adorno and J.M. Bernstein, 162–170. London: Routledge.

Aitchison, Cara. 2003. *Gender and Leisure: Social and Cultural Perspectives*. London: Routledge.

Allen-Collinson, Jacquelyn. 2011. Feminist Phenomenology and the Woman in the Running Body. *Sport, Ethics and Philosophy* 5 (3): 297–313.

Andrews, Hazel, and Les Roberts. 2012. Introduction: Re-mapping Liminality. In *Liminal Landscapes: Travel, Experience and Spaces in-Between*, ed. Hazel Andrews and Les Roberts, 1st ed., 1–17. New York: Routledge.

Appadurai, Arjun. 1996. *Modernity al Large: Cultural Dimensions of Globalization*, 1. Minneapolis; London: University of Minnesota Press.

Badischer Sportbund. 2014. *Mitgliederstatistik*. http://www.badischer-sportbund.de/ DERVERBAND/Wirueberuns/Mitgliederstatistik/. Accessed October 6, 2014.

Barnett, Lynn. 2005. Measuring the ABCs of Leisure Experience: Awareness, Boredom, Challenge, Distress. *Leisure Sciences* 27: 131–155.

Bauman, Zygmunt. 2013. *Does the Richness of a Few Benefit Us All?* Cambridge: Polity Press.

Boecker, Lars, Martin Dijst, and Jan Prillwitz. 2013. Impact of Everyday Weather on Individual Daily Travel Behaviours in Perspective: A Literature Review. *Transport Reviews* 33 (1): 71–91.

Bolte, Karl M. 1990. Strukturtypen sozialer Ungleichheit: Soziale Ungleichheit in der Bundesrepublik Deutschland im historischen Vergleich. In *Lebenslagen, Lebensläufe, Lebensstile*, Soziale Welt Sonderband 7, ed. Peter Berger and Stefan Hradil, 27–50. Göttingen: Schwarz Verlag.

Bundesagentur für Arbeit Statistik. 2015. *Strukturdaten und -indikatoren Agentur für Arbeit Mannheim*. http://statistik.arbeitsagentur.de/Statistikdaten/ Detail/Aktuell/iiia4/zdf-sdi/sdi-644-0-pdf.pdf. Accessed August 7, 2015.

Carmichael, Fiona, Joanne Duberley, and Isabelle Szmiging. 2015. Older Women and Their Participation in Exercise and Leisure-Time Physical Activity: The Double Edged Sword of Work. *Sport in Society* 18 (1): 42–60.

Chavez, Deborah. 2000. Invite, Include and Involve!: Racial Groups, Ethnic Groups and Leisure. In *Diversity and the Recreation Profession: Organizational Perspectives*, ed. M.T. Allison and I.E. Schneider, 179–191. State College, PA: Venture Publishing.

COMFORT. 2014. *Comfort City Ranking*. http://www.comfort.de/fileadmin/ user_upload/COMFORT_ab_2014/teaser_und_banner_ab_2014/ COMFORT_City_Ranking_TOP_15.pdf. Accessed September 10, 2014.

Corsín Jiménez, Alberto. 2003. On Space as a Capacity. *The Journal of the Royal Anthropological Institute* 9 (1): 137–153.

Cortis, Natasha, Pooja Sawrikar, and Kristy Muir. 2008. *Final Report: Participation in Sport and Recreation by Culturally and Linguistically Diverse Women.*

DeLuca, Jaime R. 2016. Like a "Fish in Water": Swim Club Membership and the Construction of the Upper-Middle Class Family Habitus. *Leisure Studies* 35 (3): 259–277.

Fox, Kate. 2014. *Watching the English: The Hidden Rules of English Behavior.* 2nd ed. Boston, MA: Nicholas Brealey America.

Freitas, C.R.de. 2015. Weather and Place-Based Human Behavior: Recreational Preferences and Sensitivity. *International Journal of Biometeorology* 59: 55–63.

Führer, Christian. 2013. *Memories of Mannheim: Die Amerikaner in der Quadratestadt seit 1945* Nr. 40. Heidelberg, Ubstadt-Weiher, Basel: Verl. Regionalkultur.

Gilroy, Paul. 2004. *After Empire: Multiculture or Postcolonial Melancholia.* Abingdon: Routledge.

Gramsci, Antonio. 1992. *Prison Notebooks: Volume I.* With the assistance of Joseph A. Buttigieg and Antonio Callari, 3 vols. New York: Columbia University Press.

Hahn, Hans P. 2012. Introduction: Urban Life-Worlds in Motion. In *Urban Life-Worlds in Motion: African Perspectives,* Global Studies, ed. Hans P. Hahn and Kristin Kastner, 9–27. Bielefeld: Transcript.

Hannerz, Ulf. 1980. *Exploring the City: Inquiries Toward an Urban Anthropology.* New York: Columbia University Press.

Harman, Lesley D. 1988. *The Modern Stranger: On Language and Membership* 47. Berlin; New York: Mouton de Gruyter, c1987.

Hartmann, Maximilian. 2014a. *Shoppingparadies Mannheim?* http://mannheim.at/shoppingparadies-mannheim/. Accessed September 10, 2014.

———. 2014b. *Ist Mannheim schoen?* http://mannheim.at/ist-mannheim-schoen/. Accessed August 6, 2014.

Hatzfeld, Ulrich. 2001. Freizeitsuburbanisierung—Loest sich die Freizeit aus der Stadt? In *Suburbanisierung in Deutschland: Aktuelle Tendenzen,* 81–95. Opladen: Leske + Budrich.

Huizinga, J. 1940. *Homo Ludens: Versuch einer Bestimmung des Spielelementes der Kultur.* 3th ed. Basel; Bruessel; Köln; Berlin: Akademische Verlagsanstalt Pantheon Verlag fuer Geschichte und Politik.

Isengard, Betinna. 2005. Freizeitverhalten als Ausdruck Sozialer Ungleichheiten oder Ergebnis Individualisierter Lebensführung? Zur Bedeutung von Einkommen und Bildung im Zeitverlauf. *Kölner Zeitschrift für Soziologie und Sozialpsychologie* 57 (2): 254–277.

Klehr, Christian, Magdalena Ringeling, and Verena Scholze. 2007. *Trends und Lifestyle in der Metropolregion Rhein-Neckar.* Neustadt an der Weinstrasse: Neuer Umschau Buchverl.

Kommunale Statistikstelle. 2015a. *Einwohnerbestand 2014 in kleinraeumiger Gliederung: Statistische Daten Mannheim, N 1/2015.* https://www.mannheim.

de/sites/default/files/page/2407/d201501_einwohnerbestand_2014.pdf. Accessed August 6, 2015.

———. 2015b. *Einwohner mit Migrationshintergrund in kleinraeumiger Gliederung: Statistische Daten Mannheim, N 3/2015.* https://www.mannheim. de/sites/default/files/page/2188/d201503_migrationshintergrund_2014. pdf. Accessed August 6, 2015.

Lamont, Michèle, and Sada Aksartova. 2010. Der alltägliche Kosmopolitismus einfacher Leute. Strategien zur Überwindung von Rassengrenzen zwischen Männern der Arbeiterklasse. In *Ethnowissen*, ed. Marion Müller, 257–285. Wiesbaden: Springer Fachmedien.

Longa, Jonathan, and Kevin Hyltona. 2014. Reviewing Research Evidence and the Case of Participation in Sport and Physical Recreation by Black and Minority Ethnic Communities. *Leisure Studies* 33 (4): 379–399.

Metropolregion Rhein-Neckar. 2015. *Rhein-Neckar in Zahlen.* https://www.m-r-n. com/start/investieren-und-wirtschaften/rhein-neckar-in-zahlen.html. Accessed August 6, 2015.

Michael, Janna. 2015. It's Really Not Hip to Be a Hipster: Negotiating Trends and Authenticity in the Cultural Field. *Journal of Consumer Culture* 15 (2): 163–199.

Müller, Marion, and Darius Zifonun. 2010. Wissenssoziologische Perspektiven auf ethnische Differenzierung und Migration: eine Einführung. In *Ethnowissen*, ed. Marion Müller, 9–33. Wiesbaden: Springer Fachmedien.

Ndlovu-Gatsheni, Sabelo. 2011. The World Cup, Vuvuzelas, Flag-Waving Patriots and the Burden of Building South Africa. *Third World Quarterly* 32 (2): 279–293.

Orley, Emily. 2012. Places Remember Events: Towards an Ethics of Encounter. In *Liminal Landscapes: Travel, Experience and Spaces in-Between*, ed. Hazel Andrews and Les Roberts, 1st ed., 36–49. New York: Routledge.

Overwien, Bernd. 2004. Internationale Sichtweisen auf "informelles Lernen" am Uebergang zum 21. Jahrhundert. In *Grundbegriffe der Ganztagsbildung: Beiträge zu einem neuen Bildungsverständnis in der Wissensgesellschaft*, ed. Hans-Uwe Otto and Thomas Coelen, 1 Aufl., 51–73. Wiesbaden: VS Verlag für Sozialwissenschaften.

Ragge, Peter W. 2015, March 12. *Sorge um die Kriminalität.* http://www.morgenweb. de/mannheim/mannheim-stadt/sorge-um-die-kriminalitat-1.2148398. Accessed August 7, 2015.

Rhein-Neckar.de. 2015. *Das Wetter im Rhein-Neckar Dreieck.* http://wetter. rhein-neckar.de/. Accessed August 7, 2015.

Scheuermann, Michael. 2015. *An diese guten Erfahrungen des letzten Jahres wollen wir anknüpfen: Jungbusch feierte den 11. Nachtwandel Über 25.000 Menschen besuchten die "Busch-Nächte."* Accessed February 24, 2016.

Schimmel, Kimberly. 2014. Assessing the Sociology of Sport: On Sport and the City. *International Review for the Sociology of Sport* 50 (4–5): 591–595.

Schulke, Hans-Juergen. 2007. Fan und Flaneur: Public Viewing bei der FIFA-Weltmeisterschaft 2006—Organisatorische Erfahrungen, soziologische Begründungen und politische Steuerung bei einem neuen Kulturgut. In *Die Welt ist wieder heimgekehrt: Studien zur Evaluation der FIFA-WM 2006*, 25–71. Münster: Waxmann.

Schulze, Gerhard. 2005[1992]. *Die Erlebnisgesellschaft: Kultursoziologie der Gegenwart*. 2 Aufl. Frankfurt [Main]; New York: Campus.

Schwab, Christiane. 2015. *Die Stadt als Erkenntnisform*. In *Europäische Ethnologie in München: Ein kulturwissenschaftlicher Reader*, ed. Irene Götz et al., 167–191. Münster, Westf: Waxmann.

Spinney, Jamie E., and Hugh Millward. 2011. Weather Impacts on Leisure Activities in Halifax, Nova Scotia. *International Journal of Biometeorology* 55: 133–145.

Sport1. 2015. *DEL: Eishockey-Meister Adler Mannheim von tausenden Fans empfangen Fans feiern Meister Mannheim*. http://www.sport1.de/eishockey/del/2015/04/del-eishockey-meister-adler-mannheim-von-tausenden-fans-empfangen. Accessed March 28, 2016.

Spracklen, Karl. 2013. *Whiteness and Leisure, Leisure Studies in a Global Era*. New York; London: Palgrave Macmillan.

Stadt Mannheim. 2013. *Vom Ziel Her Denken. 2. Mannheimer Bildungsbericht*. https://www.mannheim.de/sites/default/files/page/7130/bbm_01-192_stand_06-02-13.pdf. Accessed December 11, 2014.

———. 2015a. *Daten und Fakten*. https://www.mannheim.de/stadt-gestalten/daten-und-fakten. Accessed August 6, 2015.

———. 2015b. *Fachbereich Sport und Freizeit*. https://www.mannheim.de/stadt-gestalten/fachbereich-sport-und-freizeit. Accessed August 7, 2015.

———. 2015c. *Kulturelle Vereine und Einrichtungen*. https://www.mannheim.de/kultur-erleben/kulturelle-vereine-und-einrichtungen. Accessed August 7, 2015.

———. 2015d. *Kulturelle Vereine und Einrichtungen*, viewed 7 August 2015, from https://www.mannheim.de/kultur-erleben/kulturelle-vereine-und-einrichtungen.

Statistisches Landesamt Baden-Württemberg. 2013. *Berufspendler in Baden-Württemberg*. https://www.statistik-bw.de/Veroeffentl/Statistik_AKTUELL/803413009.pdf. Accessed August 6, 2015.

Strümpell, Christian. 2008. 'We Work Together, We Eat Together': Conviviality and Modernity in a Company Settlement in South Orissa. *Contributions to Indian Sociology* 42 (3): 351–381.

Taylor, Tracy. 2001. Cultural Diversity and Leisure: Experiences of Women in Australia. *Society and Leisure* 24: 535–555.

Thomassen, Bjorn. 2012. Revisiting Liminality: The Danger of Empty Spaces. In *Liminal Landscapes: Travel, Experience and Spaces in-Between*, ed. Hazel Andrews and Les Roberts, 1st ed., 21–35. New York: Routledge.

Turner, Victor. 1974. Liminal to Liminoid, in Play, Flow, and Ritual: An Essay in Comparative Symbology. *Rice University Studies* 60 (3): 53–92.

———. 1982. *From Ritual to Theatre: The Human Seriousness of Play*. Vol. 1. New York: Performing Arts Journal Publications.

———. 1989. *Das Ritual: Struktur und Anti-Struktur Bd*. Vol. 10. Frankfurt/ Main [u.a.]: Campus-Verl.

Ulloa, Astrid. 2014. Dimensiones culturales del clima: Indicadores y predicciones entre pobladores locales en Colombia. *Batey: Revista Cubana de Antropología Sociocultural* 6: 17–33.

van Deth, Jan. 2014. Einfuehrung: Leben in einer Deutschen Grossstadt. In *Demokratie in der Großstadt: Ergebnisse des ersten Mannheimer Demokratie Audit*, ed. Jan W. van Deth, 1–22. Wiesbaden: Springer Fachmedien.

van Gennep, Arnold. 1977. *The Rites of Passage*. London: Routledge and Kegan Paul.

Veal, Anthony J. 1987. *Leisure and the Future*, 4. London; Boston: Allen & Unwin.

Velho, Gilberto. 2011. Urban Anthropology. Interdisciplinarity and Boundaries of Knowledge. *Vibrant* 8 (2): 452–479. http://www.scielo.br/pdf/vb/v8n2/ a23v8n2.pdf. Accessed January 30, 2014.

Wearing, Betsy. 1998. *Leisure and Feminist Theory*. London; Thousand Oaks, CA: SAGE.

Wetterdienst. 2016. *Klima Mannheim, Universitätsstadt—Station Mannheim (96 m)*. http://www.wetterdienst.de/Deutschlandwetter/Mannheim_Universitaetsstadt/ Klima/. Accessed March 4, 2016.

Wirth, Louis. 1938. Urbanism as a Way of Life. *The American Journal of Sociology* 44 (1): 1–24.

Zifonun, Darius. 2010. Ein, gallisches Dorf? Integration, Stadtteilbindung und Prestigeordnung in einem, Armenviertel. In *Ethnowissen*, ed. Marion Müller, 311–327. Wiesbaden: Springer Fachmedien.

CHAPTER 3

The Meaning of Leisure

3.1 Excursus

T. was 26 years old when I met her. She was born and raised in Mannheim as part of a native family that was settled in the area of Casterfeld, one of the counties in the district of Rheinau. Her sister, parents, and grandparents all live in the outer city districts as well. At the time of the interview, T was living alone in a one-bedroom apartment in one of the more renowned neighborhoods close to the city center called Schwetzinger Vorstadt. We met for the interview there, in one of the trendy cafes of the Seckenheimer Strasse. We met, as was the case for most of the interviews, on an evening of a workday. She came after work dressed in business style, wearing a suit and blouse, silver jewelry, and a dark coat. (Later she told me she likes to shop at MANGO, Zara, and Peek & Cloppenburg.) By looking at her, one would think she matches physically the stereotype of a German: she is blond, blue-eyed, around 1.80 m (5 foot 9 inches) tall, and thin. She tells me that, like her parents, who also have a background in sales, she works as a customer service representative for a large insurance company, even though she originally trained to be a bank clerk. Her job requires that she is sometimes at the office but she is also often on the road meeting clients. She always carries her gym bag in the car, in case she decides to stop at the gym and do a course or two of TRX (suspension training) or "belly, butt, and thighs." Practicing physical activity is generally important to her for gaining energy and taking care of her appearance. She takes time to exercise twice or three times a week for one or two hours after work. Sometimes she

© The Author(s) 2017

V.L. Sandoval, *The Meaning of Leisure*, Leisure Studies
in a Global Era, DOI 10.1007/978-3-319-59752-2_3

coordinates with a friend or her sister so that they can train together, but most of the time she goes alone. She actually enjoys team sports, like volleyball, much more than fitness, but they require fixed training schedules to which she cannot commit due to work.

On the other nights of the week, she meets up with friends to have cappuccinos or latte macchiatos. Mostly, they meet at the trendy Kult or Lido cafes located close to her home. On other occasions, they meet and cook dinner, generally Asian cuisine, but she always takes care that she does not return home too late, so that she can sleep for seven or eight hours. She says she organizes these dinner nights because she loves to cook but hates to do it for herself. She has known these friends for a long time: they were childhood neighbors and classmates from primary school. It is with them that she spends most of her leisure time, regardless of the activity in question. She highlights how, nowadays, it is easy to meet up because none of them is currently involved in a relationship.

Weekends are, for her, the most important part of the week. On these days she never participates in sports. As she sees it, sports are pursued for physical and mental health purposes. In her case, it is because her job consists mostly of sitting in front of a desk and her body needs to release energy and stress. But true leisure is when she goes out, for example, on Friday nights to have some cocktails around the Wasserturm square with her friends at, for example, Dolce Amaro, and then head out for the dance clubs like Blue Tower or any other club with mainstream and house music. She sees partying not only as enjoyment but also as a tool to meet a potential husband with whom to fulfill her wish to have children. Due to the long party nights, she wakes up around noon on Saturdays and dedicates her first few conscious hours to cleaning and tidying up her apartment before she goes to buy groceries locally or in the city center. On Saturday nights she usually meets up again with friends for dinner and drinks. Sundays are her family days, when she goes to her sisters', parents', or grandparents' home and spends the whole day with them. For her, leisure is about sharing a nice moment with family and friends. She does not enjoy free time alone. If she happens to find herself alone at home, she likes to read comedy books or anything that will free her mind of any problems she might be having.

When she takes vacations, she likes to travel. She has been to Miami, New York, and Istanbul with her friends for short trips. She considers herself a city dweller who likes to explore urban areas. In general terms, she speaks of wanting to know about other cultures and wanting to experience living abroad. Despite this, she typically avoids certain areas of the city, such as the area known as Little Istanbul around the marketplace, that make her feel uncomfortable and unsafe.

At the time of the interview, she said she was satisfied with her life-style. However, in the course of a year, she decided to follow up on her wish to travel and live abroad. She left Mannheim to participate in a work and travel program in Australia. She left her job and her apartment and embarked on this new phase of her life, which took almost half a year, after which she returned to Mannheim to start an entirely new job and to find a new apartment and love relationship. Within 18 months, her life had experienced dramatic changes and so, too, did her leisure.

Leisure can be defined as consequence of class differences, as an activ-ity, as inner experience, or as a combination of activities and psychological states. In this section, we explore how leisure is perceived by this group of women in Mannheim. In order to better grasp how they subjectively think of leisure, I focus first on the understanding of free time and leisure as sep-arate categories from work and then on two different dimensions of their concept of leisure specifically: the practical one and the ideal one. The practical one includes a myriad of factors, from physical and psychological recovery, to external conditions and the social components of leisure and includes, additionally, the fluid boundary between free time (autonomous time away from work) and leisure time. The ideal one presents some simi-lar characteristics but has additional nuances that are not always found in practice.

First, we consider the concept of free time as a separate area of life. As has been said, each of these women has nearly identical amounts of free time due to their regulated, paid working time. They are all full-time employees, which means that, on average, they each work 40 hours a week, from Monday to Friday. Most of them work in the typical time period between 9 am and 5 pm. This regulated time separating paid work from free time is important because "work" is actually perceived as work by the informants. Even though work is not the subject matter of this study, drawing from the discourses of these women, it can be stated that they do not generally have a leisurely experience, or "*Muße*," dur-ing their workdays. In fact, they report dissatisfaction with their working environment and conditions, their income, and work tasks and rhythm. Some of them also expressed concerns about job security. Generally, they appreciate their jobs because they gain from them an income and a sense of being productive, but they do not experience fulfillment through their paid work. In fact, in most cases, my informants perceived work as a necessary annoyance. When asked about what leisure means for her (the final question of all the interviews), respondent A. said, by way of example, that it was "The time when I don't speak or do anything related to my job" (February 14, 2015). However, this statement does not only show the separation between work and leisure in their minds; it also hints at a universal definition of free time, as Granger (2014) has pointed out. Such public views on leisure could stem from historical processes and their propagation by the state and political actors among the population (s. Granger 2014, p. 302). This definition of free time is nonetheless in harmony with leisure practices and ideals of these women, as will be seen in the following sections.

Such perceived shortcomings of work life are some of the reasons why leisure time holds a great meaning in the women's lives. In informal conversations, many described conflicts with colleagues and bosses and issues with monotonous tasks or insufficient income. As countless authors have argued, (cf. Appadurai 1996; Scheuch 1972) paid work can be demanding and can, due to the nature of the tasks and their structures, rob individuals of their individuality, which can drive them to seek it in other areas of life.

Furthermore, even for the couple of informants who were completely satisfied with their current employment situation and how their careers had developed until now, there was still a clear distinction between the areas of work and free time. The reason behind this is fairly obvious: work and free time are institutionally divided areas, differing in essential questions such as time autonomy and purpose. Additionally, it is possible that the nature of work, as mentioned by Stengel (1998, p. 31), affects how the areas of life are perceived. For example, office jobs such as the ones practiced by these women could have less potential for leisure than creative or handcraft jobs. Many of the arguments highlighting the fluid boundaries between women's work and free time have been based on the family lives of married women and/or women with children and assumed that these women experience agency by having leisure during nonleisure activities (s. Wearing 1998, p. 149). However, it could be argued that for the group of women who were the subject of this report, there is no need and no desire to experience worklike activities as leisure. In other words, they experience agency when they have leisure experiences, something they accomplish mostly through thorough organization and planning. They choose and act following their own ideas and goals regarding lifestyle and leisure.

In contrast, it has been argued that the increase in the division of work and free time areas is capitalist and a product of Western history (s. Veblen 1924; Wearing 1998) and that leisurely work can be more easily found in nonindustrialized societies, where work is not removed from everyday life but is rather part of the general social life (Dobler 2014, p. 57). In this context work, free time and leisure have also been considered masculine categories (s. Wearing 1998) because of the gender dynamics present during the development of those separate categories. By this reasoning, women are trapped in the reigning categories of work and leisure, having internalized structures that have existed before them, an argument that follows Bourdieu's thoughts (s. Bourdieu 1984).

Furthermore, there is also an emotional aspect to the division between work and free time for these women. They do not easily experience joy and fun during work. Free time and in particular leisure time are for them the main times in which these feelings are experienced in everyday life, one of the reasons why leisure is highly valued. The time available for potential leisure is scarce, however. This perceived scarcity of free and, specifically, leisure time is one of the reasons, as mentioned in the methodology section in the introductory chapter, why it was complicated to organize and conduct the interviews. In practice, and somewhat ironically, participating in the interviews required the informants to relinquish potential leisure hours. As we will see, scarcity of free time influences how leisure is organized and executed in everyday life.

The conceptual division between work and free time can also be seen in a concrete example. One important symbol of leisure for these women is alcohol and its consumption. Free time and leisure can exist without alcohol consumption, but alcohol definitely is not a part of work. Alcohol, for these women, is something that is completely absent from work and is prominently present in leisure. Alcohol often marks the start of free time in contrast to work. Having a beer after a long day at work, for example, is the symbol that the "*Feierabend*," or the weekend, has started. It is also present in many of the other leisure experiences of these women. Kovac and Trussell (2015, p. 205) have argued that alcohol can be a facilitator of the leisure experience when consumed in controlled amounts. Although patterns of alcohol consumption were not a themed subject of the interviews, it was a fact that was supported by participant observation and conversations. The presence of alcohol is closely related to the leisure activity and the social context it is being done in. Alcohol is almost always present in leisure situations in which enjoyment is the priority before recuperation, particularly at later times of the day and in the evenings and nights. Although some women do mention the taste of particular drinks, in many cases it seems that alcoholic beverages are just part of the learned behavior or part of the habitus because they are an unreflected component of social life. Types of alcoholic drinks are also associated with certain social classes and age groups as well.

Spracklen (2013, p. 144) also argued that alcohol consumption is a cultural practice that can help to differentiate people but that can also help to integrate foreigners. Indeed, most women talked about alcohol being consumed socially in the company of others. In this sense, the migrant women of the study are also integrated in terms of the relationship between leisure and alcohol consumption. However, different leisure experiences might be associated with different drinks. For example, mulled wine is very common during Christmas time and colder wintry evenings, cocktails and mixed drinks are very common at bars or clubs during dancing nights, beer is very common during summer barbecues, wine is common during dinner, and so on. What is important to highlight here is the relation between the work–free time distinction as well as between leisure experiences, enjoyment, and alcohol consumption.

Despite work and free time clearly being experienced as different areas of life, the differentiation between free time—meaning, for these women, time away from work—and leisure is more fluid. Free time and leisure intertwine in practice in complex ways that can change from individual to individual and situation to situation. The many facets of leisure, such as relaxation, diversion, and social participation, are all highlighted by Dumazedier (1967, pp. 16–17). Taking a look, for example, at the recovery function of free time and how it is perceived by these women, one can see the intermingling of free time and leisure experiences, as when resting at home alone suddenly becomes leisure if the inner state of the individual allows it to.

An example of how free time and leisure can be difficult to differentiate is the issue of one constitutional element of both. Although there are individual nuances to elements of leisure, it was possible to identify common aspects shared among the interviewees. One key component of free time and leisure is the fulfillment of the recovery function. In this respect, from the emic point of view, free time and leisure have, in harmony with functionalist approaches to leisure (s. Opaschowski 1996, p. 82), a recovery function on both the psychological and the physical level. This aspect is highlighted by most of the informants, both in the interviews and in general conversations. As a matter of fact, it is something that is highlighted not only by the group studied in this case but in everyday conversations. Recovery during free time and/or leisure is a topic that can be heard anywhere and at any time in the city. Complaints about tiredness and enervation due to work are common, and so are the expressions of wishes and longing for rest and recovery. Among my informants specifically, it is the psychological recovery aspect that is emphasized.

> It is a way of freeing yourself, to free your mind. You are at work all the time, from eight to five and sometimes you carry along your work in your thoughts. So, dancing and these kinds of activities allow you to think about something else, to concentrate—not on your thoughts but on what you are doing with your hands, legs, feelings: it is a change of atmosphere. (Respondent A., February 3, 2015)

> I would say that spending time with people that you like [and] just free your mind maybe instead of thinking about work, lectures or whatever: just get your mind free and do things which are fun for you, or which make you happy—even better if you are with people whom you really like. (Respondent S., May 10, 2015)

> Ironing. I think ironing is cool. I just turn on the TV and iron and watch my series and free my mind. (Respondent C., December 10, 2014)

These quotes demonstrate the aspect of separation of work and free time as well as the need to recover psychologically during free time, more specifically through leisure. The last quote also constitutes an example of how free time and leisure can be difficult to separate, as the division between chores and leisure experiences fades. As is seen here, leisure is constructed in a discourse of "freeing the mind." During leisure, individuals experience psychological recovery from the perceived burdens of work. However, recovery must not be equated directly with rest or recovery in the physical sense. Recovery can coexist with or even result from physically demanding activities, chores, or social encounters.

The relation among recovery, chores, and social encounters is also situational. How cooking is perceived, for example, can change depending on time schedules. As respondent S. said on May 10, 2015:

> Yeah, I must say that at the moment it would be a dream if I came home and there was a meal ready. That would be a dream. When you are so hungry and then you must go grocery shopping first and cook. Sometimes I wish… But on the weekends I really enjoy it when I have time, I want to cook and really enjoy it, but during the week I'd rather not.

Fig. 3.1   Mannheim Paradeplatz (Picture taken October 1, 2014)

Cooking also changes for the women depending on the social environment and whether it is a shared experience: "I enjoy cooking for friends, when I invite friends over I'll cook something and really enjoy doing it," respondent J. said on May 22, 2015. In practice, many situations have the potential of being leisure. Leisure is individual. The channels by which it is found by these women are varied, and the boundaries between leisure and chores during free time can be flexible and sometimes difficult to distinguish. For example, everyday life can have a leisure if can take place in a series of events where it is difficult to determine when a chore ends and leisure begins (Fig. 3.1). As I wrote in a field note on September 8, 2014:

> I'm walking through the city center on a Saturday morning, the weather is good and I can see many people on the streets, people alone, in pairs, in what seems to be families, or in groups. I can see that many are buying groceries at the market or supermarket, or come from the drugstores like DM and Müller. Some carry bags in their hands filled with what they've bought. From the pace of their walk I assume they are relaxed, they don't seem in

hurry. Many are walking around with an ice cream in their hands; some others are sitting down at the benches, probably enjoying the sun. I am also enjoying the sun, even though I am here for different reasons.

This field note also shows that, for an ethnographer who is involved in participant observation in the city center, given the right conditions, a leisure experience can take place. Dobler (2014, p. 56) has written that a satisfying feeling of *Muße* can come from watching other people work (or not work, in this case). It is the contrast between other people's busyness and the own person's lack of busyness that provides a different focus to the actions. Observations as well as entries in the women's weekend diaries show that leisure can take place in close alternation with chores (free time) but also confirm that leisure is a state of mind or inner experience that can be independent of the activity being pursued, even though certain activities and conditions do foster leisure experiences. A case is made for warm and sunny weather conditions fostering leisure experiences, something that will be addressed when we consider leisure spaces and seasons of the year.

However, what is important to highlight is that, in everyday life, these women have agency; they make necessary shopping trips for goods, such as groceries and hygiene items, enjoyable by combining or alternating it with spending time within social relationships or taking time to please themselves by consuming enjoyable things, such as ice cream and coffee. For Wearing (1998, p. 149), by having leisure experiences while doing chores, women show their agency. This idea could be applied to all individuals, not only women, and it can reflect an alternation in a sequence of events in practice and not when considering one isolated segment of time alone.

One further important channel for recovery is physical activity. In fact, sports and physical activities play important roles in the leisure of these women and occupy a large amount of their time, as will be seen later. Klein (2009) has pointed out that sedentary jobs, such as the ones pursued by these women, foster high participation in physical activities during leisure, an idea that can be confirmed in the informants' stress of the need for balance and use of the body in the quotations given and in many conversations as well. The narratives of sports and physical activities often mention the aspect of freeing the mind as well. These kinds of activities are an interesting case because, even though they fulfill the "freedom of the mind" aspect of leisure, they also have a compulsory character to them. The issue of sports and physical activities will be addressed in due course. Other activities that are physically demanding but that are also pursued in order to recover or "free" the mind include, for example, dancing in nightclubs and shopping trips.

Nonetheless, these women also free their minds in different ways. Various forms of entertainment are used for this purpose, such as watching television series and movies; reading "light" books, such as thrillers and comedies; and social encounters with or without the consumption of alcohol. These kinds of activities have been deemed, for example, by Stebbins (2014, pp. 30–37) as "casual leisure" because they bring only "superficial" and not "real" happiness. But these kinds of activities are chosen consciously. For example, in the case of TV series and movies, new technologies make it possible to choose specifically what one will watch and when. Watching common TV (national channels), on the contrary, is not a typical way to free the mind, something that is attributed mostly to low-quality programs. National channels are almost never watched, and, when they are, they run in the background while parallel activities, such as correspondence via social media or chatting and talking on the phone, are taking place. Moreover, the expectation the women have from these kinds of activities is not delivery of happiness; it is being entertained and consequently being able to free the mind temporarily from other thoughts. Happiness for these women is related to an overall evaluation and reflection upon their projection of the self beyond one single segment of time. Subjective expectations from activities and leisure experiences are essential issues because leisure must meet the expectations of the people involved in it and not the researchers' expectations.

Qian et al. (2014) have found significant differences in the ways in which men and women deal with daily stressors, with women showing dramatically reduced levels of stress during leisure. In other words, these authors argued that women are able to use leisure as a coping mechanism to stress, something that is important for general psychological well-being, much more effectively than men (Qian et al. 2014, pp. 15–16). This could also explain the subjective importance of psychological recovery through and in leisure these women express. In this context, the women have referred to leisure activities as "turning off your brain." They seek to be drawn into an experience that engages their senses and stimulates their mind just as Schulze (2005) has argued, although, according to Qian et al. (2014), women might be more easily drawn into leisure experiences than men. However, one of the reasons why psychological recovery might be placed in the foreground in comparison to physical recovery might be their age. Age has been recognized as one crucial variable for lifestyle in general (Gans 1999, p. 94), and it is something that can make these women more able to tolerate high levels of physical activity. Yet, more than chronological age, the way individuals might perceive their own bodies as strong, tired, and healthy also influences leisure experiences (s. Hancock and Hancock 2014; Gunaratnam 2013, pp. 21–64). It is not possible, however, for them to survive without physical recovery as well. As respondent J. said on October 25, 24: "...but there are weekends when I really don't want to do anything. I tell myself No! You are staying home this weekend, recover from the week and that's it."Physical recovery can be experienced alongside psychological recovery, as respondent M. said on March 19, 2015: "I'm very happy if my cellphone is not ringing or doing anything on a Sunday morning. I'm just lying on my back and being by myself."

Thus in the everyday lives of these women, physical and psychological recovery coexist. Some specific leisure experiences have for them a high potential for psychological and physical recovery. For example, visits to wellness centers, saunas, and thermal baths are beloved leisure activities for these women, particularly in times of rainy weather or in the colder seasons. Most of the women talked about their fondness for saunas and other wellness activities and the positive effects they had on them in terms of their relaxation and health. However, such activities generally are pursued on just a few occasions each year, due to financial constraints. As respondent R. explained on September 26, 2014: "A spa weekend. I've done that and would like to do it again. I really liked it. I went to Strasbourg. There was sauna, massage and so on, it was nice, I would like to be able to spend more money on that."

All in all, two concepts are also strongly related to the view on free time and leisure when associated with the dimension of recovery and relaxation. First is the concept of coziness, or *"Gemütlichkeit,"* which Schulze (2005, p. 151) also mentioned and to which he related mainly the *"Harmoniemilieu"* (Harmony milieu) to a type of people searching experiences that bring mostly comfort, people who, according to him, engage in "trivial" activities. These women, especially while describing Sundays, often used the word "cozy"' to describe typical recovery leisure. They used the term "coziness" repeatedly as an important adjective describing an atmosphere or a mood during leisure. As respondent S. explained on November 4, 2014: "Sunday evenings are cozy with friends when I just say Hey! Come around! Something cozy. Sundays; I'm always a little bit, it is the peaceful day, so that you can relax."

Although Schulze (2005, p. 151) argued that coziness is social and that it cannot be achieved alone, in this case coziness is generally related to a home and a couch, and was not related to being by oneself or with family and friends. Coziness depends on the atmosphere, not on the presence or absence of company. It is relaxed in the sense that it is quiet and informal and in a comfortable setting. Coziness often includes in practice the wearing of comfortable clothing, such as sweatpants, and consuming some type of "comfort" drinks and food, such as hot tea, beer, or pasta.[1] As it does not only involve physical comfort but social comfort, too, coziness with company means those social relationships in which the individual feels able to relax. From the descriptions, it can be concluded that the type of social relationships these women can feel "cozy" with are those in which they can be what Turner (1982) would call the individual (themselves) instead of being forced to "act" a certain way (as a person) (s. Turner 1982, pp. 113–115). They can express feelings and moods freely without being bound by social norms. From the narratives, it can also be concluded that coziness includes external aspects, such as an ideal temperature and a feeling of safety.

The second concept that is strongly related to free time and leisure as recovery is rather opaque. It is the frequently mentioned idea of "doing nothing." Doing nothing is a phrase commonly used in everyday conversation to describe evenings, weekends, and vacations. The phrase "I did nothing" is quite popular in the context of narratives on typical evenings during the week or on Sundays; it is very common within conversations of the everyday life in Mannheim as well. It is a vague description, but it is expected that the conversation partner will know more or less what is meant by it. "Doing nothing" is also a category used in the research of leisure and lifestyle and is associated with a group of "passive" activities, such as watching TV and playing video games (s. Harring 2010, p. 126) or when conceived as passing the time doing nonserious, nonproductive activities in which people engage to avoid boredom (s. Fuller 2011). A similar state of "doing nothing" when in the context of sociability has been called by Foley (2017) "wasting time."

Just like coziness, women used "doing nothing" to describe leisure but not exclusively so. The range of activities that are subsumed under "doing nothing" is great. The assigned description has not necessarily something to do with doing nothing per se but about activities whose importance is disregarded, activities that could easily be substituted with something else. As respondent J. said on September 19, 2014: "Sometimes it is nice to spend a weekend at home and I can chill or watch TV or clean or so. I'm never at home yeah? Mmm, just do nothing, so to speak."

Doing nothing and coziness often go hand in hand. When asked explicitly what they meant by doing nothing, subjects described different kinds of activities, from watching TV, to social media, to face-to-face conversations, drinking coffee, reading, and the like. Respondent F., for example, said this on June 16, 2015: "...well I talk to my mother, to my siblings, or when the day is nice I'll sit outside on the swing and eat something, an ice cream or such."

Therefore, while Harring (2010) has used the variable "doing nothing" in similar way to other researchers, for my informants, doing nothing involves all kinds of different activities. But "doing nothing" is more complex and has more layers than merely describing or summarizing meaningless activities. Thus, as a researcher, one could ask: When does "doing nothing" turn into "doing something"? Or in other words: when is the leisure experience important enough to be subjectively perceived as such? Doing nothing is also a good example of the blurriness between free time and leisure. Also, this state of doing nothing cannot be confused with the "doing nothing" related to meditative or contemplative states, as described by Greek philosophers (s. Grazia 1972, pp. 58–59). Doing nothing is also closely related to boredom, and subjects always take care that the "doing nothing" does not transform itself into being bored. As someone once said to me jokingly during fieldwork: "To chill is the art of doing nothing without getting bored." Avoidance of boredom is for these women easily achieved nowadays, though; most of the time, it is done by going online to social media or entertainment sites or by contacting social relations directly via different apps. Indeed, contemplative or meditative states are almost nonexistent in practiced leisure for these women.

One possible explanation as to why these activities are disregarded as doing nothing are the theoretical works highlighting social pressures on the individual to be productive, to engage in useful leisure, or to consume (s. Dumazedier 1967, p. 8; Adorno 1991, pp. 163–165; Bauman 2009, pp. 61–64; Veal 1987, p. 166). By saying "I'm doing nothing," the individual is acknowledging the "uselessness" of his or her way of spending time and socially apologizing or gaining the acceptance of the social environment. Using "doing nothing" could also relate to a lack of seriousness in the activity, demarking a playful nature, a lack of practicality (s. Huizinga 1940, pp. 13–36). Fuller (2011) has argued that the similar term "passing the time" covers a considerable range of meanings because it varies in duration and in the activities it is describing. For Foley (2017), in contrast, "wasting time" as seen for people engaging in slow tourism, a form of tourism generally related to full enjoyment of the senses, can be a form of rebellion against a capitalist system that pushes individuals to be "entrepreneurial selves" and to have purposeful leisure activities. However, "doing nothing" for these women is more related to what they are experiencing in terms of concentration levels and general engagement of the mind; thus, it is similar to the notion of "freeing the mind" but also to what they are experiencing emotionally. It could be said that for them, "doing nothing" is an emotional middle ground between being bored and being excited with and in a leisure experience. "Doing nothing" can be leisure in practice or it can be just part of free time and can under certain circumstances be the ideal leisure, but the phrase emphasizes that the leisure experience is not at its peak, either currently or when reflected upon afterward.

Consequently, leisure can manifest itself in the form of relaxation and recuperation. Relaxation and recuperation can entail "doing nothing" and being cozy or can be achieved through relaxing experiences offered by the leisure industry, as in the case of wellness centers. However, it is important to highlight that coziness and "doing nothing" do not always have to be leisure in practice. Leisure, as Schulze (2005) pointed out, is an inner reaction: it is subjective. Other factors also contribute to considering an activity to be leisure or to having a leisure experience; for example, the pleasure and enjoyment factor pointed out by Brosius (2010, p. 173) and Whillans (2014, p. 188) were also constantly highlighted during fieldwork. Certain activities, such as going dancing at a nightclub and having a night out with friends, have a high potential for generating enjoyment and are an important part of the total leisure experiences of these women.

I have argued that the difference between work and free time is quite defined for these women; the boundaries between leisure and nonleisure within free time can be less clear, however. To mention additional examples, the interviews with these women took place in venues generally used for leisure, such as cafes or bars, during free time after work. They were enjoyable and often were followed by a pleasant, informal conversation; but is this type of experience or activity considered leisure? A similar example would be a night out with colleagues, an activity in which many of these women engage a couple of times a year. These two occasions share similar characteristics, in the sense that they have similar external settings in which, often, leisure takes place, sometimes even with the "leisure symbol" of alcohol consumption, but the individuals involved are not necessarily emotionally close. Often in these cases, it might not be clear whether the individual considers it leisure or not, even for the individual herself. As respondent I. explained on December 16, 2014: "Yes, they are colleagues. I was, for example, in a birthday party this Friday and yes, but do we do a lot together? No, we meet maybe once a month and hang out *but that's it*. Otherwise I just go out with my friends."

This quote shows that she is describing an activity that takes place during free time, a birthday party on a Friday evening. Yet different details in her narration point out that such an activity is not considered leisure or at least not *ideal* leisure. First, the social distance in the word "colleague" is highlighted in comparison with the word "friends." This distinction between activities with colleagues versus activities with friends is one that is accentuated regularly in everyday conversations (not only by these women), in the sense that while it is possible to have fun with colleagues, there are plenty of behaviors individuals would not allow themselves to engage in while with colleagues, which again highlights the issue of the performance of the social person. Friends, in contrast, are seen as people with whom the individual does not face social pressures to behave in a certain way. Friends are often described as the people "I can be myself with." The amount of alcohol consumed, for example, tends to be much less with colleagues than with friends. Additionally, the "that's it" from the quote, which was accompanied by shrugged shoulders and pressed lips, also implies that the informant is not attaching much meaning to those encounters and that there is emotional distance between her and the other participants. The same could be argued for the interview situations that are "only" meetings with an ethnographer. It could be drawn from this differentiation of situations that the perceived social and emotional distance between the people sharing the leisure moment is an important factor in how situations are experienced and perceived after their occurrences. Some authors have introduced the concept of work- or leisure-like activities in order to categorize such activities that cannot be easily put into a group (s. Veal 1987). Even though there might be individual and situational nuances as to how such activities are perceived, in general, using this conceptualization, it could be said the informants experienced free time with colleagues and the ethnographer as "leisure-like" activities because of the lack of the ideal social environment in which to fulfill leisure.

Here it would be possible to ask if the women's perception of activities as leisure-like or leisure is constant or whether it depends on other factors, such as if the individual was having a bad day, which particular colleagues were there, and others. In other words, do the women always have leisure with their friends and leisure-like experiences with more socially distant people like colleagues? Or is it also possible to have leisure-like experiences friends? Taking into consideration these kinds of practical experiences where it is not subjectively clear for the individual (and for the analysis) if it is leisure or not, it is useful to turn to an analysis of overall leisure ideals. Until now some of the components or concepts that have been highlighted are issues that play a role, in practice, in everyday free time and leisure. But the difference between leisure in practice and ideal leisure is important. Beyond experiences of leisure in practice and the different components or elements women associate with them, what is their subjective ideal of leisure? Gerhards (2008, p. 736) pointed out that there is a difference between preferences and restrictions. If these women experience leisure through different channels and in different situations within the framework or restrictions they have, in terms of the availability of time and money and the presence of social obligations, what would their preferences be if there were no restrictions?

First, one of the key components of leisure, according to theoretical approaches, is freedom of choice (s. Grazia 1972, pp. 58–59; Richter 2005, p. 41). Indeed, many leisure experiences are chosen by these women by their free will. Freedom of choice can be expressed positively when an individual chooses something, or it can be expressed negatively when the individual feels that there is a possibility of saying no and not attending or participating, although Schulze (2005, p. 178) also pointed out that choosing something can be a decision against something else.

However, freedom of choice can be more complicated than mere possibility. Opaschowski (1996, pp. 85–96) stressed that the compulsory character of activities can be hidden and often not be visible to the researcher. By way of example, we return to the case of a night out with colleagues, a situation where it was actually possible to decline invitations and not participate in the event. However, as these women pointed out when asked about their motives for attending, declining an invitation more than once and not participating enough could have negative social implications for their working environment. Social relations could grow more distant or deteriorate, causing conflict, and thus affect the harmony or solidarity at work. This shows an underlying social pressure surrounding such "leisure-like" occasions. Similarly, but less emphasized, be the case for the interview situation. As mentioned in the methods section, I used the snowball principle to find informants, which means that a friend or acquaintance recommended others to the study. Consequently, individuals might feel obliged to accept in order to avoid conflict or frictions with the individual who recommended them.

Additionally, individuals and situations can also change by the means of signing a contract to start a membership. Once an activity is chosen at will without social pressure, it can transform into a social obligation. This is the case, for example, with a few of my informants who are members of sports clubs (team sports). Being a member of such organizations requires attendance at set times, and there are social controls when commitments are broken. This is why not every woman I talked to was willing to make such commitments and add social obligations. For those who do, committing to a team can have different motivations: it can be a form of compensating for a lack of self-discipline in order to train regularly, a form of enhancing enjoyment through sharing a collective experience, or just a channel to be able to practice a preferred type of activity. Nonetheless, social obligations like this are not always be perceived to be such. Certain factors that were mentioned as affecting how easy or difficult it was to comply with the training or match commitments were weather, mood and energy, conflicts in the team, relation to the trainer, and other members of the club. Such factors, therefore, have an influence on whether the motivation is intrinsic or extrinsic at a given time.

These kinds of situations, however, are why Scheuch (1972, pp. 30–31) described an area of life deemed to contain "social obligations" that includes activities "essential to functional roles," for example, as siblings, sons and daughters, colleagues, and teammates. Nonetheless, while, for these women, this considerations on functional roles applies in the case of colleagues and it almost never applies to the case of friends, in the case of family, there are significant individual differences. Family reunions and activities constitute an interesting case because they are perceived as social obligations that vary depending on the occasion, individual, and mood. One of the main factors that affects whether they are perceived as leisure is the aforementioned social distance. Some women might be very close with their parents, siblings, grandparents, and other relations and might be able to enjoy and relax in their company, while others might not. As respondent B. explained on October 3, 2014: "I love to talk on the phone with my family, and sometimes I go visit them, especially my sister and her children."

Unlike the case with colleagues, family meetings might be "essential to functional roles," but the experience itself can be a leisure-like or a full leisure experience. Therefore, in the case of family, the fulfillment of a function must not eliminate the leisure character of the experience. In contrast with the cases of colleagues, where all of the women found interactions to be leisure-like, family activities are often described as complete leisure experiences. Emotional attachment to family and emotional fulfillment drawn from sharing experiences with them were the main reasons given for considering these experiences leisure. This is true even though some family situations might not be complete leisure, as respondent J. described on May 22, 2015, in the case of a family wedding:

> ...it is a lot of work [laughs]. I mean, okay, it is leisure but not really because I didn't choose it myself. There is some obligation, of course. It depends who from the family is getting married, if I like them or not, if I really must go or not. Yeah, so it's the same when it's a birthday or so: it depends on whether it really is the family or if I go because I must go, because one should go, it is somehow leisure still.

The type of relationship the individual has with the social environment therefore determines to a large extent whether something is considered leisure or not. Frye (2016) also established a connection between relationship closeness and leisure activities; in her case, couples who engaged in shared high-risk experiences together presented higher relationship closeness than couples where only one partner pursued the activity. Whether the shared activity was the cause or the symptom of the closeness needs further clarification, however.

It is essential to consider the time horizons: even if a particular family reunion is annoying in the short term, having a good relationship with family members in the long run is truly important for the women in this study. Indeed, familial relationships are considered lifelong relationships (as are some friendships), which influences the women's overall view on leisure, family, and friends. Relationships with colleagues are considered important mainly for the present, as these women are likely to change jobs several times during their professional lives. A few of these women have, however, developed close friendships with ex-colleagues after changing jobs.

All in all, considering leisure from the viewpoint of freedom of choice requires a closer look at the hidden layers of meaning that such choice might contain. The individual might be free to choose, as in these cases, but choice is affected by a myriad of factors that the individual takes into consideration. Social pressures in these cases do not eliminate freedom of choice but force the individual to analyze situations in terms of gains and losses. In the context of the leisure of these women, therefore, the ideal of freedom of choice exists only when they can choose or not choose something *without expecting negative social repercussions.*

Until now I have highlighted different situations in which leisure and free time might present blurry boundaries. The interviewees were also conscious that there are many different types of leisure experiences in practice. It is precisely in the combination of such different experiences that they see an ideal pattern of leisure. Well-being is associated with avoiding being saturated of one activity or experience. For example, someone who enjoys spending time with the family might also need a variation or balance with other kinds of activities. As respondent B. explained on October 3, 2014:

> And at a family reunion it's like that, of course you always have to help, it's normal, but it is no stress for me. But in the sense, if you were to have every weekend full with family or friends, yeah it would be too much, then I would tell to myself okay no way.

What this and the previous quote show is that there seems to be more nuance to social obligations during free time than the strict scholarly differentiation between leisure and social obligation might allow. Individuals enjoy many types of leisure experiences, some of which overlap with their fulfillment of functional roles. It is the amount of and the balance with other activities that is also important. So it could be said that for these women, another ideal of leisure alongside "true" freedom of choice is variety.

Alternation can be planned; in fact, as will be seen later on, a lot of thought and reflection is invested in fulfilling the alternation ideal. Nonetheless, in close relation to the ideal of alternation is another ideal that contradicts this careful planning: spontaneity. Spontaneity is an additional ideal characteristic of leisure among these women often constructed in a discourse of freedom. Freedom to be spontaneous, not needing to exercise strict control over time can, be essential for leisure:

> Essentially, it is about doing what I want to do at that moment. I don't know what I will do tomorrow, for example. If I have free tomorrow, I don't know what I will do but if suddenly something comes, for example my mom calls and wants to go somewhere or a friend or so, that's leisure for me, that I can decide freely. (Respondent I., December 16, 2014)

> ...the best vacation is always when you just jump in the car, you know you have vacation and you know you can just go somewhere and just drive. (Respondent C., December 10, 2014)

This ideal is seldom fulfilled in practice, though, because, the limited amount of potential leisure time and the wish to share leisure within different social relationships leads to a high degree of planning. It is important to highlight that all women report being satisfied with their leisure time. However, there are different ideals of leisure besides spontaneity that exist despite the fact that they cannot be translated into reality. During the interviews and conversations, these ideals sometimes came up spontaneously or in response to a direct question on wishes or ideal leisure. An aspect that often was brought up concerns weather conditions. Even if ideal weather perception can change according to what activity one is planning or wishing to engage in, the general ideal weather for leisure for these women is a weather that is ideal for outdoor activities: not too hot and not too cold, around 22 °C (72 °F). According to respondent A. on May 12, 2015, "...leisure for me is definitely relaxing, ideally sitting somewhere in the sun with friends and have a conversation and a coffee." This affirms the study of Freitas (2015, p. 62) that the ideal atmospheric conditions for outdoor leisure (observed by length of stay) are being warm with a few clouds and not too windy

Additionally, material resources, specifically money, are also a condition for ideal leisure. Even though these women do not present themselves in a narrative of material need—they often highlight the fact that their basic needs (i.e., food, clothing, housing, and healthcare) are covered—they still consider themselves to have insufficient means by which to participate with or consume all the things and experiences they would wish to consume.

> Mmm, something that I love is sushi, but I seldom eat it because it is a bit expensive, I really like doing it [laugh]. Sushi is awesome, but you cannot do it every week right? Yeah, that's really it. (Respondent A., December 4, 2014)

> I equate leisure with living, because work is just work. You have to work so that you can afford some things, leisure is for me really living, enjoying that which I can afford thanks to my job, just be free within my possibilities, just be able to do whatever I want if I feel like it, that's leisure for me. During the week when I'm working, someone else decides [about] my time, that's why leisure is actually living. (Respondent M., March 19, 2015)

These quotes show that financial constraints play a role and that freedom of choice is limited as a consequence. Harman (1988, p. 161) pointed out that not everyone is as free to consume all that is on offer. Freedom to consume is relative to one's resources, not only in financial terms but also regarding aspects such as education, social skills, race, and gender.

A further example of how financial constraints affect leisure in practice, presenting a barrier to ideal forms of leisure, is the case of vacations and traveling. Having enough money to be able to access certain types of leisure is particularly experienced as hindrance by the women in the case of traveling, as traveling is *the* primary ideal leisure experience in this case study. For the women, vacation time constitutes extended free time; prolonged potential leisure time and traveling constitute the most beloved activity during vacation time. Like other leisure activities, traveling is associated with recuperation and enjoyment and freeing the mind from bothersome thoughts. However, almost all of these women perceived a lack of financial resources as a barrier to accomplishing their travel wishes. During conversations after or at the end of the interviews, I often asked, "What would you do if you had no financial constraints at all?" Interestingly, and without exception, all the informants' answers involved traveling, going somewhere else. Discursively, they narrated their desires to experience difference, to know different landscapes, to learn about other cultures, to try new foods, and to meet new people. This agrees with the argument that the educated middle classes are omnivorous in their tastes and interested in a multiplicity of things, cultures, and experiences (Peterson and Kern 1996) but it also confirms, to an extent, Schulze's (2005) theory regarding the constant search of new experiences because of the women's search for new destinations, their will to visit different destinations every year, and their desire not to return to a place they have been already. (Visiting friends and family are exceptions.) Traveling is subjectively conceptualized to have a high experience value (s. Schulze 2005, p. 59), something that is ratified by the subjective perceptions of this particular group.

In practice, and because seeking new experiences through travel is typically limited by financial constraints, a prioritization of destinations in the women's minds takes place that forms part of organization. Interestingly, the preferred destinations that were mentioned were almost entirely locations in the United States, followed by Australia, New Zealand, and European countries such as Italy and France. Why these specific countries were considered ideal travel destinations was not very clear. Women expressed different reasons for their choices, such as sunny weather, having an interest in the culture, nature, or the fame of the place (particularly in the case of New York).

In general, and regardless of their origin, these women already had many travel experiences. They all had visited many European countries, and some also had visited countries in Africa, Asia, and South America (besides their own countries of origin). Those who were not migrants themselves often expressed the desire to have a long-term experience of living abroad, seeing it as a potential opportunity to have a fuller experience and allowing them to learn new things. As was seen in the chapter dealing with the city of Mannheim and women's relation to it, women experience cultural differences in ways that can translate into discrepancies between what they are willing to consume "omnivorously" as leisure experiences during a vacation and what they do for leisure and where they do it in their everyday lives.

Yet nonmaterial resources also comprise part of the ideal conditions of leisure, particularly the aspect of time. The wish to travel, as with other desires related to leisure, is impeded not only by financial barriers but also by time barriers. The issue of time poverty and its relation to well-being was pointed out by Reisch (2001). Women are aware of this and explicitly express the notion that ideal leisure has to have time and that they do not often have enough time for *ideal* leisure to take place. Even though the amount of time that is necessary is subjective and perceptions of time poverty or richness can vary, this was an aspect on which the informants agreed.

Additionally, they are very aware of the changing nature of leisure and leisure perception in the passing of time or during different life phases. Not only are they aware that there are ideal kinds of leisure for different age groups, they are also aware that their own ideals of leisure have changed through time:

> Yeah, nowadays I don't go partying every weekend, no, no, I'm out of that age. (Respondent C., December 10, 2014]

> Now I often spend my Sundays with my family or with friends with small children. (Respondent N., January 8, 2015]

The women often emphasized that their ideal leisure had changed. For example, as the quotes show, the amount of leisure they spend engaging in nightlife activities, such as clubbing and drinking, had been reduced while leisure activities during the day had taken priority. In some cases, this is due to the changing composition of their social networks. For example, when friends have children, their interests might, understandably, shift and so with them the interests of the group in general: their shared leisure experiences change. In other cases, ideal leisure changes intrinsically due to individual changes in interests, which the body and bodily awareness, and perception often influence. The women often spoke about changes in their bodies, in terms of energy and recuperation needed, which, in turn, affected how they thought about leisure. Their bodily awareness, they said, helped them to understand which activities they should or should not do: the body is important. For example, if was frequently mentioned that a night out with friends, dancing and drinking until 4 or 5 in the morning, was easy to do when in their late teens and early 20s: the physical recuperation time afterward was short, there was no leg or feet pain, and hangovers passed quickly. However, nowadays they feel that the required recuperation time increased and, because they have other activities they would like to pursue in their leisure besides recuperating, these kinds of activities have been pushed to the background. Nonetheless, it is important to highlight that bodily perception is also a cultural construction (s. Allen-Collinson 2011, p. 310) and that these women are not isolated from societal norms that cause them to gravitate toward "proper" leisure for particular genders and age groups. But these types of changes were often constructed during the discourse in a context of energy and recuperation, and not in the context of social norms.

However, these women were very conscious of life being dynamic and changing and saw it as part of life that their leisure in practice, as well as in the ideal, would continue to change. Part of the awareness of generational differences is also seen in the perceived distance between different generations or age groups in their social environment and the different ways in which these groups engage in leisure. Some age groups might not be perceived as a hindrance to the women's leisure while others were considered a hindrance, and there is potential for conflict. For example, some of the women complained about students and avoided venues popular with students, and they described students' behavior at these venues as "childish" and "drunk." Therefore, different age groups can have colliding ideals of leisure and be thus perceived as impeding each other's leisure. Ideal leisure, therefore, can include the absence of groups of people perceived as annoying. Different authors have talked about class rivalries (Bourdieu 1984), milieu rivalries (Schulze 2005), and gender rivalries (Wearing 1998) that can apply to these types of situations. How groups and spaces relate to each other in leisure in Mannheim in particular, and how these women construct their leisure in this context, is considered further in due course.

Ideals and perception of leisure, though, cannot be fully separated from overall lifestyle ideals. Leisure can be considered as just one area of life that is interconnected with all the others, and individuals can have a plan or project of the self, as Giddens (1991, p. 5) called it, that they wish to fulfill in their lives. The awareness for potential change in leisure is in this case related to an awareness of the dynamism of life. Situations can change or individuals can enter different life phases. In general, all of the informants younger than 35 years of age expressed either concrete plans or vague desires of family and family activities in the future. It can be concluded, from their narratives, that they are experiencing this time of their lives as a transitional period between being a trainee, or a student, and being a parent. The advantages of this life phase are financial independence, a lack of parental or family control, a lack of commitments, and few responsibilities: generally, a freedom to construct life as desired. Even though they mention in their discourse the advantages of being independent, some still wish for a family life, despite the commitment it demands. As respondent T. explained on September 28, 2014: "I've been single for two years already and at one point you wish for a boyfriend again, one with perspective because you are getting older and want to go in the direction of a family."

In some cases, this feeling of need or these wishes are accentuated by the fact that people in their social environment, such as friends and siblings, might already have entered this different life phase of parenthood. Just as with the aspect of freedom of choice, it is difficult to grasp the origin of such desires, whether they are intrinsic to the individual or whether they arise from social contexts. What is important to emphasize here is that such future desires or even concrete plans are related not only to leisure ideals but to ideals in general about the lifestyle they would like to lead in the future. Take, for example, the following statement respondent J. made on September 19, 2014. She wishes to have a quiet life in a village: "I could not imagine that when I marry and have children, that I would bring them up in Mannheim, that would be, no it would be a nightmare."

Nevertheless, even though it is not possible to dig further into the origin of such life wishes here, it is crucial to highlight the fact that women do not express feelings of being under social pressure regarding this matter. Even if questions such as "When are you having children?" might come up in the social environment for women over 30 years old, this is a kind of pressure the women face and still do not change their plans. On the contrary: through the freedom of choice they have in this life phase, they are able to shape their lives according to their plans and desires.[2] The issue of children and creating a family was not part of the interviewing guidelines, but it often came up when talking about certain leisure activities and future plans. When asked about it, some women said they did not wish to have children while others said that they were not in a rush to have children and that the right conditions in terms of income, or partner, must be present.

All in all, the current state in which they are financially independent, with stable incomes but with few family responsibilities, is one of the reasons why these women value leisure so highly when they reflect on it (after the fact). Whillans (2014, p. 187) called men and women in this stage "independent singles," people who are in the middle-class demographic and who have full control over their resources and are focused on establishing a career before having families. So, I would argue here that how ideal leisure is perceived and which channels are chosen for leisure in practice are also affected by the life stage in which the individual perceives herself to be at a particular moment. While leisure is perceived to be scarce at present, there is a firm belief (for those who desire to have children) that it will become even scarcer in the future and more constrained due to family obligations. In other words, while the amount of free time might remain the same in the future, leisure time might decrease. This idea often fosters the maximization of the experiences they are seeking to have at this stage of their lives. In this context, Gans (1999) mentioned the importance of age for leisure, but it is possible that, rather than chronological age, it is life stage that influences taste toward certain activities and leisure as well as their intensity and perception a posteriori. These aspects have been mentioned by authors who have recognized the enormous influence of children on leisure (Scheuch 1972, pp. 30–31) or the particularities of singles' leisure (Whillans 2014), which are influences quite present in the informants' self-evaluations. However, the self-evaluation of leisure activities in the narrative must not be directly equated with the motivation behind the choices for those activities. Even though the women are aware of the different life stages and different types of leisure that might accompany them, the main motivation behind their leisure choices is guided by the current ideals they have of leisure, the ideals that have been addressed in this section. Considerations about future leisure time and channels can foster or accentuate certain behaviors and contribute to explaining them in the narrative, but they are not the priority when considering leisure. For example, a woman who goes dancing and drinking in nightclubs until 5 am is doing so because she can free her mind, have fun, and have a particular bodily experience in the present. The fact, however, that she believes she might not be able to do this as often when she has children might affect her self-evaluation of this activity and in turn affect the number of times or intensity with which she engages in the activity in general.

It can be said that despite differences between these women's ideals of leisure and how they experience leisure in practice, they experience no cognitive dissonance (s. Bernard 2006, p. 64) because their ideals and practices are not in direct contradiction; they are not incompatible. Despite barriers that make leisure ideals difficult or impossible to obtain in practice, there is a consistency between decisions and beliefs that will be clearer when I deal specifically with leisure planning and execution in the following chapter. The issue of general ideals of leisure and ideals of leisure in practice everyday is, as we have seen, closely linked with what individuals expect from each specific activity and each specific experience. In fact, dissatisfaction comes when such expectations are not met, whatever they might be (emotional, physical, etc.). The important issue to be highlighted is that there is not *one* ideal of *one* leisure but different ideals for different kinds of leisure. A multiplicity of leisures or leisure types is what is associated with well-being and happiness overall by these women as part of an overall lifestyle. The question then is not whether there is "true," "good," "serious" leisure but rather whether individuals feel that their overall leisure patterns sustain a state of well-being and happiness. In the case of these women, the main question they pose themselves to determine whether they are happy with leisure thus could be, for example: Is my leisure varied enough? Other questions also essential to the women's evaluation of the variety might be: Do I have enough cozy time?, Do I have enough time to do nothing?, Do I have enough physical activity?, Do I meet all of my friends, family, and acquaintances?, and Do I travel enough?

In summary, in this section we have looked at different elements that belong to leisure subjectively, some of which are more applied in practice, some of which are rather abstract ideals of leisure. These subjective perceptions, as we have seen, refer to a myriad of activities, such as eating and drinking with friends, clubbing, cooking, shopping, and traveling. Yet there is a type of activity that requires special attention due to the fact that it occupies a high amount of the total free time these women have and because it has great importance for them subjectively: sports and physical activity.

3.2   SPORTS AND PHYSICAL ACTIVITIES: LEISURE?

The differentiation made between sports and physical activity by Cortis et al. (2008) seems useful for understanding the different levels of intensity and organization with which these types of activities are pursued. Sports are practiced formally—for example, in a club and in the context of tournaments—while physical activity is less formal and typically involves no competition (p. 31). Despite the fact that many of the characteristics of leisure are shared by sports and physical activities, there is no unanimous opinion by social scientists on whether these activities can be considered leisure or whether they are an area separated from it. Differences of opinion regarding sports and physical activity as leisure also relate to whether leisure is being analyzed with a focus on subjective experience or social function. Additionally, Cortis et al. (2008, p. 33) argued that, whether these types of activities are considered leisure or not, they can also be influenced by culture, and perceiving sports as leisure is a Western construct. The question here, however, is whether this particular group of women considers sports and physical activity leisure subjectively. With the exception of two informants, who do not engage in any form of sports or physical activity, I argue that it is. First, these activities contribute immensely to the aspect mentioned in the previous section of freeing the mind:

> Yeah, just really to get fit because during the week with desk jobs you need a balance otherwise you'll go crazy, so I try to go running or go to the gym. (Respondent I., December 16, 2014)

> ...training is, for me, just to free the mind, listen to music and just power out for two hours. Afterwards I'm a very sociable person. These are these phases when I'm not a team player, I'm just a lonely fighter. (Respondent M., March 19, 2015)

Besides being an enormous and relevant channel through which women find psychological well-being by means of physical effort that is not present in their paid work, sports and physical activity can be enjoyable and fun experiences. As respondent C. explained on December 10, 2014: "I enjoy it. I really enjoy playing soccer, I've been playing for 15 years and I just like it, the team, to have fun with other people, for me is not so important to win, of course I also like to win, but no it's fun."

Besides team sports, such as soccer, volleyball, and handball, running is a beloved physical activity. Running is one of the activities half of informants mentioned as playing an important role in their routines. Theories of milieus have actually associated running with the segment of the population to which these women theoretically belong: under 40-year-olds with higher education and with life philosophies centered on the "I" and self-fulfillment (Schulze 2005, pp. 279–330). However, running is done with different levels of regularity and intensity. It is also practiced by those who engage in team sports and other physical activities that have been associated to other milieus (s. ibid.). Therefore, running, as well as other sports, such as soccer, cannot be associated exclusively to a milieu or sociodemographic group. Running is in fact an activity that is pursued by many people in Mannheim, as can be seen by the shores of the river on any given day, particularly on weekends. Runners along the Rhine and Neckar shores comprise people from all ages, genders, ethnicities, and physical conditions. The popularity of running can also be seen in the running events that take place in and around the city, such as the Mannheim/Ludwigshafen Marathon, which takes place every year in the spring. For example, I was a participant observer during the women's run in Mannheim on Friday September 12, 2014. This event hosted around 1370 women, who completed a 7-kilometer (4.3-mile) run through the city of Mannheim, within the area of the Luisenpark and Neckar shore (Fig. 3.2). According to my field notes of September 15, 2014:

The weather was fresh, around 13 degrees [°C; 55 °F], and it was raining but no one seemed bothered by it. Before the start some were warming up, but most of them were having conversations with whomever they were there. I was doing the same but I couldn't help but notice how many people were smiling, it seemed much more than usual. When they announced we should get ready, we all walked to the starting line and the music got loud. The DJ motivated us to sing and jump to the tune of Pharrell Williams's "Happy" and Helene Fischer's "Atemlos," the crowd was really excited. Finally, the starting signal was given and we started running. I had this strange feeling that I was not running but that the crowd was carrying me but as the kilometers passed and the crowd dispersed due to different tempos, I actually had to start putting in some effort. I started to feel my legs and the speed of my breath. It didn't matter, though, some women were singing, some were motivating each other, the viewers on the outside were clapping and cheering. I was having fun and like everyone I was smiling and enjoying the moment. Running towards the finish line, the crowds got louder, the public

Fig. 3.2 Frauenlauf (Picture taken September 12, 2014)

cheered on, the DJ mentioned the names of the finishers. People kept on smiling and talking while drinking the refreshment beer and eating their bananas. Then most of us walked to the changing areas and picked up our bags or change of clothes. Some women were picked up by their boyfriends or husbands and children, but most of them were just there with a group of female friends. While changing and waiting in line, many were talking about how they felt during and after the race, the word "*Spaß*" (fun) must have been used 1000 times. At about 1930 I took the tram back home with many of the other participants. We were all muddy, cold, and tired but somehow still excited and talking about all the details of the run.

The experience of this event presents an example of a situation in which sports can be both a collective and an individual leisure experience. Such events are exceptions, though. Running and other types of physical activity take place in everyday life mostly individually or in smaller groups of people. The particular characteristic of such events is that they can not only enhance the leisure experience due to their special characteristics (presence of music, viewers, number of participants, etc.), but they can also play a role in the context of local identity and relationship to the city as leisure space, as we see in Chapter. On an individual level, such events can also increase the individual's motivation to keep on practicing physical activities and consequently cement routines that are related to such activities. Indeed, many participants of this run spoke about their future training and how they could improve their times for the next year. Social media and other platforms pertaining to these topics also play a role in exchanging information and motivating people.

One of the remarkable aspects of the practice of sports and physical activities for these women is that, in contrast to other types of leisure activities, participation has been strongly influenced by socialization through family and, especially, parents. The participation in sports and physical activity is a consistent biographical aspect in most of these women's lives. This finding is consistent with the results from the study of Cortis et al. (2008, p. 34) who, through their research into sports and physical activity among culturally diverse women in Australia, found that activities from their childhood remained familiar to them in later life and that, generally, individuals had biographical continuity in their lives. Carmichael et al. (2015, p. 54) also highlighted the importance of previous experience during school years for women's current exercise participation. In the case of my informants, the origin of this interest and participation is traced back to parents who encouraged or even imposed physical activities on them during childhood as extracurricular activities besides school:

> I've always enjoyed practicing sports. I was in [to] judo a bit. I've always practiced sports. With my friend, she was always looking for something. I was in gymnastics, yoga, but even earlier I was always in something. I was in swimming lessons because I couldn't swim [laughs] and my mother tucked me in, I had to do a backstroke and I hated it, but I had to go. (Respondent C., December 10, 2014)

I think it would have been really weird if I didn't, if I had nothing to do with soccer, it wouldn't have worked out, because we always watched my older brother play, we always went with the entire family, my mom was there, we were all at the field on the weekends, and watched him. At some point we were three playing so they had to divide themselves. My mom went to watch my little brother and my dad went with the big one so yes, it was always about soccer. (Respondent J., September 19, 2014)

Three of the women had no contact with their fathers, either growing up or as adults. In those cases, it was their mothers in particular who encouraged them to take on these sports activities. However, some of the women who started practicing sports through the initiative of their parents changed disciplines along their lives. Some would have liked to have continued their childhood sports but were forced to quit due to injuries or other health issues. Others keep practicing the same activity they had done since childhood, such as soccer or dancing. Similarities between all the women were seen with some physical activities that are consistently taken up in the late teen or in post-teenage years, such as fitness classes, strength training at the gym, and running. Women have decided on these types of activities themselves, based on their own interest, while friends have had a great influence on new team activities in which they currently engage. Friends and acquaintances help to connect women to a particular activity and/or team; by themselves, these women otherwise would not have participated.

The choice of sports and physical activity is often driven by a combination of factors, including personal taste, time and availability of money, social relations, and the purpose or reason why the individual would like to participate in sports. For example, some women remarked that they liked practicing sports in order to meet new people, while, for others, the priority was physical fitness or psychological release. Often a variety of sports and physical activities combines to serve one or the other primary purpose. For example, many women attend group fitness courses at which they have met friends and acquaintances but they also go running by themselves. The same applies for women who practice team sports but attend gyms to do strength training on their own. The aspect of meeting new people is particularly important for women with a migrant background, independent of internal or external migration. The group of women who were new to the city consciously pursued team or group sports and physical activities in order to gain new contacts among individuals with similar interests. However, this participation is also important for native women from Mannheim who are seeking to expand social circles and to gain new social contacts:

> In a team you learn new people from different age groups, from different professions, people you otherwise wouldn't get to meet, I find that really important. You learn team spirit and cohesion if you want it and do it properly. That's what I think are the main points, I just think is great to be part of a team. (Respondent I., December 16, 2014)

As we have seen in the context of leisure, generally, conscious choices are an important part of participation in these types of activities. In the case of my informants, they were able to explain their decisions and the motives behind them. However, freedom of choice is, as previously mentioned, a difficult issue to address. For example, all of the informants highlighted the health and the aesthetic benefits of participation. This could be contextualized with the already mentioned arguments regarding societal pressures on individuals and their leisure, in the sense that there is a high societal pressure to engage in physical activity because this leads to a more productive and healthy workforce. Yet in some cases, the practice of sports and physical activities can contradict gender ideals or that other leisure activities can have priorities within the social constructions of gender. For example, Katz-Gerro and Meier Jaeger (2015, pp. 424–426) found in their study of siblings that women participated more in cultural leisure activities related to art and music while men participated more in sport-related activities. The difference between men and women in general was the same as that between brothers and sisters; it showed a gender gap that has nothing to do with family-to-family discrepancies.

Nonetheless, it is also possible that gender ideals foster physical activity, which is the case, for example, with the ideal of thinness (s. Bojorqyez-Chapela et al. 2014). In order to comply with this ideal, many women might self-impose the practice of sports and physical activities. Indeed, many women mentioned their desire to be in shape and look good as one of the most important motivations for their practice. Schor (1991, p. 85) argued that just because an activity is enjoyable does not mean it is not work. Yet, subjectively, these activities are considered leisure for the women of this study, which shows that leisure must not necessarily be effortless or, in other words, not all effort is work. Another issue, however, on the topic of gender ideals, sports, and leisure is that gender ideals do not only affect the total absence or presence of such activities; they can also influence which type of activities are pursued. Aerobics and figure training are considered feminine, while team sports and sports in clubs are accepted for youth but are not seen as compatible with life of a grown-up woman (Rastetter 1998, p. 59). This means that, while women might avoid participating in team sports organized in clubs because of the level of commitment they require, it is also plausible that the social perception of what a woman should do in a particular life stage also affects their decision. The statistics of the regional association of sports clubs supports Rastetter's (1998) argument, in that women are overly represented in "feminine" sports, such as gymnastics and horse riding. However, the largest number of women of all ages can still be found in sports like soccer, handball, and athletics (Badischer Sportbund 2014), which refutes this generalization, because most women members of sports clubs are found (at least in this region) in "nonfeminine" sports, which leaves open the question of what "feminine" sports might mean.

Cortis et al. (2008, p. 33) pointed out that some cultural contexts might have different perceptions regarding the relationship between women and sports. Unfortunately, the regional statistics do not gather information about the members' backgrounds. In the case of my informants, women with a migrant background predominantly participated in physical activities that could be considered "feminine," such as dancing, different fitness courses, and running. At the same time, there was a predominance of women without a migrant background among the soccer players, a fact that I also saw during my observation at many women's soccer tournaments and matches of the women's district league. Yet the majority of nonmigrant women also pursued activities like dancing, fitness classes, and running. This was also confirmed by the much higher rate of women's participation that was observed in the fitness courses, such as spinning and chore muscles training, in comparison with men's participation in weight-lifting and machine training in adjacent rooms. This was the case in each of the five gyms I visited on several occasions during the course of the fieldwork.

Some authors (s. Wearing 1998; Carmichael et al. 2015; Cortis et al. 2008; Sikes and Jarvie 2014) and also people with whom I have talked, including a city council representative for sports and leisure, seem to believe that migrant women have larger barriers to face, in terms of sports participation, due to gender ideals stemming from their own cultures. However, gender ideals affect all women in the context of sports and physical activity. For example, my informants expressed their subjective belief in a higher presence of lesbians in soccer, basketball, and rugby than in other, more "feminine" sports. Whether this is the case or not cannot be assessed here, but it shows how ideas of femininity and womanhood influence people's perceptions. During the observation phases, such ideals were very tangible when, for example, high-quality female players were complimented by comparing them to men and, conversely, calling boys' and men's skills female or ladylike was a criticism. In agreement with this, Spracklen (2013, pp. 115–119) argued that sport is a space in which heterosexual masculinity reigns—issue that is very tangible in spaces such as soccer fields and fitness studios.

While both of the city representatives I talked to associated the lower participation of women with a migration background in sports to their strict adherence to cultural rules and to the high cultural pressure they are under, which discourages women's sports participation, I could not entirely confirm this assessment. In fact, other authors (s. Cortis et al. 2008) have highlighted that there exist different barriers for sports participation among migrant women beyond those coming from their cultures of origin; one of them is, for example, the required dress codes and uniforms, which might not conform with cultural or religious dress codes. As I wrote in a field note on August 13, 2015:

> I was sitting on a stationary bike when two young women in their early 20s walk into the gym. They stand at the reception talking to the chief trainer in charge of registrations. I can overhear and see them from where I'm sitting. They ask for information about subscribing to the gym, such as pricing and the courses offered. From their gestures and way they are taking they seem to be very interested in joining. But suddenly the face of the trainer changes as if he has realized something, I can see the discomfort in his gestures when he apologetically says: "but there is a thing, it is forbidden to train with a headscarf." The women, visibly disappointed, ask for the reason, to which he replies: "sorry it is the dress code." To which they reply with a short oh!, thank him for the information, and leave.

This episode exemplifies how such barriers present themselves in everyday life. The women left without joining and participating as a result of a constraint, both gendered and cultured, in the form of a dress code. Even though it is possible to train in different gyms, such as the couple of women-only fitness studios in the city, they can be inaccessible due to geographical distance or cost.[3] This same dress code, which is a stipulation of the contract, also forbids men to show too much skin by, for example, wearing tank tops and muscle shirts. Women are allowed to wear anything but headscarves. This is not a unique dress code; it is similar to ones in other locations. Although the dress code for men is generally explained in the context of hygiene or annoyance of other customers, the prohibition of headscarves has been challenged unsuccessfully in German courts on grounds of safety while using the machines (s. WeltN24 2013). Whether this reasoning is justified cannot be addressed here. However, what can be seen is that women's and men's bodies are being treated differently and that there are fixed assumptions about how their bodies should be in the context of physical activity, which, in practice, means the exclusion of some. Women might want to choose a particular channel for leisure, they might want to pursue a leisure experience through sports or physical activity, but this might not be possible due to societal constraints. These constraints also may come from the host society and not exclusively from cultural/ethnic codes, as exemplified by this dress code.

Sports dress codes could be flexible in order to include different individuals. For example, some women's soccer teams from the district league around Mannheim allow team members to play wearing headscarves and long tights and T-shirts beneath the uniform. As the woman is adopting some traits of the dominant culture (playing soccer), while keeping some others of her own, this could be a form of selective acculturation (s. Chavez 2000, pp. 183–184). Yet many teams involved in different sports do not allow such "transgressions," and as a result potential members are excluded. Another example of barriers to sports participation occurs in the case of winter sports. Among all my informants, only those without a migrant background practiced winter sports, such as skiing or snowboarding. Aside from the barrier of cost, women with a migration background often perceived an incompatibility between their ethnic or racial identity and such sports (such sports being perceived as "white" sports and the women feared being treated like outsiders). Chavez (2000, pp. 183–184) called this the "perceived discrimination" barrier to participation, when ethnic groups feel unwelcome and willingly choose not to participate. Nadel-Klein (2010) mentioned that ethnic groups have different stereotypical views of what other groups do for leisure, with outdoors or winter sports being then subjectively perceived as "white" sports. Thus, the issue of being welcome or not is also an issue of power relations, as the circumstances and historical backgrounds under which people are encountering each other and under which their concept of leisure has been generated must be considered. Winter sports are another example where there are currently no strategies or policies of inclusion.

However, Hudson (2013, p. 148) argued that, in fact, these are cases of self-constraint because the individual is consciously extracting the self from a possible experience on an intrapersonal level by thinking "I am not white enough to go skiing" or on an interpersonal level, "I will look foolish to others." It is important to remember that, even though individuals have the agency to surpass or eliminate this self-constraint, the cultural setting still exercises an influence. The issue in these cases is not whether women from various cultural and religious backgrounds consider sports and physical activity leisure. The issue is that when they do and want to translate this ideal into practice, they encounter a higher number of barriers or constraints to participation than their nonmigrant counterparts.

Leisure spaces dedicated to sports and physical activities are also gendered spaces. For example, the fitness centers and gyms have areas that are dominated by male members and areas dominated by female members. Many women I spoke with explained how they felt uncomfortable going to the "male" areas alone or even being in gyms with male members, often due to unwelcomed comments, approaches, or glances. In these instances, the women would choose to go to female-only gyms. It could be argued, therefore, that perceived discrimination, where minorities choose not to participate (s. Chavez 2000, pp. 183–184), must apply not only to different ethnicities but also to differences in gender because of unwanted treatment. Perceived discrimination might just refer, as argued earlier, to power inequalities in the use of space; being unwelcomed or being too welcomed (e.g., good-looking women) by the ones who hold the power over space is what makes the difference. This is in harmony with the description of gender experiences of women in gyms by Fisher et al. (2017), who highlighted that gyms are not necessary safe and inclusive spaces and often perpetuate gender relations.

The argument is that gender and ethnic issues are intertwined with participation in sports and physical activity in practice, while ideally, differences might not be as large. The understanding of the ideal of sports and physical activity as leisure is not something that can be taken for granted, but, beyond structural constraints, it is important to highlight the meaning sport and physical activity holds subjectively for the individual when it is actually translated into practice. Physical activity is often self-imposed, in the sense that it requires disciplining oneself by generating routines and habits. As respondent I. said on December 16, 2014: "I go directly after work, because until I leave work and I'm at home…no then I won't feel like it, I try to get at least one hour of sport in, otherwise my evening, my day is done."

Iso-Ahola (2015) mentioned the unconscious automatisms people incurr in for good and bad leisure. Sports and physical activity mean effort but, generally, the true effort for these women, as can be inferred from the quote, is surpassing their own tiredness or laziness, as they themselves describe it. Despite the fact that most of these women have been practicing physical activities for many years, some of them even for their whole lives, training is still not automatic or a nonchoice, as Iso-Ahola (2015, pp. 301–305) pointed out. Practicing sports and physical activities is a choice, one that is made again and again. The women talk about overcoming the own lazy self, or "*Schweinehund*"; however, it could be argued that they are in fact reacting consciously and subjugating the subconscious when they go to practice these activities a couple of times a week and, as Iso-Ahola (p. 300) pointed out, reinforcing their own conscious freedom. In fact, aspects, such as weather conditions, can have a great influence on how much will and determination individuals have to exercise to go through with their choice. As respondent J. said on May 22, 2015: "I'm very lazy in terms of sport in the winter, I tend to do more when spring starts to come, I spend more time at home in the winter, and then start to do stuff in spring and summer."

The weather can be, therefore, an acceptable excuse for the subconscious mind to override the will to do the activity:

> Inclement weather conditions can pose a barrier to leisure activity participation by negatively influencing mechanical or thermal comfort, and can also act as a physical and perceived barrier for accessibility and mobility to out-of-home leisure opportunities. (Spinney and Millward 2011, p. 134)

What must be highlighted here is that deciding upon how to react in face of the weather conditions is a situation or inner conflict that precedes the leisure experience. While the moment of overcoming oneself and the travel time to the activity might not be leisure, sports and physical activities are perceived as leisure as they are being completed. Consequently, as Klein (2009, p. 2) pointed out, these types of activities are not (only) pursued with the priority of performance but with a focus on leisure, despite the fact that they might be practiced "seriously," in Allen-Collinson's (2011, pp. 307–308) sense of routine and improvement. The physical effort required during exercise is not an effort that is bothersome or tedious. As respondent S. explained on November 4, 2014: "Spinning, I love spinning, you can release so much pressure […] that is the best way to get relaxed for me, during sport, spinning, that is for me pure relaxation even if it's difficult to believe."

In some cases, the key is to keep the drive for competition, the pressure, low, which is why some of these women contrarily keep practicing (noncompetitive) physical activities. This is also the reason why women often avoid enrolling in sports clubs, which are often too focused on competition and self-image (success). Respondent A. explained on May 12, 2015, by way of example, that she had quit riding competitively: "I want it to be fun for the horse and for me, I don't want it to be hard work, but real leisure."

In this case, the experience of leisure during such types of activities could be considered a state of "flow"' because of the balance between the challenge and the feeling accompanying it, which includes the faster passing of time (Csikszentmihalyi 1991). The relationship between flow and sports has already been addressed by different authors (s. Demontrond and Gaudreau 2008) who have shown how by the nature of these experiences, the purpose of the practice is forgotten. Some authors highlight the importance of the concept of the body and take the body as a social construct into account in all types of analysis (s. Segura 1997; Allen-Collinson 2011; Gunaratnam 2013; Walseth 2015). According to this line of thought, sports and physical activities might be experienced bodily in a flow state, but they also have additional purposes related to the body and its social perception. So sports and physical activities have multiple purposes including ones closely related to moral imperatives and bodily image, as has been mentioned, but during their practice, such goals can be absent from the minds of the women. Nonetheless, what is certain is that, if looked at empirically, in the case of these women, as Mannell (2014) proposed, sports and physical activities are conceptualized as leisure, are experienced as leisure in the "immediate conscious experience," and are perceived as leisure in "post hoc satisfaction" self-analysis (s. Mannell 2014, pp. 3–7).

Therefore, sports and physical activities can have different dimensions as well as different functions. For example, regarding experience, a kickboxing class can help one free the mind and feel a bodily rush of energy due to the production of endorphins. On a functional level, the activity helps participants lose weight and look attractive to others, even if this effect is forgotten during the 60-minute class. It can also be a time spent with friends or a way to meet new ones, and it can be understood as a learning possibility to improve body motor function or coordination.

All in all, these types of activities and experiences are great and prominent examples in these women's everyday lives of the complexity of their leisure processes and experiences. Although leisure experiences can be spontaneous as one of the ideals of leisure states, more often than not they are preceded by, or made possible through, thoughtful considerations, choices, and actions by the individual. A great number of aspects exist that the individual can take into consideration, such as, for example, previous experiences, costs, weather, body perception, and health. Additionally, there are different ideals of leisure and many channels to have leisure in practice. For some, sports and physical activity can be a form of leisure but not the ideal form because, for some women, the ideal form still has to be related sense to relaxation and recuperation. As respondent C. explained on December 10, 2014: "It is wonderful, I don't like to swim. I mean, I like to swim but it is not like that, for leisure I have to feel good, I like to go to the sauna, that ohh sauna once a month, yeah I go once a month and love it."

Finally, the ideal and practice of leisure can vary from one person to the next, and it can also change according to the situation or with the passing of time for an individual. In general, it could be argued along with Fastenmeier et al. (2003) that, from a subjective perspective, leisure can encompass different qualities: it can be spontaneous or planned, social or individual. Leisure must not be exclusively defined in any one way (p. 16). Nor should sports and physical activities, which are considered leisure by almost all my informants, even though, for some, they might not constitute ideal leisure. However, Figal (2014), who dealt with the term "*Muße*" and highlighted it as a state of mind, a quiet state of dedication to one thing only, also invite us to consider that this term applies to these women's experiences during the practice of sports and physical activities. This is because, when narrating their experiences during these types of activities, they often emphasize the coexistence of the effort, concentration, and peace of mind; thus, "flow" could apply to some types of activities such as yoga, which encourage awareness and slow pacing. In contrast, other leisure activities overlap with others (multitasking) or they might not require such a degree of concentration and effort, such as, for example, watching TV and chatting on WhatsApp or talking to family on Skype and watching a movie. How exactly the activities and experiences are distributed in everyday life and how everything is organized and takes place is covered in Chap. 4.

NOTES

1. Studies on comfort food have shown its emotional importance as well as what is perceived as comfort food is related to age, gender, and culture. All in all, these types of foods share common characteristics such as high calorie, fat, and sugar content. For more information, see, for example: Laurette Dubé, Jordan L. LeBelb, and Ji Lu. "Affect Asymmetry and Comfort Food Consumption," *Physiology & Behavior* 86, no. 4 (2005): 559–567.
2. The possibility to form life according to the project of the self (even if not called like that) is a deeply rooted belief. Awareness of unforeseen circumstances, such as illness and death does not stop them from pursuing the steps on their project of self.
3. Additionally, women's fitness studios in the city are not open 24/7 policy as some mixed gyms are, and often they are not open on weekends.

REFERENCES

Adorno, Theodor W. 1991. Free Time. In *The Culture Industry: Selected Essays on Mass Culture*, ed. Theodor W. Adorno and J.M. Bernstein, 162–170. London: Routledge.

Allen-Collinson, Jacquelyn. 2011. Feminist Phenomenology and the Woman in the Running Body. *Sport, Ethics and Philosophy* 5 (3): 297–313.

Appadurai, Arjun. 1996. *Modernity at Large: Cultural Dimensions of Globalization*, 1. Minneapolis; London: University of Minnesota Press.

Badischer Sportbund. 2014. *Mitgliederstatistik.* http://www.badischer-sportbund. de/DERVERBAND/Wirueberuns/Mitgliederstatistik/. Accessed October 6, 2014.

Bauman, Zygmunt. 2009. *Leben als Konsum.* 1 Aufl. Hamburg: Hamburger Ed.

Bernard, Harvey R. 2006. *Research Methods in Anthropology.* 4th ed. Lanham, MD: Altamira Press.

Bojorqyez-Chapela, Ietza, Claudia Unikel, Maria-Eugenia Mendoza, and Fabiola de Lachica. 2014. Another Body Project: The Thin Ideal, Motherhood, and Body Dissatisfaction Among Mexican Women. *Journal of Health & Psychology* 19: 1120–1131.

Bourdieu, Pierre. 1984. *Distinction: A Social Critique of the Judgement of Taste.* 2010th edition. Translated by Richard Nice, with a new introduction by Tony Bennett. London/New York: Harvard University Press/Routledge.

Brosius, Christiane. 2010. *India's Middle Class: New Forms of Urban Leisure, Consumption and Prosperity.* London: Routledge.

Carmichael, Fiona, Joanne Duberley, and Isabelle Szmiging. 2015. Older Women and Their Participation in Exercise and Leisure-Time Physical Activity: The Double Edged Sword of Work. *Sport in Society* 18 (1): 42–60.

Chavez, Deborah. 2000. Invite, Include and Involve!: Racial Groups, Ethnic Groups and Leisure. In *Diversity and the Recreation Profession: Organizational Perspectives*, ed. M.T. Allison and I.E. Schneider, 179–191. State College, PA: Venture Publishing.

Cortis, Natasha, Pooja Sawrikar, and Kristy Muir. 2008. Final Report: Participation in Sport and Recreation by Culturally and Linguistically Diverse Women.

Csikszentmihalyi, Mihaly. 1991. *Flow: The Psychology of Optimal Experience*. New York: HarperPerennial.

Demontrond, Pascale, and Patrick Gaudreau. 2008. Le concept de "flow" ou "etat psychologique optimal": etat de la question appliquee au sport. *Staps* 79 (1): 9–21. De Boeck Universite.

Dobler, Gregor. 2014. Muße und Arbeit. In *Muße im kulturellen Wandel: Semantisierungen, Ähnlichkeiten, Umbesetzungen*, 54–68. Berlin: De Gruyter.

Dumazedier, Joffre. 1967. *Toward a Society of Leisure*. New York; London: Collier-Macmillan.

Fastenmeier, Wolfgang, Herbert Gstalter, and Ulf Lehnig. 2003. Was empfinden Menschen als Freizeit? – Emotionale Bedeutung und Definition. In *Motive und Handlungsansätze im Freizeitverkehr: Mit 17 Tabellen*, 13–29. Berlin: Springer.

Figal, Guenther. 2014. Musse als Forschungsgegenstand. La Villa.

Fisher, Mary James, Lisbeth Berbary, and Katie Misener. 2017. Narratives of Negotiation and Transformation: Women's Experiences Within a Mixed-Gender Gym. *Leisure Sciences* 0 (0): 1–17.

Foley, Carmel. 2017. The Art of Wasting Time: Sociability, Friendship, Community and Holidays. *Leisure Studies* 1 (36): 1–20.

de Freitas, C.R. 2015. Weather and Place-Based Human Behavior: Recreational Preferences and Sensitivity. *International Journal of Biometeorology* 59: 55–63.

Frye, Nancy. 2016. "Let's Do What Together?!" Shared Activity Perceptions and Relationship Closeness. *Leisure Sciences* 0: 1–13.

Fuller, Chris. 2011. Timepass and Boredom in Modern India. *Anthropology of This Century*, 1. http://eprints.lse.ac.uk/38021/. Accessed June 16, 2016.

Gans, Herbert J. 1999. *Popular Culture and High Culture: An Analysis and Evaluation of Taste*. Rev. and updated ed. New York: Basic Books.

Gerhards, Juergen. 2008. Die kulturell dominierende Klasse in Europa: Eine vergleichende Analyse der 27 Mitgliedsländer der Europaeischen Union im Anschluss an die Theorie von Pierre Bourdieu. *Kölner Zeitschrift fuer Soziologie und Sozialpsychologie* 4: 723–748.

Giddens, Anthony. 1991. *Modernity and Self-Identity: Self and Society in the Late Modern Age*. Stanford; CA: Stanford University Press.

Granger, Christophe. 2014. Children of the Otium. How the French Got Leisured (since 1900). In *Muße im kulturellen Wandel: Semantisierungen, Ähnlichkeiten, Umbesetzungen*, 279–303. Berlin: De Gruyter.

de Grazia, Sebastian. 1972. Der Begriff der Muße. In *Soziologie der Freizeit*, ed. Erwin K. Scheuch and Rolf Meyersohn, 56–73. Köln: Kiepenheuer & Witsch.

Gunaratnam, Yasmin. 2013. *Death and the Migrant: Bodies, Borders and Care.* London; New York: Bloomsbury.

Hancock, P.A., and G.M. Hancock. 2014. The Effects of Age, Sex, Body Temperature, Heart Rate, and Time of Day on the Perception of Time in Life. *Time & Society* 23 (2): 195–211.

Harman, Lesley D. 1988, c1987. *The Modern Stranger: On Language and Membership.* Berlin; New York: Mouton de Gruyter.

Harring, Marius. 2010. *Das Potenzial der Freizeit: Soziales, kulturelles und ökonomisches Kapital im Kontext der Freizeitwelt Jugendlicher.* 1 Aufl. Wiesbaden: VS Verlag für Sozialwissenschaften.

Hudson, Simon, Gordon Walker, Bonnie Simpson, and Tom Hinch. 2013. The Influence of Ethnicity and Self-Construal on Leisure Constraints. *Leisure Sciences* 35: 145–166.

Huizinga, J. 1940. *Homo Ludens: Versuch einer Bestimmung des Spielelementes der Kultur.* 3rd ed. Basel; Bruessel; Köln; Berlin: Akademische Verlagsanstalt Pantheon Verlag fuer Geschichte und Politik.

Iso-Ahola, Seppo E. 2015. Conscious Versus Nonconscious Mind and Leisure. *Leisure Sciences* 37 (4): 289–310.

Katz-Gerro, Tally, and Mads Meier Jaeger. 2015. Does Women's Preference for Highbrow Leisure Begin in the Family? Comparing Leisure Participation Among Brothers and Sisters. *Leisure Sciences* 37 (5): 415–430.

Klein, Thomas. 2009. Determinanten der Sportaktivität und der Sportart im Lebenslauf. *Kölner Zeitschrift für Soziologie und Sozialpsychologie* 61: 1–32.

Kovac, Laura, and Dawn Trussell. 2015. "Classy and Never Trashy": Young Women's Experiences of Nightclubs and the Construction of Gender and Sexuality. *Leisure Sciences* 37: 195–209.

Mannell, Roger C. 2014. Leisure in the Laboratory and Other Strange Notions: Psychological Research on the Subjective Nature of Leisure. In *Contemporary Perspectives in Leisure: Meanings, Motives and Lifelong Learning,* ed. Sam Elkington and Sean Gammon, 3–17. Abingdon; New York: Routledge.

Nadel-Klein, Jane. 2010. Cultivating Taste and Class in the Garden. In *Mutuality and Empathy: Self and Other in the Ethnographic Encounter,* vol. 5, 107–121. Wantage: S. Kingston Pub.

Opaschowski, Horst W. 1996. *Pädagogik der freien Lebenszeit.* 3, völlig neu bearb. Aufl Bd. 1. Opladen: Leske + Budrich.

Peterson, Richard, and Roger Kern. 1996. Changing Highbrow Taste: From Snob to Omnivore. *American Sociological Review* 61 (5): 900–907.

Qian, Xinyi L., Careen Yarnal, and David Almeida. 2014. Using the Dynamic Model of Affect (DMA) to Examine Leisure Time as a Stress Coping Resource: Taking into Account Stress Severity and Gender Difference. *Journal of Leisure Research* 46 (4): 483–505.

Rastetter, Daniela. 1998. Freizeit braucht freie Zeit: Oder: Wie Maenner es schaffen, Frauen die (Frei-)Zeit zu stehlen. In *Freizeit in der Erlebnisgesellschaft: Amüsement zwischen Selbstverwirklichung und Kommerz*, ed. Hans A. Hartmann, 2 Aufl., 45–66. Opladen: Westdt. Verl.

Reisch, Lucia A. 2001. Time and Wealth: The Role of Time and Temporalities for Sustainable Patterns of Consumption. *Time Society* 10: 367–385.

Richter, Rudolf. 2005. *Die Lebensstilgesellschaft*. 1 Aufl. Wiesbaden: VS Verlag für Sozialwissenschaften.

Scheuch, Erwin K. 1972. Die Problematik der Freizeit in der Massengesellschaft. In *Soziologie der Freizeit*, ed. Erwin K. Scheuch and Rolf Meyersohn, 23–41. Köln: Kiepenheuer & Witsch.

Schor, Juliet. 1991. *The Overworked American: The Unexpected Decline of Leisure*. New York: Basic Books.

Schulze, Gerhard. 2005[1992]. *Die Erlebnisgesellschaft: Kultursoziologie der Gegenwart*. 2 Aufl. Frankfurt [Main]; New York: Campus.

Segura, Denise. 1997. Chicanas in White-Collar Jobs: "You Have to Prove Yourself More". In *Situated Lives: Gender and Culture in Everyday Lives*, 292–310. London: Routledge.

Sikes, Michelle, and Grant Jarvie. 2014. Women's Running as Freedom: Development and Choice. *Sport in Society: Cultures, Commerce, Media, Politics* 17 (4): 507–522.

Spracklen, Karl. 2013. *Whiteness and Leisure. Leisure Studies in a Global Era*. New York; London: Palgrave Macmillan.

Stebbins, Robert A. 2014. Leisure, Happiness and Positive Lifestyle. In *Contemporary Perspectives in Leisure: Meanings, Motives and Lifelong Learning*, ed. Sam Elkington and Sean Gammon, 28–38. Abingdon; New York: Routledge.

Stengel, Martin. 1998. Freizeit als Restkategorie: Das Dilemma einer eigen-staendigen Freizeitforschung. In *Freizeit in der Erlebnisgesellschaft: Amüsement zwischen Selbstverwirklichung und Kommerz*, ed. Hans A. Hartmann, 2 Aufl., 19–44. Opladen: Westdt. Verl.

Turner, Victor W. 1982. *From Ritual to Theatre: The Human Seriousness of Play*. Vol. 1. New York: Performing Arts Journal Publications.

Veal, Anthony J. 1987. *Leisure and the Future*, 4. London; Boston: Allen & Unwin.

Veblen, Thorstein. 1924. *The Theory of the Leisure Class: An Economic Study of Institutions*. 8th ed. London: George Allen & Unwin.

Walseth, Kristin. 2015. Sport within Muslim Organizations in Norway: Ethnic Segregated Activities as Arena for Integration. *Leisure Studies* 35: 1–20. doi:10 .1080/02614367.2015.1055293.

Wearing, Betsy. 1998. *Leisure and Feminist Theory*. London; Thousand Oaks, CA: SAGE.

WeltN24. 2013. *Gericht Erlaubt Kopftuchverbot im Fitnesstudio.* http://www.
sueddeutsche.de/panorama/urteil-in-bremen-kopftuchverbot-im-fitnessstudio-
ist-rechtens-1.1705639. Accessed December 16, 2015.

Whillans, Jennifer. 2014. The Weekend: The Friend and Foe of Independent
Singles. *Leisure Studies* 33 (2): 185–201.

CHAPTER 4

Leisure Practices

4.1   EXCURSUS: PROFILE NR. 2

R. is a 33-year-old woman, originally from Cameroon, who has since become a German citizen. She came to Germany as a student and pursued studies in international management. Her parents also work in businesses back in Cameroon. Upon completing her studies, she has been working in a big company as a customer service representative. She lives in a small flat with her brother, whom she supports while he pursues his own studies. When I met her she was dressed in business-casual attire, wearing a colorful blouse, black pants, colorful earrings, and a big leather handbag. She is very friendly and talks calmly and openly. We met on a weekday after work at Cafe Sammo in the city center, a place that was good for her as it was located between her workplace and her home.

When she talks about her childhood and teenage years, she speaks about riding bicycles, playing team sports with friends on the streets, and enjoying pool parties, but she emphasizes that the activities always were spontaneous and informal. In her experience, parents and children would live in separate spheres of life. Consequently, she does not feel influenced by her parents on what she did then and what she does now for leisure. When she was a child, she did not know what her parents were doing for leisure either. The activities she has pursued as an adult relate to her interests, specifically her interest in her own well-being and the possibilities presented by her social environment.

© The Author(s) 2017
V.L. Sandoval, *The Meaning of Leisure*, Leisure Studies
in a Global Era, DOI 10.1007/978-3-319-59752-2_4

On weekdays, she enjoys an average of 15 leisure hours, meaning approximately three hours a day, while, on weekends, she has around 10 hours of leisure a day. On weekdays, she arrives at work at 8 am and leaves at 5 pm or sometimes later, depending on the amount of work there is. She then takes the tram directly home and makes herself something to eat. Afterward, she likes to spend her leisure time in various ways. When alone, she likes to take long walks in the park or forest (except for when it is raining) and then read a book (she enjoys reading biographies) and write in her journal. She watches TV before going to bed. Sometimes she manages to make time to visit friends to have a cup of coffee or to cook together. She is the one who has to visit them because most of her friends have children, so it is more difficult for them to get out and about. In general, she does not meet much with people during the week.

On the weekends, she often drives to see her boyfriend, with whom she has a long-distance relationship. When they are together, they like to meet friends for drinks, go to the movies or go spend time at the pool or lake. Aside from the expenses of rent for her flat, her food, heat, and electricity, she spends the highest amount of the money on drinking and eating out with her boyfriend or with friends. She occasionally allows herself to go out to eat sushi, which she loves, despite it being expensive for her. If she stays at home during the weekend, she typically uses Saturday mornings to go grocery shopping and then does some yoga or Pilates at home. If she has been out with friends until late the night before, she stays in bed until late on Saturday, until noon or later. She also spends a lot of time on the weekend talking on the telephone or chatting with her family and friends who do not live nearby. She would like to physically meet with her friends and family more regularly, but she emphasizes the difficulties of people finding free time at mutually agreeable times.

Once a month she has a special date, in which she meets with friends from her country to cook Cameroonian food and to eat together. She is also involved with a charity organization that supports poor people in her hometown or people from Cameroon who are experiencing difficulties living in Germany. Otherwise, she does not really have much contact with Cameroonians or cook many recipes of this type of cuisine in her everyday life. She enjoys cooking lasagna and eating Würstchen (sausages) but she says jokingly she is not "Germanized" enough to like asparagus.

All in all, a big issue that influences her leisure is her health. When she is not feeling well, she cannot take the daily walks around the park that she would like to. These walks are very important for her because she likes to disconnect from technology and breathe fresh air, which she does not get to do at work or during the rest of her leisure time because she is constantly connected to her phone. The goal of keeping her weight down and staying in shape is also important for her. Sometimes she walks around the city doing some window-shopping, which is both entertaining and good for burning calories. But health issues have in the past also affected her vacation plans and work routines and have prevented her from moving to a better flat. They are a constant factor that she has to deal with despite her young age.

Asides from her health and the financial constraints that impede her, and not being able to fulfill some of her wishes, such as more spa weekends or sushi dinners and vacations abroad, she sees no major problem with her lifestyle; in fact, she is satisfied. In the near future, if everything goes well, she will spend her next vacation visiting an old school friend in Canada whom she has not seen for many years: "I like visiting all the people I know who are scattered around in the world."

4.2   Leisure Segments and Pace of Life

Until now, the focus of this work has been on how these women think about leisure and what it means for them. It emerged in the findings that leisure is perceived to be scarce and a limited resource. In practice, leisure has many different characteristics and components. For one, despite spontaneity being one of the ideal features of leisure, it not necessarily something that can be translated into practice. Additionally, another of the ideal features of leisure is the presence of close friends or family, whom the individual enjoys being with and for whom leisure time is also limited. Thus, spontaneity and the wish to spend time with loved ones are not always compatible. In order to succeed at having leisure with social relations, organizing and planning are important steps. In other words, social relations often trump spontaneity in practice. The word "organization" here should be understood as being aware of time: dividing, assigning, and prioritizing time slots. I refer to planning in regard to deciding on specific activities that take place in those time frames. Planning and organizing go hand in hand, as a plan cannot be achieved without proper organization. Organizing time and planning leisure occupies an important amount of the respondents' free time. Planning and organizing typically involves reflecting, texting, talking on the phone, arranging dates, booking activities, making reservations, buying tickets, and the like. How activities are planned is influenced by how time is perceived, so, in turn, organization, planning, and execution affect the pace of life.

Perception of time goes hand in hand with time scheduling. Thus, time schedules and personal organizers play an important role in the lives of these women. In terms of schedules, or patterns of how time is organized, the biggest influence is paid work, which mandates for all of these women an average of 40 hours of work from Monday to Friday. Due to the nature of their work, none of them is required to work in shifts so they have a relatively constant working schedule, generally between 8 am and 5 or 6 pm. However, as the women mentioned in the questionnaires distributed after the interviews, the amount of time perceived as leisure during the week varies from five hours (one hour a day), to 25 hours (five hours a day). On average, these women report having around 14 hours of leisure during the week. In contrast, they stated that around seven or eight hours of leisure a day were available during the weekend. When asked to clarify their answers, it was noted that obligations and chore activities were almost always excluded from their calculations. One of the reasons for variances was transportation times. With a few exceptions, where some took public transportation, these women drive their cars to work every day.

The perception of the amount of leisure time available, in comparison to the amount of disposable hours after paid work, shows the importance of distinguishing between leisure time and free time. These findings are similar to reports of Scheuch (1972, p. 30) who, more than 40 years ago, pointed out that, regarding weekdays, workers perceive only about three hours of leisure time and, during the weekends, just seven to eight hours. Indeed, free time as time away from paid work and not spent sleeping is not equal to leisure. However, it is important to highlight that there might be differences regarding the perception of the amount of leisure time available. For instance, previous experiences with state infrastructure, institutions, and bureaucracy can have an influence on the amount of perceived leisure time available. Having a lot of free time might not be perceived as useful if it will be needed for running errands that take a long time. If activities that are commonly done during free time, such as going to the doctor, buying groceries, or other types of state/institution-related activities, take a long time, the potential leisure time will be less. Consequently, the perception of time is influenced by a myriad of factors, including gender and previous life experiences (s. Boecker et al. 2013, p. 87; Hancock and Hancock 2014).

Different segments of time can be considered potential leisure time and are perceived as such. As Opaschowski (1996, pp. 85–96) pointed out, pauses during work, time after work, weekends, and vacations can all be considered leisure segments. In the following sections, I concentrate on the three main segments of leisure time for these women, namely (after work) leisure during the week, weekends, and vacations. These segments are essential to the perception of time overall, the sequences of activities engaged in, and their pace.

4.3   THE WEEK

> First, I cook and eat. I mean, I'm really free after 6 pm—then I'll go about twice a week to the gym, mostly on the evenings or during the weekend. Meeting with friends it's almost non-existent during the week: it is something for the weekend, meeting friends yeah. Otherwise during the week sport as I said or just relax at home or at my boyfriend's home. (Respondent S., May 10, 2015)

Regarding everyday leisure during weekdays, Scheuch (1972) argued that all social classes use this time of the day similarly. Individuals use this time to watch TV, read, talk to family, and "do nothing" (Scheuch 1972, p. 32). Even though the scope here does not make it possible to address similarities or differences between the social classes, this assumption is partly confirmed by my informants regarding their similar use of time. The three to five hours of leisure women perceive to have on weekdays are in fact mostly used for relaxation at home, including activities they classify as "doing nothing," such as viewing Facebook pages, checking Instagram images, or entertainment like series watching. Another large portion of the weeks' leisure hours is invested in sports and physical activities. For all the women involved, except for the two who do not practice any, physical activities occupy two to eight hours of the weekly allotment of leisure hours. Physical activities are prominent in the everyday schedule, and they are generally done on alternating days—for example, Mondays, Wednesdays, and Fridays. During weekdays, social activities seldom occur but, when they do take place, entail what are called "quiet" social activities, like meeting up for coffee or dinner. They are considered quiet because they might not require physical effort, involve a small circle of social relations, and do not extend late into the evening. But "quiet" is also a relative term that indicates that there is less noise and less excitement of the senses (e.g., through alcohol) than in other types of activities left for the weekend.

The types of sports and physical activities in which these women engage during the week vary greatly. The most common activity they engage in is training in fitness studios, whether taking part in classes, such as spinning or Zumba, doing chore muscle workouts, or just strength training in the machine rooms. This type of activity is often pursued in conjunction with other types of sports and physical activities, such as soccer or dance training. When fitness studios are chosen before other activities, it is mainly because they allow a high degree of flexibility regarding attendance times. Most of the fitness studios of the city are open 24/7 and offer a variety of courses that commence almost every hour up to 9 or 10 pm each day. The specific fitness studios the women attend were chosen primarily because of their geographical distance to and from either their home or work locations, despite most of them owning a car. Additionally, many fitness studios are chains so it is possible to attend alternative centers in the city or in other locations.

For those women who attend fitness centers as their only source of physical activity, the variety and schedule of courses offered, as well as infrastructure and personal attention received, affect the decision to go to a center more than the cost involved. Price does play a role upon signing the contract, with the monthly fee being paid to the gym being one of the incentives mentioned to actually attend. For those respondents who also practice other activities, such as team sports or dancing, location and price seemed to be the most important factors affecting their choices. However, additional aspects are considered bonuses. The women pay attention to the kind of clientele that attends the center, whether it is too old or too young, too muscled, too loud, and so on.[1] For example, one woman explicitly changed centers to a women-only center where she felt more comfortable and did not have to be confronted with unwanted approaches by men, even though the women-only gym had much restrictive opening hours.[2]

Going to the fitness studio is something that is generally done alone but, on rare occasions, the women will go with a friend or partner. Whether this activity is done alone or with someone else can change according to situation; for example, it can depend on one's mood. As respondent S. explained on May 10, 2015: "… sometimes I want to be left alone. I want to be alone. Sometimes I feel like talking to a friend while walking on the treadmill and sometimes that's nice but, for me, it really changes." Or whether the activity is done in solitary or with company can change, depending on the company. Respondent S. also explained:

> … when I go with my friend we'll do some cardio or we'll go to a class together. When I go with my boyfriend I'll do exactly the same as when I go alone because he also trains with the machines so we each train for ourselves and then in between we'll have a short chat, or I'll go to him and do some of the exercises he's doing and then go back. Yeah, with my friends we'll just run or go to a course.

What she is describing here is something that was corroborated by my participant observation in different gyms at different hours of the day: mostly people attend gyms alone. Even though there is a higher ratio of men to women, both attend predominantly alone. Being left alone, as mentioned by S., is something that most people seem to want, particularly in the areas of cardio, weight-lifting, and strength machines, where many people are listening to music via headphones (despite the fact that gyms also have music). Moreover, as S. describes, for those who are there with company, there are observable gender differences. Women tend to complete activities or circuits together, while men (either with other men or with women) independently complete activities and socialize in between sets. In general, there is little to no interaction between people who do not know each other, with the exception of classes or courses, which were (with the exception of spinning) attended mostly by women and in which social interaction with strangers was common. In contrast with the main training areas, people interact in the classrooms in, for example, the form of greetings and questions and comments about the class. These types of interactions are not without meaning as they present the opportunity for creating new social relations, something that will be discussed further in later sections.

So while attending fitness studios (and engaging with activities like running) is something that these women generally do alone, they occasionally manage to coordinate with friends or family to meet up during weekday evenings or afternoons in the already mentioned "quiet" meetings. During interviews and conversations, it became clear that a few locations were commonly visited by all of these women, and observation showed that many people in the city generally visit them. One of these trending locations is a cafe/bar called Bolands, a cafe/lounge that is popular among customers choosing to drink coffee in the afternoon. It was often mentioned in interviews and conversations, so I engaged in participant observation at the location.

Participant observation at Bolands on different days of the week and different times of the year showed that this venue is not visited solely by this group of women or people who share their sociodemographic characteristics. It is a well-known place in the city, frequented by people in all age ranges, even though the majority are adults from their 20s to their 50s. Just like the diverse social demographic of the city, its clients spoke different languages and wore clothes in different styles, from casual, sporty, to formal office clothes. One of the reasons it is so popular is probably its location in the city center, close to the shopping area, the university, and many office buildings. Besides its convenient geographical location, other reasons for its popularity given by my informants were the atmosphere and the quick self-service system. In general, people in groups stay in Bolands for up to two hours at a time, while individuals alone sat generally for a maximum of one hour. These people having coffee or beer alone were, on all occasions, men. Women sitting alone were waiting for company to arrive. At the time of the participant observations, which was between 4 and 7 in the afternoon, almost all of the patrons were drinking coffee. The majority of women drank latte macchiatos or cappuccinos, while the men's drinks varied more often. The preference for this type of mixed coffee was also shown during the interviews, in which interviewees also consumed these drinks. The consumption of coffees mixed with milk, cream, and other ingredients is partly related to gender ideals. For example, I was often jokingly referred to as "tough" for drinking black coffee without sugar. Although these comments from informants and other social contacts were not reproaches, they point to deeper views on gender and taste. (Such comments would not be made to a man.) In this case, the comments associate bitterness of flavor with toughness, which in turn is not associated with femininity. In the context of the coffee shop, notions of femininity are often reproduced by these women through the consumption of "soft" coffees (with sugar and/or milk), the highest representative of which is the coffee with flavored syrups, which I heard referred to as "*Mädchenkaffee*" (girls' coffee). All in all, is important to stress that eating and drinking are the consumption practices closest to the body and that they are the most prone to habituation because of the difficulty of having patternless bodily regimes (s. Appadurai 1996, p. 67) and because gender is part of how bodies are constructed (s. Allen-Collinson 2011), gendered consumption is also part of everyday life and its patterns. In this case, the coffee consumption practices of my informants were in harmony with observed patterns of behavior of other women in that context as well. As such, through leisure practices such as meeting friends for coffee, choosing a particular drink and being seen consuming it, these women reinforce (or contradict in some cases) gender ideals without even noticing it.

However, exceptions to the coffee consumption were on warm days where the consumption of drinks tended to shift toward the colder variety, such as Coke, beer, or energy drinks. In general, when talking about drinks and food preferences, informants constructed their choice in terms of taste, but observations showed that the drink and food selection of the social circle also exercised an immediate influence on the individual. For example, if one member of the group chose an alcoholic beverage, it is more likely that the others would do so too. Being the only one drinking alcohol is not socially acceptable, which is often seen in negotiations about the choice of drink, asking what the others are having, commenting in a tone of reproach "Well, if you are all having that, I'll have a [...]." If someone does finally express the desire to have an alcoholic beverage, someone else (who had initially chosen something else) will decide to join.

Fig. 4.1 *Bolands* terrace (Picture taken Wednesday, October 1, 2014, 1730)

Bolands is one of the many examples of a city venue where there is a mixed clientele, where people coexist in groups of different age groups, gender, and origin, contradicting reports from other authors. Keim (1995), for example, highlighted that in neighborhoods in Mannheim, every group of the population had its own venues and made use of its own spaces. Students, foreigners, and natives were all in different public spaces, according to Keim (1995, p. 45), but this cannot be confirmed in this case. The activity of meeting for coffee or drinks after work on weekdays (concentrated especially in some venues) seems to be something shared beyond certain demographic groups, venues, and events, as was seen in the second chapter which dealt with Mannheim as leisure space. However, it is important to note that the city center, where Bolands is located, may attract more varied clienteles in general than venues such as neighborhood bars or coffee shops, which the women described as being full of either older people or unemployed people they did not wish to be around. By observing such venues, it is also possible to see not only the different demographics but also differences in atmosphere (decoration, space use, music, smell, etc.) and products offered. All in all, these other venues were not attractive enough for these women to spend time in.

What must be highlighted here, in the context of social meetings for coffee, drinks, and dinner and regarding the organization of leisure, is the validity of Reisch's (2001) argument concerning the importance of the availability of time and its different dimensions. These types of weekday activities—meeting for coffee in the city, meeting for dinner with friends, and others—are highly valued by the individuals because they offer the possibility of enjoyment and also emotional support in times of difficulty. For example, say a woman has had a hard day at work and wants to talk about it with a friend during the afternoon coffee. If she actually manages to leave work as scheduled, if she has free time (chronometric dimension), if the cafe is open (chronologic dimension), if she has decided that she will take the time to have that coffee (personal time autonomy dimension), the remaining key issue will still be coordinating with the friend or friends that they also will have time (synchronic dimension) (s. Reisch 2001, pp. 377–378), and this is often the most difficult task. Due to schedules, which come with being a full-time employee, living in the city (e.g., traffic), and having multiple interests and social networks, people lead busy, fast-paced lives. Additionally, the family, friends and acquaintances of these women often have small children, which is a known further influence on leisure (s. Isengard 2005). In some other cases, romantic relationships can also affect organization of leisure:

It has decreased [meeting with friends], because many of my girlfriends are now in a relationship and have less time, or they want to spend an evening with their boyfriends at home, so at the end is less. (Respondent J., May 22, 2015)

I think that if my family wouldn't live so far, or if I had a partner I wouldn't spend that much time doing extracurricular activities, it would be more limited, one has to manage the time. (Respondent A., March 2, 2015)

All in all, the hours that can potentially be used for leisure are limited. Within those limited hours, many are already set aside for routine activities, particularly for sports and physical activities, which, as already discussed, and once the conscious mind has overridden the "lazy" subconscious mind (s. Iso-Ahola 2015, p. 300) and the decision to do the activity is taken, actually are experienced as leisure. In the remaining time, even though there is always some room for spontaneous action, planning and organization is required to increase the chances of success of a desired meet-up taking place. Synchronizing time and schedules is crucial and is something often done days or weeks in advance. Here is where time schedules and organizers gain importance.

Technology plays a central role in facilitating such synchronization of time with social relations, particularly technologies, such as social networks and cellphones. The use of WhatsApp is, in general, a constant characteristic in these women's lives. The participant diaries show that contact with family and friends through WhatsApp is an activity that extends throughout the entirety of each day, excluding the time spent sleeping and working. (WhatsApp is used during breaks at work.) During the weekends, it is an activity that takes place in parallel to many other activities, and it is present for almost 12 hours a day, even if its role may shift to the background or foreground, depending on the situation. WhatsApp facilitates organization of activities because of its speed and reach and also through its functionality, such as group chats, which allow planning of group activities. All of my informants make use of this app and use it to have written or spoken (voice message) conversations with family and friends. Almost all of them are also members of different groups: groups with families, groups with friends, groups with colleagues, and so on. However useful and enjoyable the use of WhatsApp might be, some informants also reflected on the fact that people seldom call each other anymore and that contact through these kinds of apps is far less personal. Aspects such as hearing a voice in real time was something that they seemed to miss and which was compared to the way in people used to manually write cards prior to the prevalence of e-mail. However, the women highlighted the practical uses of the WhatsApp tool.

Tazanu (2012, p. 258) pointed out that cellphones are a tool for sociability that can keep families and friends connected and help maintain social proximity in the presence of physical distance. Nonetheless, smartphones and applications like WhatsApp are important not only in the context of migration, where physical distance is considerable and may last for long periods of time; they are important also with all ranges of physical distance and duration of separation. These tools help connect individuals who might live in the same country, city, or even household. They are a means for communication that helps users to share specific information and organize leisure and other type of activities. Other apps with different functions also play a role, albeit less impactful than WhatsApp. For example, apps are also used to engage in video conferences; some are used to find and meet new people or love interests and to coordinate phone calls or meetings. Indeed, some apps are used in the context of presenting oneself as the "best good" in the dating context, which resonates with Bauman's (2009, p. 13) argument that people nowadays must create themselves as interesting goods. This the women do, or have done when they create highly thought through personal profiles which are a performance of the self in order to gain a date or a relationship. These profiles are also taste performances, as Liu (2008) argued, containing information about music preferences, hobbies, and other interests. Yet the virtual space, such as the WhatsApp space, can also be leisure or working space, depending on the situation. When it is impossible to meet in person, for example, a WhatsApp group can be a leisure space or "virtual neighborhood" shared with friends. Spending leisure time in virtual spaces cannot be considered "bad leisure," as online activities can also facilitate empowerment and social participation on a global level, through expressing opinions and providing a voice (Gajjala and Tetteh 2014, p. 41). For example, in the midst of the large influx of refugees to Germany, many people, including my informants, made use of virtual spaces to inform themselves about this trending topic and express their opinions about the subject, even though they did so within their own social networks and seldom made use of globally accessible modes of expression, such as Twitter. Technology can, therefore, be a facilitator of leisure as well as a form of leisure itself (ibid., p. 32).

The issue of space will be discussed in more detail subsequently, but it is important to highlight the importance of technology in the lives of these individuals. By this I mean technology as tool for planning and organization and also as a channel or form of leisure experiences, which is clearer in the case of TV and computers used for watching TV series and movies. Smartphones are also used for a variety of games, from many popular apps like *Farmville, Candycrush* to different varieties of card games.[3]

Technologies like these make it possible for individuals to avoid boredom, not only because of the possibilities of play (apps) and entertainment but because, through communication of leisure opportunities, there is less risk of boredom. Being bored is something all these individuals would like to avoid, and their being aware of leisure opportunities has been correlated with the reduction of levels of boredom (s. Barnett 2005, pp. 147–148). During the week there was a clear commonality in the channels used to avoid boredom. Participation in virtual spaces through mainstream social networks, such as Facebook, Twitter, Snapchat, and Instagram, plays an important part, as does entertainment, particularly in the form of TV series. There was an evident commonality in the TV series chosen; the main purposes of some trending series, like *The Big Bang Theory* or *How I Met Your Mother*, are to provide humor, while other series are categorized as thrillers or crime procedurals, like *Criminal Minds* or *CSI*. This type of entertainment is often enjoyed online and not as much on national television. These genres were also reflected in the participants' general tastes in books and movies. Only a few women spontaneously expressed interest in national and international news, either written or in other media, and described engaging with news as part of their routine. Therefore, technology is a means for pursuing entertainment as well as for organization and information.

However, the degree to which technology is used as a tool to coordinate time can vary from context to context and from individual to individual. For example, addressing again the issue of spontaneity, one of the migrant women explained the difficulties she encounters when adapting to a strict leisure plan:

> ...people plan a lot here right? I'm gonna do this today, that tomorrow, and you may say okay let's go grab a coffee tomorrow, no I don't have time tomorrow, do you have time in two weeks? So it's like well, no, I wanted something spontaneous you know? I want to talk to you, tell you something that happened yesterday, No, I don't have time, we can have a coffee in two weeks. But in two weeks I have already forgotten what I wanted to tell you. So that's what happens with people, I don't have everything planned, but they say can we do this in two months? (Respondent A., February 3, 2015)

So, while spontaneity might be one of the ideals of leisure, thoughtful organization of one's day, week, and month is the general rule to be followed in practice. In this quotation the woman sees it as a cultural issue, but strict planning can also come from structural facts, such as the way the leisure industry promotes its products. Products and experiences may require planning, such as, for example, the act of buying tickets or making a reservation, or issues such as infrastructure can affect it. Traveling, for instance, requires planning of arrival and departure times and, as we have already seen, can also affect the choices made in relation to venues visited, especially those visited routinely, such as gyms. These choices are also affected by financial considerations because planning influences price; booking many activities in advance is cheaper, and spontaneity is expensive. In this sense, once could argue contrary to Stebbins's (2014, pp. 30–37) classification of leisure activities as serious, casual, or project-based because, even though an important part of leisure is casual in the form of social conversation, relaxation, and play, it still requires a high degree of planning and coordination in order to take place. It seems as if these categories could easily overlap, making it difficult, if not impossible, to distinguish one from another. The term "casual" can also lead to misunderstandings in terms of the subjective relevance and meaning of activities like meeting with friends only to have a conversation without specific purpose beyond the meeting itself and spending time together.

Strict planning of time can also have a correlation with a person's general perception of time. Even though all of the women report to have, more or less, the same amounts of available free time, the migrant women appeared to differ in their perception of time. In general, when coming from a larger city (both from within Germany and from other countries), women perceived themselves to gain an increased amount of leisure time. A characteristic of large cities is, for instance, considerable travel distances that generate "lost time" and that, when accompanied by traffic problems, might reduce a person's available leisure time and increase the pace of life because there are no time "buffers." The contrary was the case for women coming from smaller cities or villages, who often perceived an increase in their pace of life and a noticeable decrease in their potential leisure time.

In other cases, previous experiences with structural issues or with perception of the chronologic dimension of time played a role. For example, if leisure activities were not available at the location:

... the thing is, previously I couldn't take as much advantage of time. Here [Germany], time is enough for you because you know, well, "I'll take 10 minutes to get to the gym," then you'll be there one hour, then you'll take

15 minutes to get home and you'll have time. Previously I couldn't. I left at six in the morning to go to work to be there at half past seven, I worked until five and was at home at half past seven so you didn't have time to go to the gym [...] and gyms and other activities don't open on the weekends, here you have activities on the weekends. I go to flamenco classes and it's perfect for me. (Respondent A, February 3, 2015)

All in all, previous experiences affect how time and pace of life is perceived. However, there was a general perception by the migrants from other countries that strict planning of time was a particular German trait. This would somehow support the findings of Barnett (2005, pp. 148–150) in which European American students were significantly more distressed by unplanned free time than their Hispanic, Asian, and African American counterparts and consequently were more prone to planning. However, my non-European informants displayed the same rigor concerning their organization of leisure time as their nonmigrant counterparts in practice. When asked about it, the main reason given was again the necessity to adapt to others' schedules in order to have a social life and social leisure. In other words, social life requires planning, so planning represents a huge part of making sure that the synchronic dimensions of time, dimensions mentioned above, are fulfilled. This is important because, as we have seen with in regard to the meaning of leisure, one of the most crucial aspects of leisure is sharing experiences with close friends and family. Additionally, and as it is pointed out by Barnett (p. 134), having unfilled free time can have a negative emotional response on people, which is avoided by successful organization and planning.

Yet organization and planning of leisure is not different among certain cultures or determined by urban-rural experiences. As Barnett (2005) showed, there are gender differences in the expectations that individuals have of their leisure. In Barnett's case, male students prioritized being challenged through an activity while female students prioritized anticipation, planning, and knowing what to expect from it (pp. 147–148). All in all, the activities (leisure and nonleisure) during the week can, to a high degree, be anticipated. These women know what, when, how, and with whom they are going to happen. Effective use of one's time is a high priority in this context, and, as has been described, part of the effectiveness involves choosing carefully with whom one will spend this time, which mostly translates into practice as time for oneself or close relationships. There are exceptions, mostly related to special occasions, in which other people meet during the week. These types of occasions are intertwined with the dynamics of the locality and local events as exemplified previously when dealing with Mannheim and its neighborhoods as leisure spaces.

4.4   The Weekend

On the weekends I am between a zombie and an Energizer Bunny. (Conversation with respondent M., March 5, 2015)[4]

The previous section focused on leisure activities and experiences that take place regularly and are part of people's everyday leisure, from Monday to Thursday. As it was described, the women from this study work on a fixed schedule from Monday to Friday, which means they have every Saturday and Sunday free from paid work. Therefore, in comparison with free time during the week, the weekends (which start on Friday evening) offer a higher amount of chronometric time that can be dedicated to leisure. The greater amount of potential leisure hours is one of the reasons why weekends are less strictly planned than weekdays, but it also is why weekends are valued as offering the most opportunity for emotionally fullfilling potential leisure time.

However, weekends are not completely spontaneous in practice. They are, similar to the week, also characterized by the presence of patterns. Routines can be found in relation to chores, which is an example of why not all the free time available is actually translated into leisure time. Yet time also plays a vital role. During the interviews, one of the first aspects described as a part of the weekends was sleeping longer—not just going to bed later (normally past midnight) but also sleeping longer, in terms of the total hours slept. As respondent B. explained on October 3, 2014:

I always start Fridays by talking on the phone with all my girlfriends Friday evenings because [on] the weekend is when my real relaxation starts. So, I talk to my friends and I stay awake until really late because I like it. Mmm, what do I do? I watch some TV or play something, I don't know, whatever game is trendy at the moment in the smartphone. And then I really like sleeping off on the weekends.

This was also confirmed by the entries in the weekend diaries where sleeping time on Saturdays and Sundays extended at least to 9 but mostly past 10 am. Waking up at those hours is simply not possible during the week due to work schedules. Long sleeping hours are often accompanied by later breakfasts and relaxing on the couch. During the week, necessary time for sleeping and eating (s. As 1978) is normally kept to the exact minimum required; during weekends, such activities as having breakfast, for example, can be extended, often becoming leisure-like. Having the possibility of making the breakfast experience slower and last longer increases the potential for its enjoyment: there is no time pressure. This could be conceptualized as "slow-paced leisure," having and taking time for the experience without haste (McGrath 2014), a stark distinction from meals during the week.

Despite the slowed-down pace that can occur during the weekend, the pace of life generally is perceived differently from individual to individual. As in the case of the week, there are significant differences between women who grew up and were accustomed to large urban areas in contrast with those with a rural background. Patterns of behavior and perception of pace of life during the weekend are vary between internal migrants from the rural areas of Germany and the rest of the women (including external migrants). It is important to highlight that external migrants within my group of informants have life histories that developed in large urban centers, generally capital cities, while those who are internal migrants to Mannheim come from cities or villages of different sizes. External migrants and internal migrants from large cities, as mentioned earlier, perceived a slowing of their pace of life in their lives in Mannheim. Women directly from Mannheim or from similar-size cities felt a consistency in pace of life. Women coming from small towns or villages in Germany expressed feeling unsettled with this different pace:

> I'm a kid from the village. I think I'm a typical kid from the village. I came to study here and when I was 19 or so. Really, I wasn't a kid anymore, right? But I was really overwhelmed by the noise, the many cars, the trams. Where I come from, there's not even a traffic light. That's it. When I drive through Mannheim I get really stressed: it bothers me, the traffic, the people, yeah [...] I'm not used to it. In our village, you can go everywhere with the bike but here you have a license and then you have a car. (Respondent J., September 19, 2014)

> I grew up in Odenwald with a lot of nature. As a child I was always outside, and now as an adult I would also like to be outside in nature, you have time to go take a walk or ride the bike, I have that influence. (Respondent A., December 4, 2014)

Earlier, different tools and ways in which women organize and plan their leisure were presented, and it was noted that one of the goals of organization is also to keep control of the pace of life. Avoiding a pace of life that is perceived to be too quick and stressful is important, as is avoiding a pace that is considered too slow and could become boring. One activity that repeats itself during the weekends, and which has a fixed place in plans, is categorized under chores: house cleaning and grocery shopping. These types of activities generally take a few hours in the early afternoon after time has been taken to relax and have brunch or breakfast. These activities are often left for the weekends because of the lack of time and energy typically available during the week. When these activities are done during the week, it is in a shorter, compressed version. As respondent J said on September 19, 2014: "It's nice to be finally at home during the weekend. I can chill, watch TV or clean up. I'm never at home right?"

The boundaries between chores and leisure can be fluid, as mentioned earlier, and they can become even more so during weekends. Chore activities can spontaneously intersect with leisure and vice versa. A day during the weekend or the weekend itself can be composed of a sequence of events of different natures. However, planning leisure of weekends is truly. Such planning often applies to time segments, such as Friday evenings, Saturday afternoons and evenings, and Sundays (before the evening). The range of activities that takes place in such moments is greatly varied and change from individual to individual. Additionally, in contrast with chore activities and leisure in the form of sports and physical activity, these activities often change for the same individual from week to week. As such, differences manifest themselves more markedly in the weekends, not necessarily based on class differences, as Scheuch (1972, p. 32) argued but possibly because the individual simply has more room to exercise freedom of choice or translate preferences into practice. As a matter of fact, one of the key elements of the weekends is change and balancing routines with different activities. One of the important goals of planning is not only to ensure the compatibility of schedules but also to ensure that leisure is not entirely dominated by routine. Leisure is conceived by individuals as time to vary, to be different, as a contrast to their working lives, and variation in leisure includes the different elements or types of leisure seen previously, such as relaxation and recuperation, enjoyment and pleasure, social or individual, even if, during the weekend, social leisure is predominant in comparison with during the week.

External aspects that foster variation in planning are the seasons, which, in the case of weather conditions, influence a spontaneous change of execution. For example, plans for a barbecue in the summer might be made up to one month in advance, but they may subsequently change or be canceled. This is something that confirms that weather conditions can be a barrier to leisure activities (s. Spinney and Millward 2011, p. 134; Freitas 2015, p. 60). Although weather conditions can be a barrier to the desired or planned leisure activity, they do not present a barrier to leisure in general, as the activities are substituted with something else, such as indoor leisure activities. However, there can be different degrees or forms in which seasons and weather may affect individuals. Some women expressed more annoyance with extreme weather, such as heat and rain, than others, which in turn can translate into their behavior when faced with these conditions.

It is important, nonetheless, to highlight that work as an employee with strict office hours and tasks to be fulfilled day in and day out affects these women on different levels. Although they express general satisfaction with their jobs, this satisfaction mostly refers to the general possibility of earning money and having responsibilities, but they do express problems in terms of routines and boredom, income and job insecurity, or problems with colleagues. From their narratives, one can infer that there is no experience of *Muße*[5] in their jobs or seldom a sensation of self-realization (s. Pieper 1989; Figal 2014, p. 7). Complaints about the end of the weekend or vacation time are part of the day-to-day dialogue; conversations seldom contain positive remarks about the working environment in general. In this case, it is possible that, just as Stengel (1998, p. 31) highlighted, how leisure and work are experienced is also influenced by the nature of work itself. In other words, the possibility of achieving *Muße* during work, and thus experiencing work as important for identity and general life satisfaction, might depend on the type of work being done. For example, creative jobs might have a higher possibility of *Muße* than the medium-level clerical work these women engage in. In this case, from the way individuals experience work and leisure subjectively, it does seem accurate to see leisure as compensating space, one that allows individuals to express more individuality and to follow their interests (s. Scheuch 1972, pp. 35–41). Leisure, then, has a higher degree of flexibility than the space of work, which must not necessarily be "ego-depleting," as Iso-Ahola (2015) argued but which, definitely, has a stricter frame or less room for agency, particularly when one is employed by someone else and has repetitive tasks.

Additionally, just as in the Carmichael et al. (2015) study of older, full-time employed women and their physical activity, women perceived employment as a barrier to participation in leisure activities, despite the fact that employment generally makes participation possible by providing income to cover various costs (Carmichael et al. 2015, pp. 51–57). Employment can be a barrier in the way it occupies time but also because it makes recuperation necessary, which might not be in harmony with the desired leisure. Consequently, most of these women have a more positive attitude toward leisure than they do toward work. As Fastenmeier et al. (2003, p. 17) declared, the weekend is a time segment more associated with leisure than the week. All in all, and even more than free time during weekdays, the weekend is a key element or time frame for individual leisure. One of the ways in which the difference between week and weekend is seen is in the higher range and variety of venues and places visited during weekends in comparison to during the week. If, during the week, gyms, sports fields, and cafes are dominant leisure activities, during the weekend, the range of venues and activities expands. Also, some women practice sports and physical activities on the weekends whereas others do not something that also greatly affects leisure venues and experiences.

Nightlife, in the form of meeting at bars for drinks and/or going clubbing, comprises important activities during these women's weekends. These types of activities take place on Friday and Saturday evenings or on days followed by a holiday. Generally, drinking alcohol takes place, starting in the early evening around 9 pm, and clubbing starts later, at around midnight, and lasts until various hours in the morning. It can last only until 3 am in the morning if the person is tired or not enjoying the party, or it can continue until 5 am, when most of the clubs close their doors. Women do not only invest time in these types of activities; they also invest a significant part of their income in food and drinks during weekend nights. The frequency with which the women engaged in such activities varied from almost every weekend to a couple of times a year. In particular, for clubbing, the tendency is for women are not in a relationship to go more often than those who are not. Indeed, because clubbing is a leisure activity pursued by some with a functional intent, it can be used as a way to meet potential love interests, as pointed out by respondent T. on October 28, 2014: "I'm single at the moment, so I go out so that I may meet someone." Just as activities vary during the weekends, so too do the motivations behind the same activities. As respondent A. said on December 4, 2014: "…so we go. I don't go to meet someone. I go to have fun together with my friends because I like the music and dancing and I can forget about the week."

Even if some wish to find someone and form a relationship, the club is often not the place they choose to actively pursue this goal. As one woman pointed out, the "type" of crowd in a club is not what she is looking for. There is a general perception that clubs are filled with people looking to engage in casual sexual relationships, or one-night stands, and not in long-term relationships. However, the motivation behind the activity can be, in some cases, observed in the on-site behavior. For example, there are differences in the type of clothing (degrees of "sexiness"), manners and interactions (flirting, dancing, etc.), presence of a "wingman" or "wingwoman," and so on.[6] And the women might occasionally engage in casual relationships even if they have other plans for the long-term future.

Among the women, clubbing is an activity that is always done with company, never alone. Some of them engage in it with close friends and others with their so-called party friends, which, as the name suggests, are friends with whom the only shared activity is clubbing. Incidentally, these latter types of relationships are generally seen as superficial. In general, the informants' social networks are very varied and composed of various circles that may or may not overlap. Interestingly, the women who were born and raised in Mannheim did not have always have their circle of friends for longer than their counterparts. Many relationships have changed or been lost in life transitions, such as end of school, end of professional education, the start of new jobs, and others. The closest friendships, or best-friend relationships, were, in all of the cases, of the same gender and of similar age. Additionally, almost all of these relationships stemmed from childhood or the teenage years. However, the closeness of the relationships describes an emotional bond, not a physical one. In many cases, the "party friends" are closest physically and might even be met with more often than the close friends.

Party friends, or social relations whose common interest is going drinking and dancing together, do not lack importance. One of the main reasons why clubbing is an activity that these women do not do alone is safety. They have an awareness of the dangers of what has been called "liminal spaces" (s. Andrews and Roberts 2012), such as nightclubs, but also have a general perception of Mannheim (in particular certain neighborhoods) as being unsafe. Companions and the "buddy system" serve to protect women in this environment, for example, in cases of excessive alcohol consumption where they might be more vulnerable to violence against them (s. Kovac and Trussell 2015, pp. 196–205). Companions accompany each other to bathrooms, walk home together, or make sure that the other takes a taxi home, but companions are not only there for safety. Factors like social perception and social desirability also play a role. As Kovac and Trussell (2015) pointed out, appearances have a great meaning at the nightclub: here being alone or appearing to be alone can be something that fosters social judgment and exclusion. Additionally, it is possible that gender roles make it difficult for a woman to be alone at a nightclub without being judged by others as nightclubs are not free from gender role "policing," something made clear by the control of dress codes (s. ibid., p. 206).

Despite dangers and policing of gender roles, clubbing, like sports and physical activities, is often constructed in a narrative of freeing the mind and releasing tensions generated in other areas of life also. Nightclubs are very varied, and some can be more compliant with social norms than others. In general, the liminal nature of nightclubs allows clubbing to be often perceived as freedom. For example, the four women who identified themselves as lesbians or bisexuals engaged almost exclusively in clubbing oriented toward the LGBT community, such as Heaven & Friends and Himbeerparty. They felt that these types of parties, which take place regularly in nightclubs, offered them a space in which to express affection or behave as they wished, in comparison with other clubs, where they felt constrained and could potentially be target of critical glances, offensive comments, or (seldom) violence. Additionally, aspects like avoiding uncomfortable situations or even harassment by heterosexual men or meeting potential love interests also were considered in their decision for these particular events and venues. In this sense, these spaces were perceived as safe, and the buddy system was used for coming and going from those spaces. Being in a club with friends and acquaintances was not only about enjoying the presence of social relations but also was a matter of not being seen alone, as mentioned earlier.

Clubbing and going out at night for drinks with friends is a case in which, even though the individuals are looking for, choosing, and having an experience, as proposed by Schulze (2005), and consuming products in the form of entry fees, drinks, outfits, and taxi rides, like the critics of the leisure industry and consumption argue (s. Adorno 1991; Bauman 2009, 2013), there is still enjoyment and pleasure, as Brosius (2010) and Whillans (2014) pointed out. There are immense emotional and identity aspects in play in these leisure activities, besides the goal of freeing the mind. For some women, nightlife is often so important that it takes priority over recuperation. Clubbing or going out for drinks is the number one reason why weekends might not always actually entail more total sleeping hours than weekdays. As respondent C. explained on December 10, 2014: "Saturday and Sunday I sleep until late but I don't sleep too long. For example, if I arrived at 5 am at home I'll be awake at 10, then I just chill a bit afterwards." Therefore, enjoyment and having the preferred leisure experience has become, in some cases, a priority over recuperation and the necessary time for sleeping. In general, though, there are stark differences in the use of time during the weekend and venues visited during the weekend and activities seem to be more affected by social goals, music taste, clothing style, atmospheric preference, or sexual orientation of the individual. Additionally, many clubs and venues are visited because of habits or routines that are easier to follow than coming up with a new plan. As respondent S. explained on May 10, 2015: "...yeah, we go because of the atmosphere but mainly because we have been going there like forever, we know that, and I think we try to think about where we are going and end up going to the same place, somehow it's weird."

Certain "trending" venues are visited more than others. Beloved Mannheim nightclubs are, for example Blue Tower, Scheckenhof, Manufaktur, and Zimmer. These clubs have a mixture of trending songs, both charts and hip-hop. However, if the women feel unsafe in a particular club's crowd, the environment will override the appeal of the type of music being played. This was the case, for example, with the Zapatto, which was often described as having excellent Latin American music and infrastructure but which the informants avoided because they felt uncomfortable or even unsafe with the men persistently pursuing them there.

In general, Latin American–themed venues are very popular. For example, while venues for drinking and dining vary, one that was mentioned as liked and visited often was Barrios, a Latin American–themed restaurant/bar in the city center of Mannheim. Barrios is a big place with a main space, a smokers' lounge, and a terrace. It promotes itself as a place to experience Cuban flair, offering mojitos, cigars, and salsa music, and it is indeed very successful. Going to or passing by Barrios on several Friday or Saturday evenings, I found it crowded and found that reservations are often mandatory if someone wishes to sit down at a table. Barrios is decorated in a rustic colonial style of dark wood and brick walls and with paintings of Caribbean beaches. The menu is varied, comprising dishes from Argentina up to Mexico. Even though many do go to have a meal, most of the women said it was one of the places with the best cocktails in town. Barrios is often a destination for a "girls' night out" or the place to have some drinks before going on clubbing.

Some reasons why this venue might be so well attended include the quality of drinks and food and its location in the city center, but the atmosphere seems to be what completes the full Barrios leisure experience. When describing various venues that embody a vision of stereotypical Latin American bars, a phrase that is often used is: "You feel like on vacation." So, this kind of "Latin American" experience being sold by the "leisure industry" seems to be in harmony with the wishes of its clientele. Through the example of a neighborhood in Munich, Özkan (2015) showed how cultural diversity sells, in the sense that it is instrumental in attracting a particular segment of the population that is interested in foreign art, food, and cultures; the same applies here. An interesting peculiarity of Mannheim is that many of these venues, such as Barrios and Havana lounge/bar, are owned, managed, and served by migrants with Turkish origins. One can often hear them speaking in Turkish behind the bar. However, this does not seem to affect the clients' "Latin American" leisure experience. From the perspective of the owners, one of the reasons they might choose to open a Latin American–themed venue could be that the market for Turkish-themed venues in the city is already oversaturated. However, Gilroy (2004) and Spracklen (2013) have shown that there can be different associations made with different groups and that there are many hidden layers and dimensions of racism; the associations of meanings might be different for the categories "Latin American" and "Turkish." While "Turkishness" is a part of Mannheim's identity through the presence of large population groups with this migration background and their many businesses and associations, and even though "Turkish" could be also associated with vacation feelings because of the Turkish Riviera, many negative associations have been constructed historically around this group as well. Yet such reflections on authenticity do not take place subjectively in the visitors' minds; the main issue is the enjoyment of the leisure experience. Furthermore, this enjoyment is mostly given by the companions (social relations) and not primarily by the context, as it is often stressed.

In general, though, is it difficult to point out the venues where leisure is mainly organized during the weekends. The Rhine-Neckar Region is well connected and people within it commute from one place or another for different purposes. While nightlife might be concentrated on the city of Mannheim, outdoor activities or shopping activities might be planned and executed somewhere else. However, one of the key factors influencing flexibility and how much the individual moves around in the region and beyond is definitely car ownership. Out of the women interviewed, eight did not own a car. Consequently they displayed a more limited geographical area in their leisure activities, which was mostly concentrated within the city's limits. Car ownership affects people's participation in certain leisure activities (Veal 1987, p. 143), even though public transportation allows a great deal of access to a wide range of places and facilities (s. Cortis et al. 2008, p. 51). Leisure activities are organized and planned keeping this aspect in mind: venues are chosen on the basis that they can easily be reached by public transportation, or activities are planned with a car owner. In cases where close social relations, such as love relationships or best friends, are car owners, the range of regional activities also tends to be wider, but car owners spend less time in the city center, due to constraints in terms of parking lots and the cost of parking spaces. For those with a car, weekends are often used to visit other cities or towns, to see friends and family, or to go shopping in shopping malls on the city's outskirts.

Changes in social relations and stages of life can affect also leisure. Social relations, generally, have a great influence on the way leisure is organized, on which channels are used to have a leisure experience, and how it is executed in practice. There is a tendency, for example, to share the few hours of week leisure time (if they are shared) with close friends or loved ones: people with whom individuals are willing to make the effort to coordinate time and to whom they "give" their leisure time. The women must feel it will be worth it, that it will be emotionally rewarding. On weekends, the range of people who meet one another extends beyond immediacy to include family and other friends and acquaintances. As respondent J. explained on May 22, 2015:

> During the week I always meet the same friend. During the weekends I go out with other friends also but she is also there. She is my best friend. Then we are there with a bigger group, five or six people, we'll go clubbing but that changes—sometimes these guys sometimes those guys.

However, the weekend is "sacred," and it will almost never be occupied with leisure-like activities with colleagues, for example. Activities with colleagues are almost always done during the week. Additionally, social relations also influence an individual's choice for certain leisure activities. Just as mentioned with regard to car ownership and sports and physical activities, friends and acquaintances introduce women to leisure activities. For women involved in romantic relationships, these relationships also exercise a great influence over weekend leisure activities. For example, respondent F., a woman who enjoys driving and exploring the region with her boyfriend, explained on June 16, 2015:

> ...so yeah I do a lot for leisure on the weekend, not very sporty but other stuff. For example, last week we were at the Erdbeerfest. We looked around online what there was to do in the region, where we could go and walk around, with something to see, so we did that. Sometimes we go on test drives with cars that we are interested in, and we just drive around.

In general, though, the women in short- or long-term relationships emphasized that a high degree of independence was important to them. In other words, they often expressed the desire to pursue their own interests, separately from their partners. Even though the dynamic might change from relationship to relationship, in general, relationships involve a higher degree of planning because they do not involve just planning activities for oneself, they also involve group and couple activities. Respondent S. explained on May 10, 2015:

> ...mmm, so, because I don't do much with my friends during the week, mostly he is at my place or I am at his. We stay the night and spend the evening together, watch TV or cook or so. The weekends are different: I'll go out with my friends, he'll go out with his, or we'll do something together with friends that also happens, or we just do something alone the two of us.

However, during informal conversations, an issue often raised was that new relationships would affect the planning and execution of leisure. For example, women would complain about a friend with a new boyfriend, that she would not plan to spend enough time with their friends. Studies of heterosexual couples have shown that romantic relationships can act as constraints for noncouple leisure, because women prioritize leisure with their male partners (Herridge et al. 2003). However, in my research, this kind of complaint also referred to women engaged in relationships with women. Furthermore, these studies were focused on a short-term evaluation, since this "uneven" phase is perceived to be provisional and it is common knowledge that a "normal" time organization will return when either the relationship ends or the initial "honeymoon" phase has passed. One woman mentioned that one of the advantages of being in a long-distance relationship was that she specifically had time for herself and did not have to "sacrifice" her leisure time all of the time. Therefore, despite the women being satisfied with their relationships and experiencing couples' time as leisure, there is also awareness of the difference between the leisure of couples and of noncouples and an understanding of the importance of both.

Romantic relationships are also something that affects weekend activities. A compromise might have to be found between the interests of the individuals, as well as coordinating their social networks. Additionally, for the three women who had long-distance relationships, their weekends require the organization of time to travel to visit their partner or be visited. Phone calls or Skype conversations might also have to be planned. Long-distance relationships require another kind of planning and execution of leisure time, one that often carries an important extra financial and time commitment, when compared with relationships developing in the same city or in close proximity.

What the example of women entering relationships or being in long distance relationships show is that changes in life can bring changes in the organization and execution of leisure similar to the changes in perception of leisure highlighted in the section on its meaning. However, and as we have already considered, people's leisure changes not only due to changes in their lives but also due to changes in the lives of their social relations. Phases in the lives of other people close to the individual can also have an effect on their leisure. For example, the granddaughter of one woman, one of my informants, who lived in a senior residence liked to spend her leisure time with her grandmother; she would pick up some fruit from the market or some cake to share with her grandmother. This was an activity that she would repeat once during weekdays after work and every Saturday. For her, it was a nice, enjoyable, and emotionally important way to spend her leisure time. The grandmother has since passed away, which left her feeling sad and, in the long term, has made her find new ways to fill her free time. Another example is a woman who became an aunt and decided to spend her leisure time with nieces and nephews. Although many authors have highlighted the influence of children, romantic relationships, and marriage on the leisure of women (s. Huda and Akhtar 2006, p. 12; Isengard 2005), little attention has been dedicated to the effect such factors have had indirectly, when it is not the individual who is involved in such relations. All in all, it is not only the demographic characteristics of an individual that affects the way in which he or she spends leisure time but the characteristics of his or her social network too. As Respondent A. explained on February 2015:

> "...sometimes I wish I had the leisure activities I had before in Lübeck, which I don't have anymore because my friends here are married, so, for example, previously I would meet and cook together, go have dinner, etc. So yeah I don't know I wish I still had that."

But while the women may be predisposed to spend Friday and Saturday evenings with friends and acquaintances, Sundays are a unique day of the weekend because, as mentioned earlier, Sundays are mostly dedicated to recuperation and relaxation, both with and without company. Sundays are often used for family brunches or lunches or simply for staying at home. Some women stay at home after attending the gym or going for a run. While only one of my informants attends church every Sunday, others do so irregularly. However, for those who are part of sports teams, Sundays are generally match days during the season, which means that the match, preparation for it, and postmatch activities occupy almost the entire day.

Except for a few Sundays each year when shopping malls or stores are open, everything in Mannheim is closed on Sunday, which makes it a day of considerably less consumption than the others, yet experiences and bodily consumption still exist.[7] Yet this does not mean that leisure experiences and consumption does not exist during this time. In contrast with Friday evenings and nights and Saturdays, it is not particularly important for Sundays to be different and more varied. Sundays are filled with routines, such as going for a run or preparing for a match. They are also filled with what could be considered rituals, like attending church or family meals. The children—in this case the women—are "summoned" to their parents' or grandparents' home, where they eat and drink together and tell each other news about their lives or the events of the week. These events produce and reproduce feelings of belonging, which could be considered a rite of incorporation (s. van Gennep 1977, p. 29) or a form of secular ritual, which, just like birthday parties, help to express solidarity and function as a cohesive force (s. Colson 1977). However, this form of family ritual does not only exist in person, as migrant women, both internal and external, also use many Sundays to talk to their families via Skype, conversations that last much longer than they might last during other days of the week (if they even take place at all on weekdays). Skype and WhatsApp are important tools for communication and reproduction of belonging beyond spatial boundaries. While WhatsApp is very much the most present tool in everyday life, Skype is used more infrequently but also holds a great meaning because it creates the possibility to see and hear the person in real time, which, according to these women, makes it feel more personal. It could be said that while WhatsApp is an everyday app, and Skype is a weekend app—people make sure that they have enough time to use it and take the time to talk to the person they wish to talk to. Skype calls are often family rituals, just like the in-person Sunday brunches.

Nonetheless, it is relevant to mention that, despite Sundays being more stable in the sense that they are less prone to change from week to week, they are also affected by seasons and weather. For example, Sundays in the summer might be used for taking a walk and eating ice cream, while December Sundays might be used to visit the Christmas market. Sundays are typically the "relaxed" day, meaning most of the women are not willing to make what they perceive to be effort—for example, going out in bad weather. Boecker et al. (2013, p. 86) pointed out that weather perception is subjective and that it affects travel and activity behavior. Although individuals might perceive weather to be the same (as bad as in another day), they might react differently according to the time frame in which it is taking place, in this case Sundays. It seems that, on Sundays, weather conditions are more of a barrier than they are on other days and times of the week. Even so, leisure activities that have been planned with social relations, such as family lunches, seem to be less affected by weather conditions than leisure in couples or alone. For example, some of the women reported discussions with and the pressure from their mothers in particular to attend family reunions. Obligatory activities are generally less affected by weather than leisure activities (p. 78) so, even though family meetings might be experienced as leisure, their social obligation character might come to the foreground. Yet it is important to highlight that Sundays are not exclusive to family. Sometimes activities are also shared with close friends or, if present, a loved one.

One final aspect that is relevant, both for weekdays and weekends, is the aspect of self-development in or through leisure. Dumazedier (1967, pp. 16–17) saw one of the key elements of leisure the broadening of an individual's knowledge and exercising creative capacity. As mentioned earlier, some women partake in various kinds of dance lessons and others view sports and physical activities as a chance to learn social skills. Broadening knowledge and developing further social skills is done not only in formal contexts; as one woman mentioned, they also can take place in bars. However, these are not the primary motives causing these women to pursue such activities. Issues related to the experience of effort and enjoyment, fitness and aesthetics of the body as well as psychological health are the main motivation behind such activities. Other activities, in contrast, do have learning and self-development in the foreground.

Some view leisure time as a time to learn about areas of life, such as art and culture. For example, a woman expressed an interest in learning about "high culture" and focused a lot of her planning on accomplishing this goal, attending concerts of classical music and the theater. For her, it is about filling what she considers a "knowledge gap":

> In the last three years I have really developed a direction in terms of my interests. Previously I was just going out partying a lot, it was normal for me because I didn't have a stable home, my parents are divorced, my only constant is my mother, she is always there even when she is not, and, because both of my parents had their own businesses, I was alone at home, they were working, I was 20 and I was partying from Friday to Sunday yeah but now I'm learning about the nice things in life, the really nice things, art, culture, traveling. Okay, culture was always there because I come from two cultures I had a bit of knowledge about it, but so really that I would say I have a wide range of interests, that is something new. Sometimes I regret I was so stubborn, I said no I don't want to know that, nowadays I'm open to experimentation. (Respondent M., March 19, 2015)

In this case, the woman has designed her own method of learning and puts it into action. Leisure for her, during the week and during the weekends, can be used to self-develop or develop skills. However, what is remarkable is that leisure in the form of learning or developing skills is more of a wish than a practice for most of these women. More than half of the women expressed the desire to learn new languages (even migrant women who already speak more than one language fluently), Spanish being at the top of most lists, while a few expressed the desire to learn to play a musical instrument. Of all the women, only one was actively enrolled on a language course, while another was studying another career parallel to her full-time job. For the rest, similar desires or wishes had not taken the form of a concrete plan. For most of the women, it was an issue of time and scheduling. For example, one woman wishes to attend flute classes but cannot because they take place in the early evening while she is still at work. This is a problem of chronologic time: when she has time, there are no lessons (s. Reisch 2001, pp. 377–378). Yet, in most cases, it is an issue of time in the sense that the wish to learn collides with the wish to recuperate: many experience a lack of energy to "keep on thinking" after a day at work. In other cases, it contrasts with the wish to practice sports and physical activities, which, as we have seen, are some of the priorities of leisure time for many. So, self-development and learning might be an ideal way to spend one's free time and part of the project of the self, but, in practice, they do not represent an organizational priority for most.

However, it is important to differentiate between forms of self-development and learning. While those who enjoy playing an instrument in a class might consider this activity to be leisure, other forms of learning might not be for others. For those women who do formally engage in learning in their free time, these activities do not constitute leisure. The women place the activities within a discourse of climbing the occupational ladder and having better opportunities in terms of work, status, and income. In this case, self-development is described as "sacrificing" leisure for the better good of the future. Respondent M., quoted earlier, explicitly argued, for example, that she aimed to avoid stereotypes linked to her job through her activities of self-development:

> I have difficulties to say what I do for work because I am immediately put in a box: I'm a secretary. Here [in the group of friends], you can be yourself and that is worth so much. I hate it: what do you do for a living? I'm a secretary. Ah! Can you make coffee? Yeah, imagine that, it is crass, or sometimes the question is ah! Do you sleep with your boss? Absolutely, absolutely crazy. But they do not know that I have to deal with contracts worth millions, or that I have the responsibility for some projects. They only hear the title, they have no idea and judge you, so here I can be who I am. (March 19, 2015)

As Harman (1988, pp. 150–151) pointed out, identity is an interplay between how an individual has chosen to present the self and how this is received by the social environment. Choosing to self-develop during free time is a possibility to actively change the reception of the self by one's social environment, which can also include ways in which to dress or act. Furthermore, discrepancies of status in the social environment might lead the individual to rethink identity. For example, the social network of this particular woman was composed by many individuals with higher educational degrees or degrees with higher social status than hers, such as engineers and computer scientists, which might account for her subjective experience of social judgment in comparison with the other women, most of whom had social relations with similar backgrounds. How we intend to be perceived is not always how other people perceive us, and this, in turn, has an effect on how we perceive ourselves. Perceiving oneself to lack something drives one to certain decisions regarding lifestyle and leisure time.

Additionally, while, for some, learning a language might constitute an enjoyable task and so becomes leisure, for others, it might be a functional matter, not only for career purposes but to facilitate communication during vacations. In other words, although learning activities might be leisure in some cases, for most of my informants, learning activities are related to improving lifestyle in general or to facilitating leisure by providing better salaries or better environmental conditions for leisure. The particular case of vacations, which was addressed briefly earlier, is covered in more detail the next section. Even so, it is important to acknowledge that even if an activity like learning a language is done with a future goal in mind, *during* the activity the individual can experience leisure as, for example, *flow*, or *Muße*.

In general, the findings described here regarding the week and the weekend are in harmony with Whillans's (2014) study, in which she found that "independent singles" (unmarried, childless, 20- and 30-somethings) liked to spend time alone but prefer being with others. During the week, her respondents mostly engaged in leisure activities alone (e.g., gym) and what she called "low-key shared leisure practice," such as meeting with others for coffee and meals. Friday and Saturday nights were for socializing, drinking, and staying up late, while Saturday and Sunday mornings were for being alone relaxing and reading (Whillans 2014, pp. 193–198). Whillans (2014, p. 196) pointed out, in summary, that the weekend has a special status: "[...] the weekend is the primary site for sociability but it is met with the uncertainty about others' availability and the challenge of temporal coordination." Regardless of the fact that not all of my respondents are single, in the sense that they are engaged in relationships despite not being married or living together, and, despite the fact that Whillans was not focused only on women, there seems to be a great deal of common factors in leisure time organization that are similar for this demographic group. Although there are some differences, which will be discussed later, it is evident that aspects such as gender, age, educational level, income, and family structure (children) do, to a great extent, affect the perception of and the channels chosen for leisure and the motivation behind leisure activities. What I have additionally shown is that two other essential aspects influence organization of time and planning and execution of leisure:

1. The sociodemographic constitution of the social relations surrounding the individual also affects the individuals' leisure (e.g., when friends have children or own cars).
2. Execution of leisure, including family rituals, can go beyond physical presence, thanks to the enabling of meetings via technology, and individual biographies, such as having an urban or rural background, can affect not only leisure ideals, but also leisure in practice.

Whillans (2014, pp. 193–198) saw that, despite the energy that avoiding being alone requires, the respondents filled weekends with leisure activities because busyness is a "badge of honor." Yet my informants did not place the importance on busyness or filling the time properly (s. Dumazedier 1967, p. 8), nor were particular types of leisure seen to bring more or less happiness (s. Stebbins 2014, pp. 30–37). Leisure is organized, planned, and executed to fulfill the ideal of balance among recovery, enjoyment, and effort and for variety. There can be patterns in leisure. For example, in the fixed times dedicated to physical activity or fixed social meetings (but, in this case, the badge of honor would not be busyness itself), there is a balance between all types of activities, including having times when one is not busy. It could be argued that, in this sense, these individuals are "omnivorous": they are open and appreciative of all types of leisure and cultural activities (s. Peterson and Kern 1996), but they need variation in order not to overdose on the same type of experience. Too much of one type of leisure can mean, as a consequence, that it is not considered leisure anymore. For example, the badge of honor would mean in the context of this research being busy but not tired, finding the balance between excitement and calmness, having a little bit of everything. This having a little bit of everything does not mean everything at the same time, however; at has been shown, there is a time and a place for all the activities chosen by these women.

A final segment of life that I would like to briefly assess in this chapter is the aspect of the vacation. The vacation is identified as one of the leisure segments by Opaschowski (1996, pp. 85–96), even if all scholars do not strictly consider it leisure because it is not part of everyday life. However, because these women have, on average, between 25 and 30 working days per year of vacation time and because the time has an important emotional component for the informants, it seems pertinent to include vacation time in the aspect of organization and execution of leisure time.

4.5   THE VACATION

> I know a place
> Where the grass is really greener,
> Warm, wet and wild
> There must be something in the water
> Sipping gin and juice
> Laying underneath the palm trees, undone
> The boys, break their necks,
> Trying to creep a little peek at us.[8]

Few recent songs can evoke the feeling of summer and vacation as well as this 2010 hit song. As was alluded to already, for the women in my study, the vacation is related to certain ideals, views on leisure, and places some of which are captured quite well in this song text. Even though I did not follow up the vacation with participant observation, it is something that was often mentioned in both conversations and interviews. Vacations are also a highly valued segment of leisure time and are often organized and planned farther in advance, often because of financial reasons, than the everyday leisure of weeks and weekends. The amount of vacation time is specific to geopolitical areas, as pointed out by Alesina et al. (2005, p. 9), with Germany having one of the highest amounts of paid vacation weeks per year in the world.[9]

The difference between free time and leisure time also applies to vacations. Vacations, when seen as time away from paid work, are not necessarily equated with leisure. The women also use vacation time for necessary activities, such as catching up with checkups with the dentist, gynecologist, and other general medical checkups, the latter an activity mentioned often as something done during vacations, and which were considered to be a necessity. Many women also used vacation time for chore activities that extend beyond the scope of chores done during everyday free time. Generally, during vacation time, cleaning is done more thoroughly or more time is spent on household decoration and refurbishment. Vacations are also used for catching up with errands or other activities that cannot be done during the weekend because of office/closing hours. One woman mentioned that she was in the process of moving and so had spent many weekends of many weeks looking at apartments, both online and in person. When she finally found an apartment, she took two weeks of vacation time in which to pack, move, and then unpack and purchase anything she might additionally need. Vacations, just like weekends, therefore, involve activities that are deemed necessary by individuals but to which they cannot attend during their regular free time. Vacation time can give individuals more time and time at the right time, in the sense of Reisch's (2001, pp. 377–378) chronometric and chronologic time. Vacation time may remain "only" free time: "One can have a lot of free time and do many things during this time, for example, during vacations. But the space of leisure may still remain empty" (Pieper 1989, p. 28).

In contrast with leisure time during the week and weekend, sports and physical activities are not a high priority for the organization, planning, and execution of vacations. Many of the women do still practice sports and physical activities when they remain at home during vacation time, but they are not a main issue to be taken into consideration. Yet clubbing and going out at night and meeting friends gain relevance during vacation time. In general, just as with weekends, social relations play an important role during vacations. Vacation time is almost always spent with company, whether it is a time spent at home (in the same city) or traveling. When women describe their vacations in the context of "staying at home," they highlight the increased amount of time available to meet family and friends and to engage in social activities. It is easier to coordinate meetings with others because of the increased time availability of the women themselves. Additionally, the discourse on vacation time is often more intensively marked by the notion of freedom. For example, the women often mentioned that, during vacation, they could go to bed and wake up when they wanted to. Individuals feel they have more control over time to do as they wish than they typically have during the week and the weekend. Vacation time is a time where the subjective experience of personal time autonomy (s. Reisch 2001, pp. 377–378) is at its highest.

Time availability affects the practice of organization during vacation time. Potential leisure time is perceived to be greater during vacation. The week and the weekend are perceived to be less rich in time, and, as a consequence, the specific sequences of events are planned more carefully. Events consist of planned activities and a planned absence of activities. Bauman (2009, p. 111) argued that a fast pace of life, where individuals are choosing product after product or activity after activity, is one of the problematic characteristics of a consumerist society and that a successful social life depends on keeping such a fast-paced way of life. Harmut Rosa (2010) also dealt with alienation of the self through acceleration of social life in contemporary times, Western societies (and individuals therein) being controlled by time regimes. Vacation time, however, even more than weekends, gives individuals the possibility to "*runterkommen*," or slow down, making vacations a form of deceleration period. More time is taken for every activity, from necessary time for sleeping and eating to committed time to tasks related to the household (s. As 1978) and also for leisure, such as social gatherings or simply "doing nothing." Indeed, during vacation time, most of these women change their pace of life consciously and experience a "slow-paced leisure" (s. McGrath 2014, pp. 26–27), even if they are not aware of this theoretical concept. On one hand, the vacation, as institutionalized practice, can be considered part of the capitalist time regime itself, even if it is constructed as some form of short-lived "oasis of deceleration" (Rosa 2010). On the other, it can be considered as a form of liminal state that restores some amount of agency to the individuals.

What has been described thus far is vacation time that, in practice, has moments of leisure identical to those of the week and the weekend. Beyond the pace and length in which activities are pursued during vacation time, its organization and execution are not radically different. Technology is used to organize activities and to communicate with others: it is used as entertainment, and it is constantly present. Yet this is how leisure practices are in vacations that take place in the same space as every day life, or vacations "at home". This is, however, not the ideal of a vacation. All of the women associate an ideal vacation with traveling, as described Chap. 3. Traveling is an activity and experience in which a high amount of planning is invested, in terms of both time and financial resources. One common way of traveling during vacation is visiting friends and relatives in destinations that are farther away or too far away to stay just for a weekend, such as going from Mannheim to visit a friend in Hamburg, a journey of more than 500 kilometers (about 311 miles). Many of these women have friends or family in different European cities, so traveling to visit them for a couple of days at a time is a common vacation activity. Dumazedier (1967, pp. 133–134) argued that the most common place to go on vacation is the home of relatives or friends, not only because of financial reasons but also because it is a good way to tighten family ties. In general, though, such trips tend to be short and, on average, last between two days and one week. These types of trips are seen to be advantageous in several ways: seeing the friend or family and spending time with them while not spending money on accommodation and having someone who knows the city to guide them through its sights.

While vacation time spent at home can be spontaneous, as it is generally possible to take a few vacation days without having to give advance notice at work, vacations that involve traveling for longer periods require organization and planning. In the case of visiting people, this organization requires coordinating the synchronization of time with the person(s) to be visited and coordinating the necessary vacation time away from work. Some of these women have vacation time restrictions. For example, vacations during the month of December might not be permitted. In other cases, the women are bound to vacation policies in favor of employees with school-age children, making it impossible for childless employees to take vacation during times of the year when schools are closed. Therefore, time autonomy is not entirely given for vacations either.

However, there is agency and room for action within the given time frame. The tendency is to take vacation time in periods of two weeks at different times of the year. Some of those vacations will be spent at home while some will be used for traveling. The reasons attributed to this type of division varied: financially, it is not possible to use all vacation days to travel, and, physically, recuperation is needed and catching up with chores and errands is necessary. However, it is important to highlight that vacations spent in the everyday space are perceived to have higher barriers to leisure than vacations taken abroad. Some of the barriers have already been mentioned, such as chores and errands, and individuals often talked about perceiving pressure to do these kinds of activities while at home. An additional barrier mentioned was the presence of technology, the same technology that enables everyday leisure and might be a hindrance to leisure during vacation. Women complained about not being left alone by messages, calls, and e-mails: the everyday problem of always being reachable versus being unreachable as an advantage of traveling.

In general, vacations are treated as special occasions. The technology that is a hindrance during vacations can be a helpful tool organizing for them. The women report using various search engines and sites to gather information about destinations and to look for and book flights and hotels. Planning for vacations is an activity that is part of their free time during the week or weekend. For some, the planning and organization per se constitutes leisure, while for others is simply a prerequisite that enables leisure. One woman said, for example, that she enjoyed researching things to do when at the destination and in this way looked forward to the trip, while another said she did not like this aspect of the experience and, whenever possible, left this tedious task to her boyfriend. The case of vacations and their planning is in fact similar to the case of other subjectively perceived special occasions, such as birthday parties and house-warming parties, that are also planned farther in advance and organized more thoroughly than everyday leisure. However, regarding vacations, trip destinations, and company, there can be differences based on whether the women live in the same city or close to their family, in particular their parents, grandparents, and siblings. For those women who are able to see and spend time with their family on a regular basis, vacations are less focused on family than for those who normally "only" communicate through technology with their families due to geographical distances. This is an important issue that will be dealt when addressing differences between migrants and nonmigrants in the context of leisure.

So, the ideal vacation still involves traveling. But traveling must not only involve visiting people whom they know. In fact, many women empha-sized the wish to visit new places and learn about new cultures. Traveling to destinations where accommodation and meals are not available through social contacts requires even more planning in advance. Saving money for traveling is the initial means of starting to plan a vacation. Traveling is arguably one of the most beloved ways to spend money or forms of con-sumption. It is a form of consumption that is perceived as being "worth it." Traveling to places outside Europe is part of the long-term plan of each of these women. The most frequently mentioned destination was the United States, followed by Australia and New Zealand. As respondent S. explained on May 10, 2015: I would love to go to the U.S. New York and L.A. I would love to see but otherwise, of course, Australia, New Zealand—but if and when I have no idea when it will be possible. The idea or wish for such long-distance travel might be considered years before it occurs because of the time required to organize and plan such trips, not only in terms of the individual's financial and time resources:

I always try to go somewhere new. I was in Bali this year for example. It was my first big trip in many years, I'm not someone who will always go to the same place, I want to see the world. My next goal is Brazil. (Respondent J., May 22, 2015)

I'm very excited about the U.S. In two weeks we are flying there for three weeks, it will be a great tour. We'll be in New York first, then Chicago and from there to Calgary in Canada, then we'll fly to San Francisco, L.A., and

Las Vegas. So we'll be two days New York, three days in Calgary, and then we're off! We'll drive: Las Vegas, L.A. we're doing with the car. I'm very, very excited. It is my first time. We have planned a lot; it won't be a relaxed vacation because we'll drive around a lot. (Respondent F., June 16, 2015)

Travel partners must also go through the same process. The informants go on this type of vacation with a variety of people, mostly in pairs, with either their partner, a sibling, or a best friend. One of the reasons for this small vacation groups is that synchronizing vacation time can be even more challenging than synchronizing time during weekends for more participants. Coming to an agreement about what to do is also a challenge for couples and noncouples traveling together. This is one of the reasons why such types of vacations are perceived to require a great deal of social intimacy and emotional bonding. The vacation partners are either less prone to conflict or they are more resistant to it. Finding a compromise might be a dynamic that is part of the relationship, with romantic relationships, siblings, or best friends.

I'm the type who likes to take two days to do nothing but my boyfriend isn't—he always needs something to do, somewhere to go, to see, so he cannot just lay around on the beach and do nothing. But we always organize it so that it is balanced: when we have too much to do, we take one or two days to do nothing. It is part of the plan for all our trips, so when we were in Turkey one week, I said okay we'll go see the most important stuff but we don't need to see everything and so we did. (Respondent F., June 16, 2015)

Going on vacation with someone who is not close enough can be risky, in the sense that there is no previous knowledge of the kinds of social conflicts that might arise. Avoiding or surmounting stress is one of the main goals of a vacation. Social conflicts are important sources of stress in everyday life (s. Strümpell and Ashraf 2011, p. 26), and they are not considered part of leisure but rather as a hindrance to it. Vacations, as leisure, are subjectively one of the most important coping resources to counterbalance stress and so contribute to the well-being of the individual by balancing positive and negative feelings, as Qian et al. (2014) highlighted. Therefore, because vacations are so highly valued, only seldom do these informants travel with people they do not know well. However, it also depends on the length and destination of the trip.

The types of trips the women took during vacation vary greatly. Vacations outside of home are organized in many different ways, but they do have similarities. For example, while women like to save for "larger" trips that take them to distant destinations and consequently do not take place every year, they also like to take vacations in the form short city trips. These kinds of trips fulfill the women's desire to travel and "see something different" while at the same time having lower costs than longer trips to far-off destinations. Favored destinations for such short trips were typically large European cities, such as London, Barcelona, and Istanbul. For these kinds of trip, the low price of flight tickets was a common factor for choosing the destination. In the cities themselves, the leisure does not differ much from leisure "at home" during the weekends. The women describe these vacations as a mixture of shopping, walking around and sightseeing, eating and drinking, and nightlife activities.

Several women, some of whom liked to go on snowboarding vacations in the winter or canoeing and rafting in the summer, described other types of exciting vacations in terms of adrenaline rush. Other women often used the phrase the "need for sun" to explain trips to destinations directly on the sea. Some destinations often listed were places in southern Spain, Italy, and Turkey, even though ideal sunny destinations might be farther away, including the sunny and laid-back California described in Katy Perry's song at the beginning of this section. Interestingly, while city trips were framed in a discourse of "discovering" and experiencing something new and exciting, beachside trips were framed in a discourse of relaxation, recuperation, and "*Sonne tanken*" (soaking up the sun). They are almost exclusively taken when the weather in Mannheim is not good, for example, during winter. This finding is in harmony with studies that show a much higher tendency to stay at the locality of residence during good weather, while bad weather increases the chances of traveling abroad (s. Palutikof et al. 2004, p. 56).

In the context of different leisure experiences for different destinations, a visit to a particular city is seldom repeated, although the same destination can be visited year after year for sunbathing, if the location was agreeable and the price fair. In a sense, these two types of vacation can also be distinguished according to the difference between the "traveler," who is spontaneous and in search of an authentic experience, and the "tourist," who simply consumes a travel package (Spracklen 2013, p. 175). In the case of the short city trip, women seek to spontaneously discover what the place has to offer, while beach trips are generally all-inclusive trips often framed in a discourse of "not thinking, not worrying just relaxing." However, there is a great class-related stigma regarding being an "all-inclusive tourist." When asked in normal conversations about their holidays, middle-class, highly educated people in Mannheim generally respond with: "*Ich bin nicht der typische tourist*" (I'm not the typical tourist) and emphasize wanting to go to "nontourist" places in a "nontourist" way. But these kinds of statements and views are not so much related to some sort of self-reflection about artificially constructed tourist experiences and the person's own position in the world's social structure and power relations or a critical view on the "tourist gaze"[10] but rather are related to very local socioeconomic asymmetries and the need for status and distinction.

Like everyday leisure during the week and weekend, alternation and variation is fundamental for individuals during vacations. Warm weather, sun, and the beach are commonly used as vehicles for recovery; urban spaces are used as vehicles for enjoyment, excitement, and discovery. How vacations are planned and executed also shows a distinction between experienced leisure and ideal leisure. Ideal leisure often entails faraway destinations and multiple days/weeks of uninterrupted vacation and include both excitement and relaxation because the time allows for both. The women show agency in coping with financial and time barriers in that they choose a destination that partly fulfills this need and plan vacation trips that are within the limits imposed by time and financial constraints. The actual execution, every couple of years, of the "dream" vacation is also the result of the women's good organization and long-term planning.

Many women highlighted the fact that only during vacations were they able to fully enter a state of leisure that was not available to them during everyday leisure. Even during vacations, they needed a couple of days to fully free their minds from work and other worries before being able to enter into the relaxed vacation mind frame. Pieper (1989, p. 23) argued that *Muße* is a state of the soul that is not guaranteed by the vacation or the weekend. However, vacations, and particularly vacations outside of the everyday space of the individual, do facilitate leisure experiences. For example, vacations can make the individual unreachable via technology and consequently foster full concentration on and immersion in the experience. Through the lowering of stress, vacations can foster leisure that is otherwise not possible. An example of this is a woman who loves to read but finds it difficult to concentrate in her everyday life. She said that, during vacations, she was relaxed and could fully submerge herself in her books. Vacations (as travel) are the main ideal form of leisure. In other words, it is mostly during vacations that the ideal of leisure and the practice join in one experience.

This chapter has shown how everyday life can be divided into different parts of life: the week, the weekend, and the vacation, each displaying distinct characteristics and patterns. How these parts are organized and turned into practices is affected not only by the general conception of leisure held by the individual but also by time availability of self and others, working conditions, and social relations. It was seen how both routines and rituals and special occasions are important components of leisure patterns, in some cases providing comfort or excitement, in other cases providing belonging and emotional fulfillment. All in all, the perception of time and pace of life is marked by these segments that are defined by institutionalized work but also by the individual and how she makes decisions and behaves within the given framework. In the next chapter, another important factor for leisure and lifestyle in general is addressed: the issue of the locality, in this case the city of Mannheim, including relevant aspects such as special events and season or weather conditions.

NOTES

1. Women felt often intimidated or uncomfortable with "very muscled" men (weight-lifters) and complained about the loud noises and growling that such men do when training.
2. A good overview of fitness studios in Mannheim and surroundings can be found through search engines. For Mannheim alone, there were 19 different studios at the end of 2015, three of which were women-only studios.
3. As this thesis was being written, the latest trending smartphone game was *Pokemon Go*.
4. In this metaphor, the zombie moves slowly and has no brains, and the Energizer Bunny "just keeps going and going." She is referring to how she is during the day (zombie) and during the night (Duracell Bunny).
5. "Muße" even though translated sometimes as leisure, is not identical to it, neither to the concept of flow. "Muße" refers to a non-activity, peaceful, effortless and free. However, Muße is not a break. Its function is not to recover, but for the individual to find and realize him or herself (Pieper 1989:23). "Muße" can take place both during work and leisure. This is why not all Muße must necessarily be considered leisure and inversely not all leisure is Muße. Additionally, Muße is not flow. A good way to differentiate between the experiences is by taking a look at the issue of time perception and pacing, because Muße is related to a higher awareness of the self, consciousness and slowing down, while flow is more related to a kind of suspension of the self and to the flying of time.

6. Wingman or wingwoman are friends who support their companions in the quest to find potential love interests and dates. They were, for example, often seen to make the first step of greeting a stranger as intermediary or to distract the stranger's companions to enable conversation.

7. In Germany, everything is closed on sundays except for gas stations and some restaurants or small bars. It is not possible to shop for example in supermarkets, clothing stores, pharmacies, drug stores, etc.

8. "California Gurls," Katy Perry and Snoop Dogg.

9. Taking the full number of vacation days is a common practice, since the tax scheme makes the alternative (payoff for vacation days not taken) almost meaningless.

10. As analyzed in the classic work by John Urry The Tourist Gaze: Leisure and Travel in Contemporary Societies (1990).

REFERENCES

Adorno, Theodor W. 1991. Free Time. In *The Culture Industry: Selected Essays on Mass Culture*, ed. Theodor W. Adorno and J.M. Bernstein, 162–170. London: Routledge.

Alesina, Alberto, Edward Glaeser, and Bruce Sacerdote. 2005. *Work and Leisure in the U.S. and Europe: Why So Different?* NBER Macroeconomics Annual 2005, vol. 20.

Allen-Collinson, Jacquelyn. 2011. Feminist Phenomenology and the Woman in the Running Body. *Sport, Ethics and Philosophy* 5 (3): 297–313.

Andrews, Hazel, and Les Roberts. 2012. Introduction: Re-mapping Liminality. In *Liminal Landscapes: Travel, Experience and Spaces In-between*, ed. Hazel Andrews and Les Roberts, vol. 30, 1st ed., 1–17. New York: Routledge.

Appadurai, Arjun. 1996. *Modernity al Large: Cultural Dimensions of Globalization*, 1. Minneapolis; London: University of Minnesota Press.

As, Dagfinn. 1978. Studies of Time-use: Problems and Prospects. *Acta Sociologica* 21 (2): 125–141.

Barnett, Lynn. 2005. Measuring the ABCs of Leisure Experience: Awareness, Boredom, Challenge, Distress. *Leisure Sciences* 27: 131–155.

Bauman, Zygmunt. 2009. *Leben als Konsum.* 1 Aufl. Hamburg: Hamburger Ed.

———. 2013. *Does the Richness of a Few Benefit Us All?* Cambridge: Polity Press.

Boecker, Lars, Martin Dijst, and Jan Prillwitz. 2013. Impact of Everyday Weather on Individual Daily Travel Behaviours in Perspective: A Literature Review. *Transport Reviews* 33 (1): 71–91.

Brosius, Christiane. 2010. *India's Middle Class: New Forms of Urban Leisure, Consumption and Prosperity.* London; New York: Routledge.

Carmichael, Fiona, Joanne Duberley, and Isabelle Szmiging. 2015. Older Women and Their Participation in Exercise and Leisure-Time Physical Activity: The Double Edged Sword of Work. *Sport in Society* 18 (1): 42–60.

Colson, Elizabeth. 1977. The Least Common Denominator. In *Secular Ritual*, ed. Sally F. Moore and Barbara G. Myerhoff, 189–198. Assen: Van Gorcum.

Cortis, Natasha, Pooja Sawrikar, and Kristy Muir. 2008. Final Report: Participation in Sport and Recreation by Culturally and Linguistically Diverse Women.

Dumazedier, Joffre. 1967. *Toward a Society of Leisure*. New York; London: Collier-Macmillan.

Fastenmeier, Wolfgang, Herbert Gstalter, and Ulf Lehnig. 2003. Was empfinden Menschen als Freizeit? – Emotionale Bedeutung und Definition. In *Motive und Handlungsansätze im Freizeitverkehr: Mit 17 Tabellen*, 13–29. Berlin: Springer.

Figal, Günther. 2014. Muße als Forschungsgegenstand. La Villa.

de Freitas, C.R. 2015. Weather and Place-based Human Behavior: Recreational Preferences and Sensitivity. *International Journal of Biometeorology* 59: 55–63.

Gajjala, Radhika, and Dinah Tetteh. 2014. Relax, You've Got M-PESA: Leisure as Empowerment. *Information Technologies & International Development* 10 (3): 31–46.

Gilroy, Paul. 2004. *After Empire: Multiculture or Postcolonial Melancholia*. Abingdon: Routledge.

Hancock, P.A., and G.M. Hancock. 2014. The Effects of Age, Sex, Body Temperature, Heart Rate, and Time of Day on the Perception of Time in Life. *Time & Society* 23 (2): 195–211.

Harman, Lesley D. 1988, c1987. *The Modern Stranger: On Language and Membership*. Vol. 47. Berlin; New York: Mouton de Gruyter.

Herridge, Kristi, Susan Shaw, and Roger C. Mannell. 2003. An Exploration of Women's Leisure Within Heterosexual Romantic Relationships. *Journal of Leisure Research* 35 (3): 274–291.

Huda, Sadrul, and Afsana Akhtar. 2006. Leisure Behaviour of Working Women of Dhaka Bangladesh. *International Journal of Urban Labour & Leisure* 7 (1): 1–30.

Isengard, Betinna. 2005. Freizeitverhalten als Ausdruck Sozialer Ungleichheiten oder Ergebnis Individualisierter Lebensführung? Zur Bedeutung von Einkommen und Bildung im Zeitverlauf. *Kölner Zeitschrift für Soziologie und Sozialpsychologie* 57 (2): 254–277.

Iso-Ahola, Seppo E. 2015. Conscious Versus Nonconscious Mind and Leisure. *Leisure Sciences* 37 (4): 289–310.

Keim, Inken. 1995. Die Westliche Unterstadt. In *Kommunikation in der Stadt: Teil 2. Ethnographien von Mannheimer Stadtteilen*, ed. Werner Kallmeyer, vol. 4.2, 42–188. Berlin; New York: Walter de Gruyter.

Kovac, Laura, and Dawn Trussell. 2015. 'Classy and Never Trashy': Young Women's Experiences of Nightclubs and the Construction of Gender and Sexuality. *Leisure Sciences* 37: 195–209.

Liu, Hugo. 2008. Social Network Profiles as Taste Performances. *Journal of Computer Mediated Communication* 13: 252–275.

McGrath, Peter. 2014. Escape From Time: Experience the Travel Within. In *Contemporary Perspectives in Leisure: Meanings, Motives and Lifelong Learning*, ed. Sam Elkington and Sean Gammon, 18–27. Abingdon; New York: Routledge.

Opaschowski, Horst W. 1996. *Pädagogik der freien Lebenszeit*. 3, völlig neu bearb. Aufl Bd. 1. Opladen: Leske + Budrich.

Özkan, Derya. 2015. Let Them Gentrify Themselves!: Space, Migration and Culture in Munich's Bahnhofsviertel. In *Europäische Ethnologie in München: Ein kulturwissenschaftlicher Reader*, ed. Irene Götz et al., vol. 42, 193–218. Münster: Waxmann.

Palutikof, J.P., M.D. Agnew, and M.R. Hoar. 2004. Public Perceptions of Unusually Warm Weather in the UK: Impacts, Responses and Adaptations. *Climate Research* 26: 43–59.

Peterson, Richard, and Roger Kern. 1996. Changing Highbrow Taste: From Snob to Omnivore. *American Sociological Review* 61 (5): 900–907.

Pieper, Josef. 1989. Arbeit, Freizeit, Muße. In *Arbeit, Freizeit, Muße: Was ist eine Universität? 2 Beiträge/von Josef Pieper*, vol. 5, 11–30. Münster: Regensberg.

Qian, Xinyi L., Careen Yarnal, and David Almeida. 2014. Using the Dynamic Model of Affect (DMA) to Examine Leisure Time as a Stress Coping Resource: Taking into Account Stress Severity and Gender Difference. *Journal of Leisure Research* 46 (4): 483–505.

Reisch, Lucia A. 2001. Time and Wealth: The Role of Time and Temporalities for Sustainable Patterns of Consumption. *Time Society* 10: 367–385.

Rosa, Hartmut. 2010. *Alienation and Acceleration: Towards a Critical Theory of Late-modern Temporality*. NSU Summertalk 3. Malmö: NSU Press.

Scheuch, Erwin K. 1972. Die Problematik der Freizeit in der Massengesellschaft. In *Soziologie der Freizeit*, ed. Erwin K. Scheuch and Rolf Meyersohn, 23–41. Köln: Kiepenheuer & Witsch.

Schulze, Gerhard. 2005[1992]. *Die Erlebnisgesellschaft: Kultursoziologie der Gegenwart*. 2 Aufl. Frankfurt [Main]; New York: Campus.

Spinney, Jamie E., and Hugh Millward. 2011. Weather Impacts on Leisure Activities in Halifax, Nova Scotia. *International Journal of Biometeorology* 55: 133–145.

Spracklen, Karl. 2013. *Whiteness and leisure. Leisure Studies in a Global Era*. New York; London: Palgrave Macmillan.

Stebbins, Robert A. 2014. Leisure, Happiness and Positive Lifestyle. In *Contemporary Perspectives in Leisure: Meanings, Motives and Lifelong Learning*, ed. Sam Elkington and Sean Gammon, 28–38. Abingdon; New York: Routledge.

Stengel, Martin. 1998. Freizeit als Restkategorie: Das Dilemma einer eigenstaendigen Freizeitforschung. In *Freizeit in der Erlebnisgesellschaft: Amüsement zwischen Selbstverwirklichung und Kommerz*, ed. Hans A. Hartmann. 2 Aufl, 19–44. Opladen: Westdt. Verl.

Strümpell, Christian, and Hasan Ashraf. 2011. Stress and Modern Work: Ethnographic Perspectives from Industries in Bangladesh. *Viennese Ethnomedicine Newsletter* 13 (2–3): 24–33.

Tazanu, Primus M. 2012. *Being Available and Reachable: New Media and Cameroonian Transnational Sociality.* Mankon, Bamenda, Cameroon: Langaa Research & Publishing; Distributed in and outside N. America by African Books Collective.

van Gennep, Arnold. 1977. *The Rites of Passage.* London: Routledge and Kegan Paul.

Veal, Anthony J. 1987. *Leisure and the Future*, 4. London; Boston: Allen & Unwin.

Whillans, Jennifer. 2014. The Weekend: The Friend and Foe of Independent Singles. *Leisure Studies* 33 (2): 185–201.

CHAPTER 5

Migration Background and Leisure

5.1   EXCURSUS: PROFILE NR. 4

A. is a 25-year-old Venezuelan who, like many other migrant women, came to Germany to study. She recently finished her degree as a medical technician and started working. At the time of the interview she had been in Germany a little over three years. When she walked into the cafe at which we had agreed to meet, I saw a tall woman with brown skin and long curly hair. Immediately after we met, she smiled and began talking in a friendly manner, as if we already knew each other. There was an immediate comfort in our conversation because of our common country of origin, even though we are not from the same city. She talked frequently and kindly about her family, especially her parents and sister. Her father is a pediatrician and her mother a salesperson, and she highlights their influence on her professional career and leisure preferences. Her mom, for example, always pushed her to take swimming and English lessons as a child and not be "lying around" the house after school.

Talking about her migration process, she says that when she first arrived, it was difficult for her. For the first couple of months, for instance, she would spend her free time in her room, just "consuming content" on her computer, as she called it. This made her feel depressed and she started to gain weight so, after a while, she decided to change her leisure activities into more physically and socially active ones. Nowadays, she goes to the gym for one or two hours from Monday to Thursday and has dance lessons on Saturdays. She praises the transport system; its reach and

V.L. Sandoval, *The Meaning of Leisure*, Leisure Studies in a Global Era, DOI 10.1007/978-3-319-59752-2_5 punctuality allows people to get everywhere quickly. All in all, she is happy that "time lasts longer here."

Yet it was difficult for her to make friends as she perceives people to be less open and talkative than what she was used to. She mentions that she believes that the reason why people drink as much alcohol in Germany is because they need to feel free and to be able to open themselves up, something they simply do not do when sober. Nonetheless, it was important to her to learn German, to meet native people and adapt to the new environment. She highlights that her courses at the gym and her dancing lessons have been a great instrument in achieving this goal. Additionally, these courses and lessons also offer her continuity with the activities she was involved with during her childhood and teenage years, when she did ballet and athletics and took guitar lessons. Continuing her guitar lessons, she says, is one of her future leisure goals.

All in all, she mentions that, for her, meeting new people during leisure time is good because she wants to talk about something other than work with people who have different tasks and problems. However, she does find it hard to plan social leisure activities weeks ahead, as do many of her friends who are from countries like Mexico and with whom she feels she shares cultural similarities. She also enjoys going to Latin American–themed parties in which she can dance salsa or Zumba with these friends. At the moment, she would also like to have a "serious relationship" but finds it hard to find someone even when she tries online dating. She is convinced that "good catches" are already married and that the others are just looking for casual sexual relationships.

Besides her weekly and Saturday activities, she says that, on Sundays, she rarely feels like going to the gym and she spends most of the time during that day at home, sitting on the couch and watching TV series (she likes *Arrow* and *Revenge*), listening to music, and talking to her family on Skype while cleaning the apartment. Another of her favorite activities is viewing images on Instagram. On Sundays she never feels like cooking, so usually she just orders some takeaway pizza, but Sundays also cause her to miss her family and their Sunday lunches and walks, even when she is in constant communication with them via WhatsApp and other social media.

She likes being visited by friends and family and, last year, bought her younger sister a ticket to stay with her for a couple of weeks. In future years, she would like to organize a trip with her parents as a present to them. Additionally, each winter she travels "back home," as she calls it, to experience Christmas celebrations with her family and to avoid the cold wintry weather of Germany. In the summer and autumn, she also likes traveling with friends on short weekend trips around Europe and around Germany, especially during the time of the Christmas markets in December.

A. stresses that she is happy and enjoys her leisure. She says she likes her job but enjoys her leisure more. She stresses this is possible only if you are a "successful migrant" and that to become one in financial and social terms is a question of individual attitude and effort.

Each of the previous chapters focused on the leisure perception and the channels chosen for leisure by a particular group of women in Mannheim. The common features in the ways they conceive, plan, and execute their leisure have been described and analyzed as a whole. Different approaches could be taken to explain the similarities among this group of women— for example, by focusing on their similar social class backgrounds and habitus (Bourdieu 1984); interaction of their social class with age (Gans 1999); income and household structure (Walker and Jieping 2007, p. 96); exposure to the same culture industry (Adorno 1991); or age and educational level in interaction with constant selective exposure within a milieu (Schulze 2005, pp. 267–279). Yet it was shown how individual nuances inform the way in which leisure is perceived and organized in everyday life. Differences can stem, for example, from the different groups the individual belongs to, groups that have different compositions and interests. The individual encounters many different situations in everyday life in which one or another identity from the "identity portfolio" might be brought to light (s. Jenkins 2008, p. 73). As Jenkins (2008) highlighted, collective identities or individual belonging to different groups and individual identity that makes the individual unique are both equally important. All in all, it has been shown how both structural characteristics and individual agency coexist and influence the formation of leisure.

The previous chapters also highlighted the importance of an aspect that fosters similarities but that is often ignored by authors investigating socio-economic or structural factors with regard to lifestyle: the local context. The importance of the local context is recognized, for example, by Miller (2010, p. 218), who stated that the role of the sociopolitical order is to enable particular lifestyles, or by Gerhards (2008, p. 737), who pointed out that preferences cannot be translated into practice without the necessary, available local infrastructure. Additional characteristics of the local context, such as weather, have a behavioral effect on individuals (Freitas 2015, p. 58). Furthermore, it could also be drawn from Geertz (1976, p. 234) that each locality has its own cultural context, which influences how lifestyles and identities are constructed and reproduced, something that has been discussed in detail when describing leisure in Mannheim. Yet this cultural context is not territorially bound: global and local dynamics influence individuals and their taste and leisure as well (Brosius 2010, p. 74).

In sum, as an important component of individual lifestyles, leisure is a complex subject in which many aspects combine to form individual patterns. However, the leisure of individuals is not static. The sociostructural characteristics of an individual might change, for example, by having children or earning more money. Additionally, as we have considered, leisure is constantly changing cyclically through the passing of seasons. Lifestyles and leisure can also change over time—for example, through the introduction of new technologies (Bonz and Wietschorke 2013) or drastic environmental changes (Palutikof et al. 2004, p. 45). In addition, individual leisure can change through migration processes and shifts in interests and belongings related to it. In relation to the topics of leisure and migration, it is important to keep in mind that the concept of leisure (as well as the different channels in which it takes place) is a cultural construct, as Taylor (2001, pp. 535–536) and Huda and Akhtar (2006, pp. 15–16) argued. Taylor (2001, pp. 535–536) stated that some leisure activities can be used to assimilate migrants into dominant cultural practices while others can help express and celebrate cultural differences. From the narratives in interviews and conversations and interpretation of the participant observation that has been presented thus far, it can be concluded that informants with a migrant background share to a great extent the concepts and practical execution of leisure of their nonmigrant counterparts. Some commonalities, as in the case of planning and organization, are the result of a necessary adaptation that makes social leisure possible. Others, like the passion for team sports, stem from common interests that preceded and followed migration. Still others come from preferences that could not be translated into practice before migration (e.g., going on a girls' night out) but are possible now due to the current local characteristics.

While some of the differences have been briefly pointed out, this chapter examines them further because, even if there are not differences with regard to leisure, some of them do have relevance for the day-to-day living of these women and how they constitute their leisure. One of the differences mentioned earlier was, for example, differences that stem from the urban–rural divide rather than general cultural differences per se. Growing up in a village can have an influence on how a person experiences the city and its life rhythm. Those women coming from rural contexts (all of whom are internal migrants in this case) expressed feelings of strangeness in their narratives about the city, their leisure ideals and activities, showing a lot of connection to nature and outdoor activities. Additionally, it was touched upon how previous experiences can affect how time is perceived. Women with an external migrant background often perceived an increase in potential leisure time due to the fact that infrastructure and institutions allowed for a quicker actualization of nonleisure activities. Things just as simple as not spending three hours in traffic getting to and from work have an immense influence on leisure and perception of time. As a result, even when the subjective amount of leisure is the same in hours for all women, the qualitative individual evaluation of whether this time is enough or not can vary according to previous experiences in other local contexts. All of these aspects show that, in some cases, individuals originating from rural areas can have more differences regarding rhythm of leisure than between migrant and non-migrants from urban areas. In other words, in some situations, external migrants and natives have more in common when it comes to their leisure if they share urban biographies. The importance of and interconnection between leisure activities and social relations has been discussed. For internal and external migrants, leisure activities play a much more crucial role for the development of new social relationships. However, and as mentioned previously, even for nonmigrants, relationships have changed or been lost, often in transitions, such as the end of school or professional education or the start of new jobs. What all the women shared was that the closest friendships were in every case of the same gender and similar age. "Best friendships," it was revealed, also stemmed from childhood or teenage years and remained so even after migratory movements. Harring (2010) used the issue of gender and inter-ethnic "best friendships" as an indicator in the analysis of the social and cultural capital of youth but, in the case of my informants, best friends were not only exclusively of the same gender but were also almost always of the same ethnicity, shared the same cultural background, and were considered best friends regardless of lack of physical proximity. This latter point is something that all the women shared, regardless of their origins.

However, it cannot be said that they lack local social and cultural capital. Interethnic relationships and friendships do constitute an important part of these women's lives and social relations. As we have seen, leisure organization often requires configuring time to allow for social activities to take place, as witnessed in the case of the migrant women who adapted to a different way of time management (something that is subjectively seen as a marker of the local culture). Furthermore, as has been mentioned, family plays a key role in the lives of all of these women. When describing weekends, both migrant and nonmigrant informants highlighted how Sundays are often a time dedicated to family. This is also the case for migrant women who can communicate with their families and friends, overcoming physical distance thanks to technology. Keim (1995) pointed out in her ethnography of one of Mannheim's neighborhoods that not all migrants are perceived in the same way. She highlighted that some migrants can be considered "noticeable" while others are rather "unnoticeable," in the sense that some are seen to be strongly attached to their cultures while others seen to be more integrated into a "German" lifestyle (ibid., p. 46). What we have witnessed up until now, with regard to the leisure of these women, is that there are many similarities between them and that individual differences are often a consequence of their interests and situations. Their leisure patterns are "unnoticeable," in Keim's (1995) terms. As is seen further later, however, ethnicity is connected to noticeability as well. Even when individuals are not seen as socially problematic by their environment, those individuals can still be perceived as an "other."

In this chapter, I aim to highlight some of the differences and some of the situations in which difference related to a migrant background play more crucial roles. Even though these women share many characteristics, including age, educational level, household composition, and local context, they present some differences that can be linked to their different experiences and their individual migrant backgrounds. In this particular case, migrant backgrounds are often interconnected with experiences and perception of ethnicity. Even though there are multiple commonalities and belongings, and despite the fact that ethnic difference does not play a role in all situations within these women's lives, this chapter focuses on the situations in which migrant background, sometimes in its interconnection with ethnic differences, plays a role in the context of leisure.

Following the same pattern of previous chapters, I also address the issue of sports and physical activities because of the important role they play in the leisure of my informants. In particular, I would like to show the "racialization" of particular kinds of sports (s. Spracklen 2013, p. 194) and how this influences the leisure pursued by these women. As Saint and Krueger (2011) found in their study of ethnic differences and types of exercise in the United States, one's education level plays a role in whether a person participates in physical activity, but ethnicity plays the major role regarding which specific activity the individual participates in. In summary of their findings, ethnic-racial differences in sports participation type did not diminish with increasing education (Saint and Krueger 2011, pp. 205–208). Spracklen (2013, p. 194) labeled sports like hiking and skiing "white" sports because of the dominance within them of white participants. This statement was confirmed by my "nonwhite" informants through their related narratives. In general, sports and physical activity in Mannheim and its surroundings were perceived as a positive environment; indeed, all migrants highlighted the high level of acceptance in sport teams and fitness studios. According to the women, these environments are often used as tools to meet new people and are subjectively evaluated as good integration mechanisms. What must be clarified, though, is that my informants and interviewees, even though they belong to different ethnicities, did not encounter barriers to participation related to clothing norms of their own particular backgrounds. They did not face barriers that are present for many migrant women, as was exemplified with the prohibition of hijabs in fitness studios.

In the particular case of my informants, however, sports as a racialized field was particularly relevant when it came to winter sports. Although ethnic differences did not seem to play a role in participation or leisure experiences derived from physical activity in general, winter sports present an exception that is important to highlight. Spinney and Millward (2011, p. 137) argued that there can be individual differences in how weather conditions affect outdoor leisure activities by taking the example of snow and mentioning that it is, on one hand, a barrier to and, on the other, a facilitator of outdoor activities. In my study, whether snow was seen as a barrier to or facilitator of outdoor activities was directly related to migrant backgrounds in relation to ethnicity. For those women without a migrant background, snow was regarded positively and as something directly related to facilitating winter sports. For women with a migrant background, it was seen as aesthetically pleasing but as a hindrance to outdoor activities. Migrants often framed winter sports in a discourse of ethnicity and ethnic incompatibility. For example, one of the women said that she would feel uncomfortable skiing because everyone would look at her uncomfortably or ridicule her because she was black, which shows the presence of perceived discrimination (Chavez 2000, pp. 183–184) as a barrier for participation.

Informal conversations with the migrant women also made especially clear the existence of other ethnic stereotypes related to leisure activities and taste, as pointed out by Nadel-Klein (2010). (For example, this happened to me when I was teased about having a "typically white" backpack [a hiking backpack] and being associated with placing practically before style). Another activity that was often associated with "whiteness," or that was seen as incompatible with other ethnicities and so did not present itself often in the leisure activities of the women, was swimming. Although going to swimming pools and lakes, bathing, and sunbathing are beloved activities for all, swimming as a "serious" physical activity (s. Allen-Collinson 2011, pp. 307–308) aimed at performance enhancement and fitness was, for the migrant women, just like winter sports and hiking, associated with a certain ethnicity. Swimming has been related to upper-middle-class habitus in the United States by Deluca (2016, p. 268), who argued that being able to swim has a cultural importance for this group and that going swimming in the club is an essential part of their "summer lifestyles." However, as Deluca pointed out, access to facilities and swimming lessons are privileges carried across generations (p. 273) and, even though he does not dig into the issue of ethnicity, social classes are inextricably linked to historical inequalities of power and related opportunities. In the case of the women of this study, swimming might be just an example of how such differences still have consequences in today's reality. Even though all of the women in this study have access to the facilities, the use of these spaces differs due to a lack of ability or internalized stereotypes about ethnicity and leisure. Unlike winter sports spaces, however, swimming spaces, such as public swimming pools and lakes, are engaged with but they are used differently. All in all, swimming and winter sports are examples that show that, as Longa and Hyltona (2014) argued, social class does not determine one's inclusion in activities and opportunities. Rather, social class must be considered alongside gender, ethnicity, income, and age (Longa and Hyltona 2014, p. 388).

Ethnic differences also play a role beyond leisure for social relations in the sense that some phenotypical characteristics are associated with particular cultural traits. Even though women did not mention it explicitly during interviews or conversations, the exoticization of some ethnicities was quite palpable during participant observation. For example, friends and social relations wanting to touch darker skin or curly hair to see what it felt like is something that did not happen invertedly. This means that white skin and straight or wavy hair is considered the norm and that there is often an invasion of private sphere that is not consensual and would not happen the other way around. Also, stereotypes about skin color and dancing or running abilities were very present in observed conversations about leisure activities. Though even if women stressed the multicultural nature of the city of Mannheim and openness as a positive factor, differences are not (yet) normalized in the sense of being perceived as nothing new and the members of society interacting with individuals without falling into ethnic stereotypes, as this short examples have shown.

Returning to the issue of summer and winter lifestyles, it has been described how physical activity increases for all the women in the summer due to additional outdoor activities that are undertaken in addition to routine activities throughout the year while winter crystallizes more differences because winter sport activities are considered "typically" white activities and participants with different ethnicities feel either not welcomed or felt these activities did not match their ethnic identity. But these differences go beyond issues of ethnic identity and leisure activities; they also relate to the family dynamics in the context of the situation that the individual is in. For example, although nonmigrant women often make use of winters to engage in weekend trips or family vacations with parents and siblings, migrant women use winters to visit their families in their countries of origin for longer periods of time. As respondent A. explained on February 3, 2015:

> So, in the summer? No, [in] the summer I stay here but I use the winter to go home because the climate is horrible here. I rather spend some time there with my family but the summer is nice here so is not worth it to spend it somewhere else, even if I'm alone, because my friends have gone somewhere.

This type of travel, which is bound to the rituals of the annual cycle, is common for people working and living in different places from their families, something that has been described in different contexts (s. Strümpell 2008, p. 370). However, regarding family dynamics, one key difference must be highlighted. In the case of the women in my study, family dynamics are different between migrants and nonmigrants, particularly in the financial sense. (For example, family skiing trips are almost exclusively paid for by parents or grandparents.) In general, nonmigrant women pointed out that family vacations, either winters skiing or summers on cruise ships, are paid for and organized by the older generations. As respondent A. described on May 12, 2015: "I was on vacation with my parents last year. They organized a cruise trip with the *Aida* so we traveled around Dubai."

Some expressed in their narrations gratitude toward their families because they would not be able to afford such trips on their own. Two women also pointed out that, even if they wanted to contribute financially to the vacation, they would not be allowed to do so. Similar comments were made regarding everyday leisure activities with parents and grandparents. Spending time with family is an important part of leisure; many women mentioned going on shopping "tours" of the mall or the city center with their mothers, with the mothers being the ones actually paying for the clothes. This is not based on a lack of money by the women themselves but on a specific family dynamic of parents of financially independent adults. Such trips and leisure activities were described in the context of family bonding and hold a great emotional importance to the women. Gifts are exchanged in the other direction as well, but women mentioned buying presents for their families only for special occasions, such as birthdays, Christmas, Mothers' Day, and other anniversaries.

In contrast, family dynamics of the migrants differed greatly. First, the parents or grandparents do not pay for vacations. In general, my migrant informants traveled to visit their families. Only on rare occasions did they travel with their families, and when they did so, they said it was a gift from them to their parents, that they wanted to take them on vacation. Furthermore, not only do migrants often use the winter months to visit their parents and families, but, when they do, they bring presents with them. One woman explained that traveling to the country of origin not only meant buying an expensive flight ticket but also bringing presents, costing "a couple of hundred euro." Tazanu (2012a, pp. 107–126) pointed out that Cameroonian migrants in Germany are expected to show material success when "going back" and that there is great social pressure from family and friends to comply with this norm. Traveling to visit parents and grandparents, though, is not the same for all migrants, as not all families and cultural contexts are the same. For example, three women highlighted the importance traveling every year to visit their families had for them and that they did so in a discourse of emotional fulfillment and happiness. Two other women mentioned that this was not as important for them and that they had traveled to their countries of origin less frequently.

Many factors can affect how migrant women perceive traveling to their countries of origin. One that can be considered is gender roles. Tazanu (2012a) also pointed out, for example, that women visit Cameroon less often because the patriarchal society is not used to economically independent women. Going to the country of origin can mean for the individual confrontation and hurtful judgment on his or her lifestyle choices (pp. 103–123). Indeed, the two women who expressed mixed feelings about visiting their home countries were originally from Cameroon, and one said that, while she felt joy to see her family, she was annoyed not to have the freedom to move around alone and to have to be constantly accompanied by her brother.

These few examples show that there can be differences not only between migrants and nonmigrants but also between migrants themselves. The way in which vacations, one of the facilitating periods of leisure, are conceived and executed is influenced by many factors, not all of which can be examined here. What must be highlighted here is that migrants use vacations more often to travel to visit their parents and families, while nonmigrants use vacations either to travel with parents and family or to travel with other social relations. Additionally, the directionality of "gifts" or exchange of goods is different: while nonmigrant women are on the receiving end, migrant women are on the giving end. This is important to recognize because such dynamics influence how the individual sets her general budget for leisure. In other words, even though all of these women might have comparable incomes because of their educational level, job descriptions, and shared local context, and even though they might share similar ideals of leisure and preferences for leisure activities, their total available "leisure budget" is not be the same because of the differences in monetary family dynamics.

An additional aspect that creates differences in leisure budgets is remittance payments or other forms of material family obligations. Some of my migrant informants send remittances in the form of money every month or several times a year; some send goods in the form of medicines and other supplies, while others are financially responsible for younger siblings who have also migrated. It is important to point out that the women I interviewed and talked to do not come from local lower classes but rather middle classes. Sending money or material support to their families is not about mere necessity but often about perceived moral obligations and relative wealth. Women are often reminded of such obligations via social media, such as WhatsApp, just like in Tazanu's (2012b) case. Other leisure budget differences can stem from different conditions of student loan payments because some of the native women were paying student loans granted by public institutions (which are payable without interest) while migrant women from outside EU countries were not granted such affordable loans until recently and thus had to take student loans from banks, which means paying higher amounts after they start working life.

However, it is important to highlight that, subjectively, the reduction of available income for leisure due to expenses related to supporting a family is not framed in a narrative of complaint or loss in relation to leisure. Leisure and this type of financial expense do not seem to overlap in subjective perception or calculations. Narratives about remittances and other kinds of support are always marked by the presence of aspects such as reciprocity, for example, in the sense of "My parents supported me, now that I can I want to help them as well," and, on an emotional level, "I want to help them because I care about them." Besides direct financial or material support and the dynamics of vacations and familial reciprocity, other expenses that have consequential budgetary effects can come from something as "insignificant" as paying a Skype flat rate that allows them to call other countries every month. The monetary differences are seen in consumption issues, such as car ownership, for example. Although the majority of the native women I talked to owned a car, the majority of the migrant women did not, often citing cost as a reason. Additionally, and similar to the dynamics of vacations, some native women received a car (or the first car) and the costly driving license as a present from their parents or grandparents. Car ownership is important because it is also a factor influencing leisure behavior (Veal 1987, p. 143). Indeed, those women with cars enjoyed a wider geographical (regional) range in their leisure; the everyday leisure of the women without cars was more locally bound.

Other aspects that affect disparities in leisure budget and, consequently, its execution can be, for example, visa regulations. For those migrants who are not naturalized Germans, traveling to other countries for vacation can involve costly visa and administrative fees. Indeed, these fees and time-consuming visa issues, as well as everyday local bureaucracy, are the main reasons behind my informants' choice to take German nationality. Half of my informants with a migrant background are naturalized Germans while the others had multiple nationalities, which allowed them to travel to a wide variety of countries without visa restrictions. What is interesting here is that naturalization was framed primarily in a discourse of leisure possibilities related to traveling and not in a discourse of identity. Phrases like "I will always be [xyz], the passport doesn't change that," or "I know I'm [xyz], this [passport] just makes things easier" often accompanied the topic of naturalization. Only in one case did a woman highlight the advantages of free travel in a discourse on the nation-state and the protection of its citizens, in particular the protection of the rights of minorities regarding sexual orientation. However, even if there is no strong identification with the nation-state overall, it is not the same for the local context. As has been shown, the women feel a strong identification with Mannheim, as the local context in which they unfold their lives.

All of these aspects, which cut the leisure budgets of migrant women compared to those of nonmigrant women, could be interpreted as a disadvantage. However, even if the migrant women "lose," in financial terms, due to their responsibilities and the financial expectations of their relatives, they might "gain" freedom, due to the distance separating them. Nonmigrant women might have a larger leisure budget, but they have less available time due to the closeness of family. Often they are more bound to activities that are not ideal leisure and that are often felt as social obligations. For example, respondent J. said on May 22, 2015:

> …mmm. Now that I don't live so close to my family, it has gotten better. Less now. I'm not so often at birthdays and so on. Well, there will be a wedding soon and I have to go with my family even though I really don't want to.

In this line of argument, it can be pointed out that migration can be a process that is perceived, subjectively, as liberating. Gagné (2013), for example, described how the Maori who migrate to large cities experience more freedom and choose to live lifestyles that are not in accordance with the traditional Maori lifestyle. Often individuals willingly adapt their lifestyle to that of the neighborhood and social class in which they are currently living (pp. 60–160). Migrating can result in the construction of new forms of leisure, which are free from the social norms that promote specific types of leisure—for example, norms that associate women with "home leisure" (s. Huda and Akhtar 2006, p. 2). These changes are subjectively felt as well. As respondent A. explained on March 2, 2015:

> So, well, I said. Now I have time, time lasts a lot because, by not having my family here, by not having to visit cousins, if I only have to work or study you really have much more time, you have more free time. So I said to myself, okay, I'll find something nice to do.

Nonetheless, it is also important to highlight that my group of informants claimed never to have ever experienced discrimination or had to face certain restrictions in their new environment, such as the aforementioned clothing restrictions that other groups of migrant women might face. Additionally, they did not felt constricted by their cultural background in the sense of dealing with barriers related to gender roles and physical activity. This might be also the result of migration processes being "freeing" in the sense that all of these women migrated alone and had a physical distance separating them from their previous social environments. The absence of such barriers on a subjective level is important because, just as Wearing (1998, p. 121) and Cortis May et al. (2008, p. 45) pointed out, they can be a detriment to women's freedom in leisure.

5.2   To Laugh or Not to Laugh: Humor and Entertainment

Up until now, I have pointed out significant differences to do with outdoor leisure and leisure budget, There are some differences that could also be seen in other leisure activities, specifically in leisure that mainly takes place at home. For this type of leisure, TV watching is one important aspect that different authors have considered. Dumazedier (1967, p. 45) highlighted the introduction of TV in the 1940s as a sort of revolution for the area of leisure and pointed out that entertainment is one of the main concerns regarding leisure for the individuals (p. 229). Scheuch (1972, p. 32) argued that watching TV as leisure during the week is an activity common to all social classes, while weekend activities would differentiate them. For Schulze (2005, pp. 279–330), watching entertainment programs on television was a characteristic leisure activity of the "self-fulfillment" milieu. Drawing further conclusions, Stebbins (2014, pp. 30–37) classified this kind of leisure as "casual" leisure and TV watching as passive entertainment, which does not bring "real" happiness.

However, the introduction of new technologies has brought new forms of viewing that go beyond the "traditional" TV watching. The video-on-demand industry has made self-scheduled, deliberate watching by individuals possible and has also given rise to binge-watching, the watching of multiple episodes in one sitting (Jenner 2015), which could itself be considered a new form of leisure activity. Even though the term "binge" usually implies excessive behavior, studies have not found social norms that help define limits to denote excess, thus binge-watching seems to be a characterization of leisure that is very individual (s. ibid.). The case of TV series is particularly interesting because it is a leisure medium that is relatively independent of costs, because the costs related to such consumption of entertainment are very low (in relation to people's incomes in some countries, such as Germany). With a flat rate or access code, endless possibilities from which to choose are available to individuals. Whereas television allowed individuals to choose from different channels, video-on-demand allows individuals more freedom in terms of schedules and access to more content. This is the case for my informants who have access and who make use of this type of entertainment. In fact, watching TV series in the video-on-demand format is part of their everyday leisure and, in individual cases and situations, so is binge-watching. Although the range of series watched mirrored the large variety available to consumers, some patterns differentiated migrants from nonmigrants. Certain differences can be observed from their discourse and practices.

For the women in this study, TV series watching plays an important role in overall leisure, as it is one of the activities often associated with "coziness" and can occupy anything from two to 10 hours or more a week, often depending on whether a series is subjectively deemed binge-worthy or not. The main reason given in favor of this type of viewing rather than watching "regular" TV was the matter of choice it presents. Furthermore, because video-on-demand series are selected, they were often less accompanied by parallel activities, like chatting or chores, in comparison with regular TV watching. Watching or binge-watching series, then, is a self-created leisure experience, in the sense that the schedule and the content is chosen by the individual as well as the place and accompanying conditions, such as room temperature, comfortable clothing, and food and drinks. However, while the schedule and self-created atmosphere was the same for all the women, differences could be observed in the type of entertainment or content. In particular, I would like to highlight the case of humor and series.

The range of programming watched by my informants is very wide, but U.S. American-produced TV series definitely dominate. For instance, there are overlapping series, the same series watched by more than one woman, which have been mentioned already. However, in one genre there were discrepancies in the migrant versus nonmigrant groups, and that is the comedy genre. This is important because this genre also is one of the most-watched genres overall by the women. All the women said comedy contributed to "freeing the mind" and loosening up. Bourdieu (1984, p. 170) placed taste in the context of the internalization of socioeconomic structures. Jenner (2015) also argued that "binge-watching"' certain series can create new forms of distinction and fan communities based on taste and perceived "quality" of content. Earlier Kuipers and Simms (1971, p. 244) brought the concept of taste and humor together and argued that not only structural factors but also cultural traditions play a role in what it is considered "good humor" and that the dynamics between such factors can form different "humor styles."

In the case of this study, women without an (external) migrant background achieved an almost unanimous consensus on issue of the comedy series and mentioned series like *How I Met Your Mother* and *The Big Bang Theory* when they expressed their enjoyment of this type of humor. Some watched it in the original language, English, while some watched the German translation. Women with a migrant background, despite their

German-language proficiency, also turned to original versions of series or turned to series or videos in their mother languages. As respondent L. explained on September 5, 2014:

> I watch mostly French television because I come from Cameroon and we speak French there so I like watching TF1, it's a French channel and I have the opportunity to have it at home so I watch some entertainment there, yeah. So, entertaining things like, in Germany, it is called "*es wird schräg*" but I watch the French one, or things like that, with comedians. I like funny stuff—even when I watch the videos online I always watch funny stuff and French movies.

Besides aspects of language, what was often mentioned was the quality of the humor. When explicitly asked about popular trending comedy series, the migrant women said that they do not necessarily find those series funny. In general, informal conversations led me to conclude that they generally have difficulty sharing the humor of their nonmigrant counterparts. Yet, when I mentioned that these were American and not German TV series, the narrative turned into a question of ethnicity, with the series being perceived as "white people's humor." This kind of subjective evaluation of particular comedy series resonates with Spracklen's (2013, p. 69) argument that popular culture and, within it, TV shows serve primarily to entertain white consumers and almost always portray a picture of whiteness and other racial stereotypes that perpetuate the status quo. In direct personal interactions, other types of humor must be shared or tolerated. Entertainment, especially the video-on-demand industry and websites like YouTube, make it possible for individuals to choose from a much larger number of choices including choosing something individuals identify with. In the case of these women, the intersection of migrant background (or lack thereof) and ethnic identity plays a role in how the content of entertainment is perceived and, consequently, which contents are chosen for leisure.

While entertainment TV might be highly influenced by the what the industry offers, as leisure, it does not have a monopoly over people's consumption, as Adorno (1991, pp. 85–92) argued. Additionally, Wearing (1998, p. 75) pointed out that watching TV is not only a passive activity, but it evokes emotional identification and gives pleasure. Nowadays the shows offered are so varied and people have access to so much content that they can translate their preferences into practice and choose channels of leisure with which they can identify. Additionally, not all entertainment comes from industry, as can be seen in the many YouTube channels, and the "traditional" entertainment industry is facing competition in the rise of a new industry of video-on-demand entertainment, led by Netflix and Amazon, which pay more attention to the wishes of viewers who are gender, ethnically, and culturally diverse (Jenner 2015). Indeed, people are choosers, as Appadurai (1996, p. 42) argued, but, contrary to Appadurai's argument, choosing should be considered a deliberate action and the individual an actor. By choosing something, individuals are positioning themselves and also deciding against a myriad of things, as Schulze (2005, p. 178) said. In this case, women are choosing a humor they share and identify with instead of other types of humor they might not enjoy. By being able to choose, they are actively forming their own leisure experience according to their preferences.

All in all, it is important to highlight how media exercises a big influence on people's lifestyles and leisure (Brosius 2010, p. 8) and how tastes for certain things, such as specific comedy series, can be the expression and also the reproduction of particular belongings. Wearing (1998, pp. 167–169) saw a close connection between leisure and humor, both of which are cultural constructs. This form of leisure shows that, on one hand, individuals are not passive and they make conscious choices regarding what to do and consume in their leisure. On the other hand, it shows that individuals' leisure choices can be influenced by their cultural backgrounds. Among my interviewees, this influence was particularly perceived and expressed in the case of humor and comedy entertainment. Although all of the women chose laughter through video content as a channel for a leisure experience, the content itself differs. This is important because what people are laughing about can say many things about their day-to-day problems, their emotional responses, or even their values, for example. Additional differences regarding interaction with entertainment media was evident in the fact that those with a migrant background showed a greater interest in news in all formats. They often mentioned reading and watching news concerning their countries of origin as well as German news as part of their leisure activities, something the native women did not mention. This could be explained on the grounds that someone who has migrated due to sociopolitical issues might be generally more interested in such topics in general.

There is one important exception that I would like to mention regarding different tastes in humor content, because it is closely related to the local identification with Mannheim (addressed in the previous chapters): the case of Bülent Ceylan. Ceylan is a nationally known stand-up comedian from Mannheim, who is probably, along with singer Xavier Naidoo, the most renowned personality from the city.[1] Half Turkish, half German, Ceylan's comedic content has influenced the city's population to a point where some of his phrases are found in everyday conversations. Phrases like "*Uffbasse!*" (watch out!) or "*Die Haar, die Haar*" (the hair, the hair) expressed in the cities dialect have a recognition value in the city. The latter is often used to tease women or men who are too vain or too focused on their hair (related to Ceylan's relation to his hair), a reference that is understood city-wide. The content of his stand-up sets often invites reflection on cultural stereotypes, such as those about Turkish migrants and current events. Interestingly, the women found this comedian good, describing his sets as smart and good. This shows that content to which individuals can relate is essential for humor and for being entertained. The local connection between this particular comedian and *all* of the women of this study serves as common ground in their evaluation of his jokes and in turn further cements their identification with the city.

5.3 SPECIAL OCCASIONS

One final aspect regarding migrant backgrounds and leisure that I would like to address briefly concerns special occasions. Just as the special events of the city have been described as events that influence the lives of people living there, whether they are participating or not, and that serve to produce and reproduce a common identity, special events also take place in the context of a shared migrant background. These are occasions that are part of the leisure pattern of every individual even though they are not a part of everyday leisure, and they include parties with a national or regional theme, meetings with friends with the same origin, and events from cultural associations. Cultural background plays a role here because participants are individuals who share the same cultural background and, based on this, feel a common belonging; special kinds of food are cooked and eaten, music is listened to, and a common language is spoken, all of which revolve around the country or region of origin. For my informants, certain occasions take place monthly or only a couple of times a year but, for them, hold an important emotional significance and are framed in a discourse of "missing" something and "identity" and sharing something that cannot be shared with other people with whom one does not share the same background.

Just like the events of the city, these occasions serve as rituals. A ritual, even one that is secular, can be a declaration and demonstration of an identity (Moore and Myerhoff 1977, pp. 8–10). If, during the migration process, the individual forms a lifestyle that is not "traditional," these types of rituals can help restore status as a member of a certain group (s. Turner 1989, pp. 184–193), and they can also be considered periodic rites of solidarity, in which common features of a group are emphasized and the unit and its members celebrate themselves (s. Colson 1977, p. 190). These are situations that highlight a common cultural and ethnic identity, which, in the case of these women, does not play a central role in their everyday lives. Indeed, these women and their occasional events with social relations who share the same ethnic and cultural background might confirm that "segregated ethnic communities" are just part-time worlds, where there is a constant shift by individuals in their belonging to groups (Zifonun 2010, pp. 312–313): their identities alternate, coexist, and are expressed in and through leisure activities.

In summary, it could be said that, while leisure plays an important role for all of these women, and while they might share similar preferences, it is possible that for nonmigrant women, those preferences can be more easily translated into practice, due to the reduced presence of financial responsibilities related to caring for family. Migrant women have less money and more time on their hands whereas native women have more money and less time on their hands. However, with the time and money they do have to spend on their leisure, they do so in very similar ways because they think about leisure in similar ways and because the channels of leisure available to them in their shared local context are the same too. Yet while some activities might look the same, such as TV series watching, the activities might hide within them different meanings and identifications, such as the perception of humor. Additionally, although they are not formally excluded from any type of leisure activities, migrant women can face barriers to leisure activities that are particularly racialized due to past or current social inequalities. Fortunately, though, for this specific group of women, such barriers are perceived as exceptions to a generally good leisure portfolio from which they can choose.

This chapter, and investigation, could not focus on specific differences between various migrant backgrounds or on generational (first-, second-generation migrant, etc.) levels because doing so would be beyond the scope of research. The goal was to gain an insight into the leisure of all these women and in this particular section to present some situations and contexts in which differences stemming from migrant backgrounds play a role in leisure. As several previous chapters have shown, in everyday life, it is more locality, gender, age, and educational level as well as individual differences that influence an individual's formation of leisure patterns. Thus it is important to stress that cultural differences between the native population and migrants must not be equated with differences that are merely a consequence of the migration process and of individuals finding themselves in another type of situation socially and institutionally. This chapter has thus focused on the latter type of differences. All in all, leisure is an area of life in which individuals can play the most with their "identity portfolios" (s. Jenkins 2008, p. 73). In a matter of hours, they can jump from being a member of the team "xyz," to being a sister, to being a TV series fan, but together those identities linked to the leisure activities and experiences (and other areas of life) all compose the individual as whole.

Note

1. His stand-up shows fill the city's largest event venue, the SAP Arena, and are sold out weeks in advance.

References

Adorno, Theodor W. 1991. Culture Industry Reconsidered. In *The Culture Industry: Selected Essays on Mass Culture*, ed. Theodor W. Adorno and J.M. Bernstein, 85–92. London: Routledge.

Allen-Collinson, Jacquelyn. 2011. Feminist Phenomenology and the Woman in the Running Body. *Sport, Ethics and Philosophy* 5 (3): 297–313.

Appadurai, Arjun. 1996. *Modernity al Large: Cultural Dimensions of Globalization*, 1. Minneapolis; London: University of Minnesota Press.

Bonz, Jochen, and Jens Wietschorke. 2013. Habitus und Kultur: Das Habituskonzept in den empirischen Kulturwissenschaften. Ethnologie – Volkskunde – Cultural Studies. In *Pierre Bourdieu's Konzeption des Habitus: Grundlagen, Zugänge, Forschungsperspektiven*, ed. Alexander Lenger, Christian Schneickert, and Florian Schumacher, 285–306. Wiesbaden: Springer VS.

Bourdieu, Pierre. 1984. *Distinction: A Social Critique of the Judgement of Taste*. 2010 edition. Translated by Richard Nice, With a New Introduction by Tony Bennet. London/New York: Harvard University Press/Routledge.

Brosius, Christiane. 2010. *India's Middle Class: New Forms of Urban Leisure, Consumption and Prosperity*. London; New York: Routledge.

Chavez, Deborah. 2000. Invite, Include and Involve!: Racial Groups, Ethnic Groups and Leisure. In *Diversity and the Recreation Profession: Organizational Perspectives*, ed. M.T. Allison and I.E. Schneider, 179–191. State College, PA: Venture Publishing.

Colson, Elizabeth. 1977. The Least Common Denominator. In *Secular Ritual*, ed. Sally F. Moore and Barbara G. Myerhoff, 189–198. Assen: Van Gorcum.

Cortis, Natasha, Pooja Sawrikar, and Kristy Muir. 2008. Final Report: Participation in Sport and Recreation by Culturally and Linguistically Diverse Women.

DeLuca, Jaime R. 2016. Like a "Fish in Water": Swim Club Membership and the Construction of the Upper-Middle Class Family Habitus. *Leisure Studies* 35 (3): 259–277.

Dumazedier, Joffre. 1967. *Toward a Society of Leisure*. New York; London: Collier-Macmillan.

de Freitas, C.R. 2015. Weather and Place-based Human Behavior: Recreational Preferences and Sensitivity. *International Journal of Biometeorology* 59: 55–63.

Gagné, Natacha. 2013. *Being Māori in the City: Indigenous Everyday Life in Auckland*, 41. Toronto: University of Toronto Press.

Gans, Herbert J. 1999. *Popular Culture and High Culture: An Analysis and Evaluation of Taste*. Rev. and updated ed. New York: Basic Books.

Geertz, Clifford. 1976. "From the Native's Point of View": On the Nature of Anthropological Understanding. In *Meaning in Anthropology*, ed. Keith H. Basso and Henry A. Selby, 1st ed., 221–237. Albuquerque: University of New Mexico Press.

Gerhards, Juergen. 2008. Die kulturell dominierende Klasse in Europa: Eine vergleichende Analyse der 27 Mitgliedsländer der Europaeischen Union im Anschluss an die Theorie von Pierre Bourdieu. *Kölner Zeitschrift fuer Soziologie und Sozialpsychologie* 4: 723–748.

Harring, Marius. 2010. *Das Potenzial der Freizeit: Soziales, kulturelles und ökonomisches Kapital im Kontext der Freitzeitwelt Jugendlicher*. 1 Aufl. Wiesbaden: VS Verlag für Sozialwissenschaften.

Huda, Sadrul, and Afsana Akhtar. 2006. Leisure Behaviour of Working Women of Dhaka Bangladesh. *International Journal of Urban Labour & Leisure* 7 (1): 1–30.

Jenkins, Richard. 2008. *Social Identity*. 3rd ed. London, New York: Routledge.

Jenner, Mareike. 2015. Binge-watching: Video-on-demand, Quality TV and Mainstreaming Fandom. *International Journal of Cultural Studies*: 1–17.

Keim, Inken. 1995. Die Westliche Unterstadt. In *Kommunikation in der Stadt: Teil 2. Ethnographien von Mannheimer Stadtteilen*, ed. Werner Kallmeyer, vol. 4.2, 42–188. Berlin, New York: Walter de Gruyter.

Kuipers, Giselinde, and Kate Simms. 1971. *Good Humor, Bad Taste: A Sociology of the Joke*. New York: Mouton de Gruyter.

Longa, Jonathan, and Kevin Hyltona. 2014. Reviewing Research Evidence and the Case of Participation in Sport and Physical Recreation by Black and Minority Ethnic Communities. *Leisure Studies* 33 (4): 379–399.

Miller, Daniel. 2010. *Der Trost der Dinge*. With the Assistance of Frank Jakubzik. 1. Auflage 2613. Frankfurt am Main: Suhrkamp.

Moore, Sally F., and Barbara G. Myerhoff. 1977. Introduction: Secular Ritual: Forms and Meanings. In *Secular Ritual*, ed. Sally F. Moore and Barbara G. Myerhoff, 3–24. Assen: Van Gorcum.

Nadel-Klein, Jane. 2010. Cultivating Taste and Class in the Garden. In *Mutuality and Empathy: Self and Other in the Ethnographic Encounter*, vol. 5, 107–121. Wantage: S. Kingston Pub.

Palutikof, J.P., M.D. Agnew, and M.R. Hoar. 2004. Public Perceptions of Unusually Warm Weather in the UK: Impacts, Responses and Adaptations. *Climate Research* 26: 43–59.

Saint, Onge, and Patrick Krueger. 2011. Education and Racial – Ethnic Differences in Types of Exercise in the United States. *Journal of Health and Social Behaviour* 52: 197–211.

Scheuch, Erwin K. 1972. Die Problematik der Freizeit in der Massengesellschaft. In *Soziologie der Freizeit*, ed. Erwin K. Scheuch and Rolf Meyersohn, 23–41. Köln: Kiepenheuer & Witsch.

Schulze, Gerhard. 2005[1992]. *Die Erlebnisgesellschaft: Kultursoziologie der Gegenwart*. 2 Aufl. Frankfurt [Main]; New York: Campus.

Spinney, Jamie E., and Hugh Millward. 2011. Weather Impacts on Leisure Activities in Halifax, Nova Scotia. *International Journal of Biometeorology* 55: 133–145.

Spracklen, Karl. 2013. *Whiteness and Leisure. Leisure Studies in a Global Era*. New York; London: Palgrave Macmillan.

Stebbins, Robert A. 2014. Leisure, Happiness and Positive Lifestyle. In *Contemporary Perspectives in Leisure: Meanings, Motives and Lifelong Learning*, ed. Sam Elkington and Sean Gammon, 28–38. Abingdon; New York: Routledge.

Strümpell, Christian. 2008. 'We Work Together, We Eat Together': Conviviality and Modernity in a Company Settlement in South Orissa. *Contributions to Indian Sociology* 42 (3): 351–381.

Taylor, Tracy. 2001. Cultural Diversity and Leisure: Experiences of Women in Australia. *Society and Leisure* 24: 535–555.

Tazanu, Primus M. 2012a. They Behave as Though They Want to Bring Heaven Down: Some Narratives on the Visibility of Cameroonian Migrants Youths in Cameroon Urban Space. In *Urban life-worlds in motion*, ed. Kastner Hahn, 101–129. Bielefeld: Transcript.

———. 2012b. *Being Available and Reachable: New Media and Cameroonian Transnational Sociality*. Distributed in and outside N. America by African Books Collective. Mankon, Bamenda, Cameroon: Langaa Research & Publishing.

Turner, Victor W. 1989. *Das Ritual: Struktur und Anti-Struktur* Bd. 10. Frankfurt/Main: Campus-Verl.

Veal, Anthony J. 1987. *Leisure and the Future*, 4. London; Boston: Allen & Unwin.

Walker, Joan, and Li Jieping. 2007. Latent Lifestyle Preferences and Household Location Decisions. *Journal of Geographical Systems* 9: 77–101.

Wearing, Betsy. 1998. *Leisure and Feminist Theory*. London; Thousand Oaks, CA: SAGE.

Zifonun, Darius. 2010. Ein 'gallisches Dorf'? Integration, Stadtteilbindung und Prestigeordnung in einem 'Armenviertel'. In *Ethnowissen*, ed. Marion Müller, 311–327. Wiesbaden: Springer Fachmedien.

CHAPTER 6

Conclusion

The issue of how women, both natives and migrants, living in Mannheim conceive of and spend their leisure time is an interesting topic, for various reasons. Focusing on leisure allows us to see how people handle structural constraints in their everyday life, which means it also informs us about possible emotional and behavioral responses when leisure time is not filled as desired and how the women interpret the choices they make and the practices they are involved in. Mannheim, as a city of people with a myriad of backgrounds, presented an excellent field site and opportunity to look at people who share structural similarities and to see how this translates into their lived reality. One of the advantages of this work is that it looks at people who are in an average socioeconomic position, enjoy a good status in society, are not marginalized, and are not often the target of research interests; difficulties involved gaining access to them and their time during fieldwork. However, understanding how these women live is important because full-time employees in service work constitute a large proportion of the working population. In other words, it could be said that the women researched are part of the mainstream. Knowing about their everyday patterns and the meanings behind them can also contribute to a better understanding of their construction and reproduction of identity. Trying to grasp how they understand and constitute their leisure activities, and if and how their migration background affects their leisure conception and patterns, was the goal of this research: going beyond everyday

© The Author(s) 2017
V.L. Sandoval, *The Meaning of Leisure*, Leisure Studies
in a Global Era, DOI 10.1007/978-3-319-59752-2_6

assumptions on difference, but also beyond scholarly assumptions about the relevance of socioeconomic factors or "primary" identities, such as ethnicity or religion.

This work aimed to grasp how full-time employed women in Mannheim understood and practiced leisure and how these two dimensions related to each other. In order to address these issues, different aspects were taken into consideration.

The book then looked at how the city as leisure space has its own characteristics, as a result of historical processes and environmental conditions, and how these women reacted and behaved in interaction with the city as leisure space. I considered how individual leisure is influenced by the city's infrastructure and events and found that special events are important on both individual and collective levels. The findings show how the city and its neighborhoods as spaces can be seen negatively or positively, situationally, and how the locality's physical characteristics, including weather and climatic conditions, influence which channels individuals choose for leisure. I found that this distinction can present itself in the form of geographical boundaries, when, for example, other cities or other neighborhoods are associated with different social classes or groups to which the individual does not feel a sense of belonging. In this case, it was important for the women to discursively separate themselves from students, tourists, and the snobs of Heidelberg and general inhabitants of Ludwigshafen and to distinguish themselves internally from people of Mannheim's "dangerous" neighborhoods. However, the research showed that the distinction is not static and has many layers, for example, when such neighborhoods are an essential space for the individual's leisure. What is problematic in "distinction" concepts is that belongings (and, with them, the need for expression of distinction) can change depending on the situation. For example, when encountering individuals from other regions, it is possible that the differences among the three cities just mentioned would disappear to give place to a Rhein-Neckar Region identity. However, this particular hypothesis has not been a focus of this study's research objective.

First, the concept of subjective leisure was examined: which practices are understood as leisure and what is the overall ideal of leisure. We saw how leisure in practice can have multiple components and multiple channels, some of which are more focused on helping the body and mind recover from the burdens of work; others of which are centered on social relations; while some are focused on fun and the leisure experience. Indeed, leisure in practice is constituted by variation in activities and experiences, with alternation and variety of experiences seen as the main leisure goal. Additionally, the study shows how the areas of work and free time are strictly separated for these women, the former being time that is not under their control and the latter being periods in which they are free to control time. Contrarily, the areas of free time and leisure can have fluid boundaries, and the general ideal of leisure for these women required certain conditions to be met, including the presence of close social relations, certain weather conditions, and the availability of time and financial resources at their disposal. Often their vacation was the common time in which such conditions were met.

The book goes on to consider how these abstract views are expressed in practice, in the organization and execution of leisure. It was seen how women make use of technology, such as smartphone apps, as a means to plan and organize social leisure, and how technology can also provide a space for leisure itself, for example, by enabling meeting and conversation with family and friends possible despite physical distance. It was seen how, in the execution of leisure, sports and physical activity played a very relevant role during the week, while nighttime activities, such as drinking and clubbing, had an important relevance for the weekends (Sundays being the exception, as a quiet family or friends' day). The vacation, in contrast, was generally planned well in advance, with the women saving time and money and being organized in order to meet the ideal leisure characteristics. As Dumazedier (1967, p. 229) wrote almost 50 years ago: "Each person becomes concerned about his own balance between relaxation, entertainment, and self-improvement along the stream of everyday occurrences." This idea very much applies to this group of women, who, even though the idea of self-improvement exists in the background, are searching for balance in their leisure practice. However, it was noted that the leisure ideals constantly influence how these leisure practices are planned and perceived afterward.

If something has been learned from how these women think, plan, and experience leisure, it is that the women are not "puerile" in Huizinga's (1940, p. 331) understanding, or numbed from so much "outer input" in Simmel's (1903, p. 187) terms. Even though they are searching for sensations and stimulating activities, they sometimes also seek relaxation and small-scale socialization. They seek a balance in their leisure and lifestyles, and their thoughtful organization includes different types of leisure and leisure experiences in an expression of this quest. Moreover, leisure presents a possibility of escaping from the seriousness and compulsory nature of work, yet it is varied and rightfully so, according to the women's understanding. It can be individual and social, cozy and calm, exciting and entertaining, or serious and playful; it can break with the rules of society or be in compliance with them. Leisure time might be considered liminal because it is characterized by choice and it is not mandatory (s. Turner 1974, p. 74). Yet, having fulfilled leisure is a "moral imperative" and a life goal for these women, which makes Dumazedier's (1967, p. 8) reflection on the individual's need to make the most out of their free time in order that they can feel and look complete to others still valid almost 50 years later. Indeed, a fulfilled leisure, understood among other things as a varied leisure, is an essential part of the project of the self. One of the goals in this project is to avoid a monotony of experiences, a monotony that is often experienced in the area of work. So leisure acts for these women as a counterweight to work, which confirms compensation theories of leisure (s. Iso-Ahola 2015). If there is an area of life in which these women, to use Csikszentmihalyi's (1991) concept, experience something such as *flow*, it is during leisure, and especially so during physical activities, where there is a full concentration on the task and when the effort (at that moment) is no longer related to the consequences of the task. In this case, women perceive leisure as their choice and not as an activity forced on them. However, as we saw in regard to gender dynamics, in particular when considering sports and physical activities, leisure is not an area in which social norms and power structures are fully absent. What must be mentioned is that leisure is not subjectively framed in the context of consumption but that, in many cases, consumption is just a facilitator or companion to leisure. The main focus of the activity or the experience is something else, with social relations and emotional and bodily fulfillment often being the main goals. Bauman (2009, pp. 61–64) pointed out the contradiction of a consumerist society in which happiness is the measure of success yet happiness is an unattainable goal because there is always something else to consume, and thus income has nothing to do with happiness. According to Schulze (2005, p. 59), there is a difference between experiential value, "*Erlebniswert*," and "*Gebrauchswert*," the value of use. The former becomes more important in the 'Erlebnisgesellschaft' event society, the current society driven by the search of experiences instead of value, and we may say that in addition to specific "things," one also can consume or buy friendships and close relationships. But nonconsuming activities like running can also have a high experience value. The reason why different activities or settings have different experience values is that different outcomes are expected from different experiences, which again highlights the importance of leisure variety. Additionally, there are so many meanings behind consumption: how "things" are understood and used and how they affect the individual understanding of self and the environment is important as well. As we have considered, consuming mulled wine at the Christmas market can be a ritual that cements feelings of local belonging and gives bodily pleasure, for example, going beyond a mere transaction of goods.

Furthermore, to address the underlying research question of whether migrant backgrounds have consequences for these women's leisure, we have seen that a migrant background is not relevant for the meaning of leisure or even for most channels chosen for leisure. What is understood to be leisure is shared, both in the women's narratives about leisure and in their practice. Channels of leisure were similar among all the women, and differences were based on individual preferences, not due to different backgrounds, except among internal migrants from rural areas who preferred outdoor activities. For the group of women studied, we have seen how (external) migrant backgrounds affect primarily the leisure budget in interaction with family dynamics and institutionalized differences, which disfavor migrants. Women with an external migrant background typically have more free time and thus potential leisure time because of fewer family-related activities, which often occur in the boundary between free time and leisure, but fewer financial resources because of family responsibilities. Furthermore, in some situations, ethnicity and migrant backgrounds interrelate to form barriers to leisure when the migrant women perceived activities, such as winter sports, as ethnically incompatible with themselves. However, and fortunately, ethnic differences generally did not play a role in their everyday leisure because of how the local context is experienced as "open" to difference, both institutionally (lack of discrimination and barriers) and socially (people are open to difference). In some cases, though, despite the meaning and channels of leisure being the same, there were hidden layers of belonging and identification, as in the case of comedy series or comedy videos, which in this case produce and reproduced cultural identities in the context of language and humor.

In the introductory chapter I tangentially showed how leisure could be conceived as belonging to the umbrella concept of lifestyle. Returning to that conceptualization of leisure as one dimension of lifestyle, we may ask: Drawing from their leisure conception and experiences, what can be learned overall about the lifestyle of these women?

According to existing theoretical approaches, these women belong to particular social classes, or milieus. For example, according to Schulze's classification, my target group would belong to the "*Selbstverwirklichungsmilieu*," or personal fulfillment milieu, because of their age and educational level. This milieu is composed of people under 40 with middle to high levels of education. For their leisure, they like activities such as going to concerts, visiting Greek and Italian restaurants, going to pubs, sports like running, and watching entertainment programs on TV. They spend a lot of time in the city center, are flexible, rarely have weight problems, and have a life philosophy that focuses on the self (and what "I" want to do). However, following the same classification, this group also shows some aspects of the "*Unterhaltungsmilieu*," entertainment milieu, especially in the taste for soccer, dance clubs, cheap clothes, and thrillers. However, this is also a milieu revolving around the "I" (Schulze 2005, pp. 279–330). Even if they share these traits, the women present individual differences that are not irrelevant in terms of their meaning, understanding of the self, and biography. Furthermore, there is a prominent use in everyday life (not only in leisure) of new technologies like WhatsApp, Skype and video-on-demand viewing. New kind of behaviors, new channels and forms of leisure and new lifestyles emerge as the result of the presence of these technologies. Thus new patterns emerge that go beyond or break with habitus, a finding that supports Bonz and Wietschorker's (2013) view that the lives of actual individuals are more complex than a concept like habitus because of the consequences of the introduction of new objects and technologies. For this reason, lifestyles, including leisure, are not only "a conglomerate of values, which one has become during socialization and behavior habits or ideas, which one proves, confirms and reinforces in everyday contacts" (Richter 2005, p. 113), but they also include rejecting or changing such habits or ideas because of changes in the environment or personal biographies, such as moving from one place to another. Individuals also can rebel against such socialization, by, for example, disputing learned gender or sex behaviors.

However, if we were to consider the issue of levels of lifestyle as Richter (2005, pp. 115–116) has done, utilizing the concepts of subtle distinction, distinction, and attributive culture, it could be said that all the women share the same nucleus of "typical" style; they all have a lifestyle that makes them, in the perception of general public and policy makers be perceived as part of Germany's general population (subtle distinction); they share views about leisure, share some habits and behaviors that distinguish them from other groups (distinction), but they still have individual styles (e.g., fashion) and consumption patterns and ways to express their lifestyle to others (attributive culture). But Richter (2005) and Bourdieu (1984) have also argued that individuals never truly break with their parents and social class habitus and the corresponding patterns of distinction. However, it has been shown how not only technological introductions but also migration processes (internal/external, rural/urban) can lead to important changes in lifestyle.

As per the findings of the empirical data, many approaches to leisure this have been marked by the absence of different aspects that have a great importance in people's lives. For example, the locality with its climatic and weather conditions, as well as events or local rituals that are a fundamental part of the locality and people's everyday lives, and which also influence taste. City events, such as the Christmas markets and city festivals, are considered yearly repetitive rituals that bring together different segments of the society and help (at least temporarily) reconcile differences and thereby reproduce and produce collective feelings of belonging to the city. These (secular) rituals provide continuity at both the individual and the collective level (s. Myerhoff 1977, p. 218). Such events are an example that milieus, if they exist empirically at all, are not isolated entities that reveal themselves only selectively (s. Schulze 2005, p. 267). The way the individuals form their lifestyles, even though that lifestyle is influenced by socioeconomic factors, is, as Dumazedier (1967, p. 229) pointed out, not a direct result of those factors. Individuals are generally resourceful, make use of what the environment has to offer, and have their own aspirations, which play a role. Leisure is composed of everyday routines that are carefully planned and executed by the individual, but it also composed of events, some of which have a ritual character. Rituals, then, are outside of routine, as Goody (1977, p. 27) pointed out, but both have a presence in leisure.

Indeed, by looking at the patterns of leisure, patterns that are repeated by the choices of the individual and are influenced by socioeconomic factors, such as location, individual biography, and interests, I would argue alongside Pauli (2012) that lifestyle can be understood as individually ritualized practices, but, although some are ritualized practices (which involve meaning, belonging, and social position), others are routinized practices. The difference is in the meaning or lack thereof behind such practices. Each individual has her own leisure and lifestyle, despite sharing structural characteristics with others, and it is routinized because there is a continuity to these practices, many of which generate, or are an expression of, particular identities for the individual. We have seen that the actions of these women do not occur randomly and that there are patterns of organization to everyday life, a big part of this being paid work. Going to work Monday to Friday, from 9 am to 5 pm, going to the gym three times during the week after work, going clubbing on Friday night, and going for family brunch on Sunday all contribute, for example, to form a pattern that repeats itself every week (with possible minor variations). All in all, each individual has a coherent pattern that is her own lifestyle (Otte and Rössel 2011, p. 13).

However, what else can be gained from this knowledge on their leisure and lifestyle to more fully understand the role they play in these women's identities and how they perceive themselves and their belonging? How does lifestyle and leisure interplay with identity? As we have seen, the relationship with and within Mannheim as a living and leisure space, including important collective rituals, serves to produce and reproduce an identity as "Mannheimer," as inhabitants of this city: people who share this space. This idea can be contrasted, for example, with an identity of "Germans," which is less marked, and is often merely a bureaucratic classification that is revived in particular events, such as soccer tournaments, and perhaps placed in the foreground in other local environments. However, there are collective identities that differ from woman to woman: identity as a member of a team, as a dancer, as a member of a social group or family, as worker of a company, as member of the LGBT community, as fan of a certain television series, and so on. Each and every one of these identities is important for them, as they constitute the women's "repertoire of identification" (s. Jenkins 2008, p. 27). The importance of leisure is that leisure activities constitute a large part of the women's identity portfolio because they often constitute the creative, free part of their lives. So, the perceived deficits of work life and the nature of their work highlight the importance of leisure in the subjective perception. Even though identities, such as profession, nationality, ethnicity, religion, and the like, are also part of their belonging and interact with other identities, their "leisure identities'" are highly important and often positioned in the foreground in life and in practice. As Lamont and Aksartova (2010, p. 262) pointed out, ethnic boundaries can be overcome by having a common profession, and I would argue that, likewise, they can be surmounted by having common leisure and leisure spaces. As the women of this study showed, this is possible, besides other factors, because of the characteristics of the social environment in which they live in Mannheim, a space they all consider to be full of leisure possibilities and with few barriers to leisure. It is a space that is shared by a collective that seems to accept many types of identities, even if there is conflict potential, for example, in the case of gender relations. Hannerz (1980, p. 113) wrote that the consequences of the anonymity of the city in which individuals must be recognized, based on general identities such as ethnicity and class, can vary among societies. It seems, then, that, for these women, the environment does not attach negative meanings to their external characteristics, which gives them considerable freedom to form their lifestyles as wish, within their financial means.

All in all, this book has presented an overview of the leisure of these women, in showing how their lived reality varies despite their shared socioeconomic characteristics, which might place them in a particular category. By engaging in ethnography, it was possible to contextualize these characteristics and see how the women evaluate and narrate their lives as well. Naturally, this group of women in Mannheim is just one segment and cannot represent the entirety of the population. But it is a good opportunity for considering individuals who are not marginalized or classified as "problematic" in public discourse but instead are part of the "mass." One of the important insights is that lifestyle commonalities can originate from the sharing of a variety of factors, including sociodemographic factors, *not just of the individual* but also of the social environment surrounding the individual, as was seen with the effects of having friends with children, *and* local characteristics and conviviality. This insight could open the door for engaging in more social network analysis when it comes to lifestyle segmentation, for example. Additionally, it is necessary to further examine the differences concerning the lifestyle of migrants and natives (and where exactly the cultural differences lie). Other discoveries might be presented by the different nature of the individual's life situation and the migrant condition in general. At least, in the case of these women, differences in leisure and therefore lifestyle were first based on individual preferences and then based on dynamics generated by the migration process in general; cultural differences and identification with the culture of origin were important for occasional special events or rituals, and not prominent in everyday life. It was also seen that internal migration generated differences with regard to perception of the environment and behavior concerning social relations as well.

This book has predominantly highlighted commonalities over differences between the women. It might be is necessary to reiterate that the women are not similar in their understanding and practice of leisure as the result of some strange magic but rather as the result of the conjunction of shared characteristics, shared understandings of leisure, and the urban space, the latter of which is so often forgotten in German lifestyle studies.

Discursive practices have an enormous importance for the molding of reality. They not only transmit but also generate meanings, and these practices fortify habitus and distinction mechanisms. It thus also would be necessary to make the target of academic inquiry the discursive practices, by both the media and scholars, that lead to public certainties, such as "Of course the lifestyles of migrants are different". Academic inquiries need to reflect on the role they themselves play in cementing those same public certainties, as is done in Germany, for example, with the countless studies on the "Turkish migrants" or the most recent obsession with refugees' misery. In a wider political context, this particular group of women might contribute to show that attributed differences are often consequence of discourses and that, when looking at topics such as leisure from an emic perspective, it is possible to grasp the commonalities in activities, experiences, and identifications that really play a role for the individuals in their everyday lives beyond stereotypes or sharply divided categorizations. Hereby, the overall taste of the individual, translates into decisions about leisure and lifestyle that have both intrinsic and extrinsic characteristics. It is necessary to keep studying and understanding the mechanisms that produce differences in lifestyle, which can include local institutionalized rules and norms and particular biographical trajectories that go beyond issue of culture, religion, or social class.

References

Bauman, Zygmunt. 2009. *Leben als Konsum*. 1 Aufl. Hamburg: Hamburger Ed.

Bonz, Jochen, and Jens Wietschorke. 2013. Habitus und Kultur: Das Habituskonzept in den empirischen Kulturwissenschaften. Ethnologie—Volkskunde—Cultural Studies. In *Pierre Bourdieu's Konzeption des Habitus: Grundlagen, Zugänge, Forschungsperspektiven*, ed. Alexander Lenger, Christian Schneickert, and Florian Schumacher, 285–306. Wiesbaden: Bücher.

Bourdieu, Pierre. 1984. *Distinction: A Social Critique of the Judgement of Taste*. 2010th edition. London; New York: Harvard University Press and Routledge. Translated by Richard Nice, with a new introduction by Tony Bennett.

Csikszentmihalyi, Mihaly. 1991. *Flow: The Psychology of Optimal Experience*. New York: Harper Perennial.

Dumazedier, Joffre. 1967. *Toward a Society of Leisure*. New York: Collier-Macmillan Limited.

Goody, Jack. 1977. Against "Ritual": Loosely Structured Thoughts on a Loosely Defined Topic. In *Secular Ritual*, ed. Sally F. Moore and Barbara G. Myerhoff, 25–35. Assen: Van Gorcum.

Hannerz, Ulf. 1980. *Exploring the City: Inquiries Toward an Urban Anthropology.* New York: Columbia University Press.

Huizinga, J. 1940. *Homo Ludens: Versuch einer Bestimmung des Spielelementes der Kultur.* 3rd ed. Basel: Akademische Verlagsanstalt Pantheon Verlag fuer Geschichte und Politik.

Iso-Ahola, Seppo E. 2015. Conscious Versus Nonconscious Mind and Leisure. *Leisure Sciences* 37 (4): 289–310.

Jenkins, Richard. 2008. *Social Identity.* 3rd ed. London: Routledge.

Lamont, Michèle, and Sada Aksartova. 2010. Der alltägliche Kosmopolitismus einfacher Leute. Strategien zur Überwindung von Rassengrenzen zwischen Männern der Arbeiterklasse. In *Ethnowissen*, ed. Marion Müller, 257–285. Wiesbaden: Springer Fachmedien.

Myerhoff, Barbara G. 1977. We Don't Wrap Herring in a Printed Page: Fusion, Fictions and Continuity in Secular Ritual. In *Secular Ritual*, ed. Sally F. Moore and Barbara G. Myerhoff, 199–224. Assen: Van Gorcum.

Otte, Gunnar, and Jörg Rössel. 2011. Einführung: Lebensstile in der Soziologie. In *Lebensstilforschung*, ed. Jörg Rössel and Gunnar Otte, 7–34. Wiesbaden: VS Verlag für Sozialwissenschaften.

Pauli, Julia. 2012. *Klasse verbraucht. Elite und Konsum aus ethnographischer Perspektive.* Lecture series: Konsum, Shoppen, Alltag, Kontrolle. Hamburg: Universität Hamburg. http://lecture2go.uni-hamburg.de/veranstaltungen/-/v/13150. Accessed January 27, 2014.

Richter, Rudolf. 2005. *Die Lebensstilgesellschaft.* 1 Aufl. Wiesbaden: VS Verlag für Sozialwissenschaften.

Schulze, Gerhard. 2005[1992]. *Die Erlebnisgesellschaft: Kultursoziologie der Gegenwart.* 2 Aufl. Frankfurt [Main]; New York: Campus.

Simmel, Georg. 1903. Die Grosstädte und das Geistesleben. Dresden.

Turner, Victor. 1974. Liminal to Liminoid, in Play, Flow, and Ritual: An Essay in Comparative Symbology. *Rice University Studies* 60 (3): 53–92.

INDEX

© The Author(s) 2017
V.L. Sandoval, *The Meaning of Leisure*, Leisure Studies
in a Global Era, DOI 10.1007/978-3-319-59752-2

The manufacturer's authorised representative in the EU is Springer
Nature Customer Service Centre GmbH, Europaplatz 3, 69115 Heidelberg,
Germany. If you have any concerns regarding our products, please
contact ProductSafety@springernature.com

Printed and bound by CPI Group (UK) Ltd, Croydon, CR0 4YY

28/04/2026

02098487-0001